STREET BIOGRAPHIES
of the **ROYAL BURGH** of
HADDINGTON
DAVID DICK

Foreword by **NIGEL TRANTER**

Clerkington Publishing Co.

ISBN 0 9530274 0 6

Printed by Kelso Graphics, The Knowes, Kelso TD5 7BH.

The photographs are by the author except where otherwise acknowledged.

STREET BIOGRAPHIES of the
ROYAL BURGH of HADDINGTON

This is a novel way of finding out about the people and the history of Haddington through its street names, monuments and some of its mansion houses. A brief biography is given for those streets which commemorate sons and daughters of the town and of others who have distinguished themselves through their service to the country in many capacities.

Who for example was Davidson of Davidson Terrace, Ross of Ross's Close or Fortune of Fortune Avenue? Who was the Ferguson who stands on top of the huge pillar at the west end of the town? Who was Hopetoun whose chimney-like monument stands in the Garleton Hills? These and dozens of others are explored in this small volume about the streets and the people of the Royal Burgh of Haddington.

Published by
Clerkington Publishing Co.,
West Lodge Clerkington,
Haddington EH41 4NJ
Tel. 0162 082 5341

CONTENTS

Foreword by NIGEL TRANTER

Here is something which I, for one, have never come across before - a book of street names, with reasons for them being so named, and the events and personalities behind so many of them, this encapsulating much of the history, concerns and notables of Haddington. And Haddington has had a lengthy and dramatic history, much more so than most towns of its size; also many distinguished citizens. It is fortunate in all this, with its own character, appearance, environment - and not least now, in having David Dick to thus make it known and appreciated by all, in this work of enthusiasm, caring and much research, by one of enquiring mind.

Not a few of the items are fascinating indeed. I was particularly intrigued by the Amisfield Park and Place excerpts. I knew about the Charteris and Wemyss connection, but had no idea that these lands had previously been given to one of Oliver Cromwell's Ironside officers, Colonel Stanfield, who then, in 1650, settled in Haddington instead of returning to England, and chose to develop the wool trade of the sheep-strewn Lammermuirs, and manufactured there woollen goods, thus becoming a benefactor to the town. He indeed became a member of the Scottish Parliament, and was knighted by Charles the Second - and all this, only to be murdered by his own disreputable son, and with the collusion of Lady Stanfield, his strangled body found in the Tyne. Material for a novel here? Another which rings a particular bell with me is Giffordgate, with its links with Sir Hugo de Giffard, the Wizard, Goblin Ha' and its legends. I have written about this extraordinary character.

These are but two of a host. I commend this work to all readers and to some who are perhaps not readers at all, and well beyond the town of Haddington itself. All history is important, for history is the memory of the race; and local history, coming closest to the individual, is not less so than the national and international sort. Read this, and you will be wiser, informed, pleased - as well as surprised - as was I.

Acknowledgements

This small volume, which is mainly about the people after whom the streets and statues of Haddington have been named, would never have seen the light of day without the help and encouragement of many Haddingtonians - members of the 'Haddington Remembered Group', 'Haddington's History Society', the Day Centre of Haddington, the Probus Club of Haddington and through dozens of meetings with other Haddingtonians.

The **'Haddington Remembered Group'** - many of whom have given me help and encouragement: the chairperson Mrs Elizabeth Nisbet, the Secretary, Mrs Pat Moncrieff, and many other members have lent me material and have willingly given me information particularly during chats and walks through the streets of Haddington.

The Haddington Day Centre in Church Street: **Mrs MacNeill** put me in touch with her sister-in-law, **Mrs Baillie**, who in turn gave me help with the life of Provost Davidson (Davidson Terrace). Mrs MacNeill also told me of **Mrs Miller** of Prora Farm, the daughter of the late Provost Hugh Craig (Craig Avenue) who kindly provided me with details of her father's life and checked the final draft of this street name.

Mrs Pamela Elizabeth Armstrong, my daughter, whose energy and innumerable ideas for the presentation and marketing of this volume have added to its attractiveness. Her enthusiasm and encouragement pushed me to get it into print without more delay.

Miss C.R. Budge, Headmistress of The Compass school, for her willing help with the history of Somnerfield House (gained from notes written by **Mrs J.D.Ferguson**) and about the work of the school as contained in Appendix II - Education in Haddington.

Professor Roger Burley for his help with the derivation of Burley's Walls gleaned over the telephone and during his excellent lecture to Haddington's History Society.

The late **Mr Matthew D Carlaw MBE** the Burgh Chamberlain of Haddington from 1950 to 1965 and Chairman of the Royal Burgh of Haddington & District Council, gave me a most interesting insight of the workings of the Town Council during his term of office. He shed light on the derivation of several street names and I am grateful for that in addition to his generous and convivial hospitality.

Victoria Fletcher, of the Haddington Remembered Group and Haddington's History Society for her help in researching the Hay family (lairds of Alderston in early 17th century).

Mr George Fortune kindly provided me with information about the life of his father, Provost Robert Fortune, the second and last to be given the honour of being made a Freeman of the town and after whom Fortune Avenue is named. I am grateful to him for lending me the photograph of his father which appears in the text.

Mrs Rita Godek gave me useful information of changes during her years at Maitlandfield and about other occupants before and after her own occupancy for which I am most grateful.

Mr Eric Groome of Haddington's History Society, Haddington Remembered Group and Haddington's Probus Club who took me on several interesting tours of buildings and streets and explained, in minute detail many features of their construction. He kindly lent me several drawings, photographs and books from his vast collection and was a constant source of advice and encouragement. To the ubiquitous Eric and his charming wife Vera, I am grateful for their kindness and hospitality.

Mr Douglas MacKenzie, MacKenzie & Moncur Consultants Ltd., Heating, Electrical & Energy Advisers, 2a Ramsay Garden, Edinburgh - for information with reference to his Great Uncle, Dr William Cossar MacKenzie of Alderston.

Mr John McGurk, Editor of the Edinburgh Evening News, for his for his good wishes and for his permission to publish an extract from an article: *Actress Wife Spotlights her Husband* by Lennox Milne which appeared in the Edinburgh Evening Despatch of 6th March 1954.

Mr John McVie, the Town Clerk of Haddington from 1956 to 1974, helped me with many dates of the naming of streets and the development of Haddington through much of its history in addition to which he lent me several useful volumes.

Mrs Veronica Marchbanks, Archives Assistant of the British Red Cross, Museum and Archives, Guildford, Surrey for information about the life of Lady Hersey Baird as President of the East Lothian Branch of the British Red Cross.

Mrs Helen Miller for her help with the life of her father, Provost Hugh Craig, and for her kindnes in lending me a photograph of him.

Mr K Minty, Divisional Roads Manager, Lothian Regional Council, Alderston House, Haddington for taking the trouble to send me architectural information about Alderston and for additional information about the stained-glass panes.

The late **Mr James Mitchell**, a hand weaver of Mitchell's Close who kindly shared with me his reminiscences of William Davidson of Davidson Terrace.

Mr Robert G Mitchell, Convenor of East Lothian District Council, who sent me details of Haddington's international rugby players - the Calder brothers, after whom Calder's Lawn was named at his suggestion to the Council.

Mr Phil Mowat of East Lothian Council who kindly permitted me to have access to Council files relating to street names. His patience, interest and active help have added much to the accuracy of this volume.

Mr Douglas Pittillo, Lothian Regional Council Property Services Department, 7/9 North St David's Street, Edinburgh - for his permission to inspect title deeds of Alderston.

Miss Margaret Pringle, a past committee member of the Haddington's History Society and a member of the Haddington Remembered Group, who willingly shared her extensive knowledge of Haddington's history and who helped me with many biographical details of old Haddingtonians. I am also grateful to her for the loan of several books and documents. Her attention to detail in proof-reading the manuscript with numerous and helpful suggestions are specially appreciated - this gave me the confidence to proceed with the publication of this book in the knowledge that it has been properly vetted. She has been a constant source of encouragement and inspiration.

Mrs Audrey Ritchie kindly allowed me to photograph several oil paintings at the Offices of East Lothian District Council.

Mrs Margaret Saunders of Inverness for information about her grandfather Dr. William Cossar MacKenzie.

Mr Alexander Fraser Spowage JP, an ex-Provost of

Haddington, generously lent me papers and photographs of the Town Council of Haddington and helped me with the life of Provosts Craig, Davidson and Fortune as well as many others. In addition he compiled the list of Provosts of Haddington from 1900 which is given in Appendix III. It was Mr Spowage who guided me on my first walk through the streets of Haddington during which I learned from him much of their history, name derivations and name changes. His knowledge of the Royal Burgh and its worthies is encyclopaedic and I only had to lift the telephone to receive the answer to almost any query. His encouragement and convivial hospitality made this project a thoroughly enjoyable one.

Dr Nigel Tranter, Scotland's greatest and most prolific historical novelist, for his superb foreword and for his encouragement for the success of this book. My meetings with Nigel Tranter were a privilege, an education and an inspiration.

Mrs M D Turnbull of Stornoway Isle of Lewis - for copies of documents and photographs relating to her Grandfather, Dr. William Cossar MacKenzie.

Mr William Taylor of Gifford who kindly shared with me his reminiscences of Provost William Davidson (Davidson Terrace). The two men worked together in the West Mill and met in London when the late William Davidson attended the coronation of George VI _____ in 1937. I am grateful too for his help with the story of Rosehall and for trouble he took to make a detailed drawing of this area as it was during and after the 1914-18 war. He kindly lent me several photographs of Mr Davidson and the West Mill. His wife, **Mrs Agnes Taylor**, kindly lent me a photograph of Provost Robert Fortune. Their kindness and hospitality added considerably to my enjoyment in this project.

My wife, Muriel - for her patience in searching and recording relevant gravestones at St Mary's Parish Church and other Churchyards, for checking the manuscript and for final proof reading. She was an unfailing source of encouragement and tolerance. It was mainly due to her insistence that I finished this book at all.

My daughter **Mrs Pamela Armstrong** for her wealth of ideas relating to the presentation and for her humorous encouragement especially in relation to design and marketing. Few fathers have the good fortune to have the genuine and continuous interest of their families - I am one of the lucky ones.

Ms Veronica Wallace of Haddington Public Library in Newton Port is due my gratitude for her unfailing courteous and willing help in my researches.

Mr Ken Whitson, Managing Director of J & G Croall Ltd, Printers and Publishers of the East Lothian Courier for his permission to publish extracts from the Haddingtonshire Courier and the East Lothian Courier as acknowledged in the text. I am grateful too for his advice and encouragement.

Introduction

A s a relative newcomer to Haddington it was with some diffidence that I embarked upon the task of writing its 'street biographies'. I need not have been even slightly nervous; the people of this Royal Burgh have given me willing help in such a way as to make the task sociable and pleasurable. Each person I approached for help was keen to talk with pride about 'our town' and after I had explained what I was about, that is writing street biographies, it was apparent that my interest in the town was considered to be a compliment given.

What then is a 'street biography?' It is, quite simply, a short biography of the person after whom a street has been named. Ideally, each one starts with a statement giving the location, the year(s) in which it was built, any redeeming architectural features and it ends with a short biography of the person after whom the street has been named.

This book is therefore substantially biographical with a taste of the history of the time of the subject. However, some streets are named after places rather than people; in such cases a brief outline of the buildings, their uses and some of the inhabitants of the past is given. I have also included the history of a few houses and their previous occupants.

I apologise in advance for any inaccuracies and omissions in the text and I ask for tolerance and understanding in the hope that those who find any errors will drop me a note so that I can improve my records. My only hope is that those good people of Haddington who have provided me with so much help and wonderful encouragement will not feel let down.

David Dick

THE ROYAL BURGH OF HADDINGTON

The name Haddington - there are several versions of the derivation of the name Haddington - one is the 'hidden town', another is an adaptation of 'Hadentun' or 'Haden's Farm' ('tun' meaning farm); Haden was an early Saxon chief. Another suggestion relates to the fact that the territory was part of the marriage dowry of the daughter of the Earl of Warren and Surrey when she married the son of David I. Her name was Ada or Hadina and the name Adington or Hadington was given to the settlement where she founded St Martin's Nunnery in 1153. She was the mother of Malcolm IV and William the Lion (12). Yet another possible derivation is from the Gaelic Chuidan, cuidan - town at a small fold.(34)

Whatever the derivation, Haddington is a Royal Burgh and the date of its charter is ancient but unknown; documents are thought to have been destroyed during one of the several sackings of the town - but then documents may never have existed at all as some authorities believe that burghal status was acquired by use and wont. However, several authorities do give indirect evidence to the existence of a burgh dating back to the reign of David I (1124-1153) - a charter of King David's makes reference to "in burgo de Hadingtoun" and another of the Bishop of St Andrews, after David's death, refers to "re Ecclesia de Hadintum" (1.p3; 2.p.202; 5.p.1; 14.p.ix).

William the Lion (1165-1214) resided in the town and his son Alexander II (1214-1249) was born on 24th August 1198 in the Palace of Haddington on the site of which the County Buildings now stands.

The town suffered its first invasion at the hands of King John in 1216, Alexander II having incurred his wrath when he joined with the English barons against King John's misrule. Henry III pursued his father's vengeance by burning the town yet again in 1241 when he attempted to compel Alexander to swear allegiance to him.

After his victory at Halidon Hill in 1333 and the fall of Berwick, Edward III sacked Haddington. This was followed by the destruction of the Franciscan Friary, 'The Lamp of Lothian', in

1356 - again by Edward III's invading English army. The clear light of its choir could be seen for miles around and was regarded by weary travellers of those ancient times as a haven of rest. The Friary was situated near the site of the present Episcopalian Church in Church Street. The designation 'Lamp of Lothian' has been adopted by St Mary's Parish Church, a collegiate church, which was built on the site of the previous church granted by David I and destroyed by Edward III in 1356. The Duke of Gloucester, who became Richard III, scoured Haddington in 1482 en-route to Edinburgh. Haddington was occupied by the English in 1548 - the famous siege which ended in 1549 with the aid of the French army. Haddington was burned down again in 1593 and yet again by Cromwell in 1650.

Haddington has suffered more than its fair share of floods. It is remarkable that almost any heavy fall of rain causes sudden swelling of the River Tyne and a flood in Haddington - a not uncommon occurrence even today. The earliest recorded flood was in 1358 when houses and bridges were washed away. Continuous rain for several days in 1421 raised the level of the Tyne so that almost every house was flooded and the inhabitants took refuge by boat in St Mary's which itself was damaged resulting in destruction of its sacristy, library and ornaments.

The 1572 flood washed down so many stones that the Town Council ordered the Treasurer "to lay to the west pier the great and small stones borne down by the flood, at the town's expense." (2. p.203). Another flood in 1673 flooded the schoolhouse and in 1775 the Tyne rose to a depth of seventeen feet; the whole of the Nungate and half the town was awash 'level with the third step of the Cross which stood about the middle of the High Street' (2 p.203). A stone was inscribed as a perpetual reminder: "On the fourth day of October MDCCLXXV, the river Tyne, at three o'clock afternoon, rose to this plate. *Quod non noctu deo gratias nemo enim periit.*" (2. p.204).

The floods of 1791 and 1797 flooded the mills and caused severe damage. In 1810 the weir at Long Cram (a section of the Tyne west of Distillery Park after which Long Cram off Pencaitland Road takes its name) and East and West Haughs were flooded. A wall plaque at the corner of Sidegate tells of another flood in 1949 when the waters of Tyne rose to flood much of the Nungate, Church Street and the High Street. Again, in 1994, Haddington was flooded, the Tyne quickly lapping over the wall on the Nungate side spreading to flood the houses on both sides.

Aberlady Road

The main outlet for Haddington's exports was the port at Aberlady and during the 15th to the 18th century this was a well-travelled road which came to be called simply Aberlady Road. It is shown on the 1819 Plan of Haddington and Nungate as 'Road from Aberlady'. This plan shows other roads such as the 'Road from Dunbar' now called Dunbar Road and the 'Road to Gifford' now Gifford Road.

The importance of Haddington with its surrounding fertile land, its mills, dyeworks, tanneries and its nine incorporated trades: baxters (bakers), cordiners (shoemakers), fleshers (butchers), hammermen (blacksmiths), masons, tailors, skinners, weavers and wrights (cabinetmakers) was evident from the trading statistics given in the Exchequer Rolls (25); the amounts shown below represent the value of exported goods from customs receipts:

Year	Haddington £	Edinburgh £
1441	220	418
1451	109	544
1479	159	1625

The 15th century products consisted of wool, fleece, hides and cloth. However by 1692 foreign trade had diminished to a few Dutch and English goods and there were no longer any Haddington ships at Aberlady but it ceased to be a port when the railway arrived at Haddington in June 1846 and two years later the Earl of Wemyss purchased the anchorage.

Alderston Meadow
Alderston House

Alderston Meadow is a new housing complex built by Cala Homes (Scotland) Ltd., in the grounds of Alderston House in 1995.

Alderston House, about 2.5 km north-west of Haddington's town centre, was built about 1790 for Robert Steuart (1765-1823), the Laird of Alderston. It is a three-storey pedimented mansion with Roman Doric columns supporting its 1820 porch. The single-storey west wing was added in 1830 but its stables date from 1760 which is the estimated date of some of the upstairs woodwork of the mansion house.(26 p.76)

Alderston House takes its name from the lands of Alderston and its Lairds, the first of whom was Thomas Hay of Alderston and Hermiston (1602-1654) whose father was Lord Clerk Register, Sir John Hay of Barra, the first baronet.(37.p.47). This accounts for the Hay family crest in a stained glass pane of a staircase window. The Hays of Alderston were a branch of the Hays of Yester, of whom John Hay was the 1st Marquis of Tweeddale.

Another early reference dates back to 1659 when the Laird of Alderston, with the Earl of Haddington, Lord Ellibank, was required to keep the 40 ft wide road (an inalienable right of the town) in good condition.(1.p.87) The Register of Seisins (Sasines) Haddington 1781-1868 (38) records that on 16th September 1789 George Buchan Hepburn sold the estate of 'Alderstone' to Alexander Tod, Captain of the 'Busbridge', Indiaman, and a further entry dated 20th July 1790 records that 'Alexander Tod of Alderston acquired the estate.'

The Alderston estate came into the ownership of Robert Steuart on 31st March 1802 and in 1819 he bought 10 acres of Meadowshot Park from Sir George Buchan Hepburn (38). Robert Steuart was born on 12th October 1765 and died on 10th November 1823. It is likely that Steuart built Alderston 'Manor' house the estimated year of which is given as 1790 (26) but it appears in the Register of Sasines of Haddington for the first time in 1828; the stables (1760), now almost derelict, were built before he was born. It is possible that this square building with its north facing Tuscan columns was the original Alderston House from which the 1760 wood panelling of the present mansion house was taken.

His son, also Robert Steuart, was born at Alderston in 1806 and on reaching his maturity (aged 21 years) the whole estate of Alderston including Meadow Shot Park passed from the trustees to him (14th July 1827) (38). He was very popular in the burgh and in 1829 he contested the parliamentary seat against Sir Adolphus John Dalrymple who was the Member for the five burghs. In the election of 1831 the Laird of Alderston won the seat by one vote, but because of the fact that some of his supporters had abducted Bailie Simpson, a Lauderdale party supporter for Dalrymple, the House of Commons chose in favour of Dalrymple.

Dalrymple's tenure of office was short and Robert Steuart stood again in the first elections of the Reformed Parliament in 1832. This time he won the seat without dispute. He resigned in 1837 on his appointment as a junior Lord of the Treasury and that year he sold Alderston 'with the consent of Maria Dalrymple his spouse' to James Aitchison (38). In 1841 Steuart was re-elected to Parliament and held the seat until 1841 when he was defeated by a slender margin of nine votes against James Maitland Balfour of Whittingehame, father of the 1st Earl Balfour (Prime Minister 1902-06). (14)

Robert Steuart's competence and popularity were recognised in his appointment as Consul-General of Colombia in South America but illness led to his early death in Bogota on 15th July 1843. Only a few months before his death his many friends in East Lothian had subscribed the sum of £400 for a testimonial to him. His public funeral was attended by many hundreds of his admirers.(14)

The Alderston Tomb in the graveyard of St Mary's Parish Church commemorates the parents of Robert Steuart who died within six days of each other in 1823. Their tombstone is inscribed:

'Sacred
To the Memory of
Robert Steuart Esq. of Alderston
Born 12th October 1765
Died 10th November 1823
Sacred
To the Memory of
Louisa Clementina Steuart
second wife
of Robert Steuart Esq.
of Alderston
She was youngest daughter
of the late John Drummond Esq.
of Logie Almond & the Lady
Catherine Murray, his spouse
Born 12th February 1771
Died 16th November 1823.'

The next Laird of Alderston was James Aitchison, a local wheat farmer, who purchased Alderston in 1837. (38) He married Janet Rennie and had three daughters, the eldest of whom, Marion, married the 2nd Baron Denman in 1871.

The 2nd Baron Denman was the only son of Thomas Denman, the 1st Baron Denman (1779-1854), who was Whig MP for Wareham and Nottingham and, in 1830, became Attorney-General in Earl Grey's government. He was Lord Chief-Justice in 1832 and defended Queen Caroline against the accusations of

George IV. His son, Thomas Denman, succeeded as 2nd Baron Denman in 1854. He was born on 30th July 1805 and educated at Eton and Brasenose College, Oxford. He followed in his father's footsteps in that he became a Barrister of Lincoln's Inn in 1833 and an associate to his father when he was Chief Justice of the Queen's Bench.(16.p.471) The 2nd Baron's first wife was Georgina, daughter of the Rev. Thomas Roe, who died in 1871. Six months later, on 10th October 1871 he married Marion, eldest daughter of James Aitchison at Haddington. By Royal licence he took the name Aitchison before Denman under the Will of his mother-in-law. He died suddenly of a heart attack at the King's Arms Hotel in Berwick on 9th August 1894, aged 89 years and was buried at Alderston (16.p.471). His wife continued to live at Alderston with her two sisters, Margaret and Helen, until her death on 27th February 1902.

The Aitchison gravestone in St Mary's Churchyard is inscribed:

'In Memory of

Marion Aitchison	.	Margaret Aitchison
of Alderston	.	died 12 March 1892
wife of Thomas	.	Helen Aitchison
2nd Baron Denman	.	died 29th November 1889
died 27th February 1902	.	daughters of the late
Thomas	.	James Aitchison
2nd Baron Denman	.	of Alderston
died 9th August 1894'		

A Notarial Instrument of May 1902 gave ownership of Alderston to Colonel William Aitchison and in December 1902 Alderston was owned jointly by the Colonel and his son William Aitchison junior. In May 1904 Alderston was sold to Francis Murray Rae of Aberdeen; he owned the house and lands for three years and sold it to Dr. William Cossar Mackenzie. (39).

A staircase window at Alderston House has stained-glass panes with initials 'MCK' above a deer head alongside which is a second crest of the Hay family. The former gives the identity of the last Laird of Alderston, William Cossar Mackenzie D.Sc., Ph.D., who owned lands in Lothian. He was a retired Principal of the Egyptian Polytechnic of Engineering in Cairo. He was born on 15th February 1866 in Edinburgh, a son of Alexander Donald Mackenzie, a Bailie of Edinburgh and partner of the engineering firm Mackenzie & Moncur. He was educated at Daniel Stewart's College and Edinburgh University where he was a distinguished scholar and gained the highest level of academic achievement - that of Doctor of Science (D.Sc.). His specialist study was in Agricultural Chemistry and he continued his researches at the University of Strasburg and Halle in Germany where his work gained him the degree of Doctor of Philosophy (Ph.D).

He was appointed in 1891 by the Egyptian Government to lecture at the College of Agriculture at Ghizeh in Cairo. He became its Principal and was appointed Principal of the Polytechnic College of Engineering for the last four years of his service in Egypt. Such was the high esteem in which he was held he was awarded the Egyptian Order of Osmanich (3rd Class) and the Order of the Medjidieh (2nd Class). His early retirement, in 1907, due to ill-health, was partly caused by attacks on university staff during the student riots in Alexandria.

With his wife, Mary Ann Sheppard, and his family of three sons and a daughter, he purchased the grounds and mansion of

Alderston and embarked upon several costly improvements. He became involved in several societies in Haddington and was particularly interested in educational matters with his membership of the Burgh and Landward School Board. The Courier of 22nd September 1911 describes him as:

'....a kindly and straightforward man who had ideas with regard to education and its organisation, and had rendered valuable service to the community.'

This was an appreciation of him following his tragic and early death, aged forty-five years, which occurred after an accident at Alderston. He had climbed on to the roof of the mansion to clear some debris from a rhone pipe when he overbalanced, striking his head on the roof of the billiard room. He died two days later on Saturday 26th July 1911. He was buried at St Mary's Churchyard where the family gravestone is inscribed:

In loving memory of
WILLIAM COSSAR MACKENZIE
of Alderston
for fifteen years in the Egyptian Government Service
Born February 15 1866
Died July 29 1911
and of his wife
MARY ANN SHEPPARD
Died February 24 1944
and their son
Allan Sheppard
who died in pow camp Borneo
March 23 1945, aged 39
also their son
John Gurney Mackenzie CMG
for 27 years in the colonial service
in Nigeria
died 12th September 1975, aged 67
also their son in law
David Charles Meehan
born 24.11.09 died 26.7.86
and their daughter
Marion Byan Meehan
19.12.09 - 12.8.86

Mrs Mary Ann Mackenzie continued to live at Alderston until 31st May 1919 when she sold the mansion and estates of 47.5 acres to the East Lothian Board of Control.

Alderston was again for sale in 1925, this time to The Scottish National Benevolent Association and it became a convalescent home for the Scottish Rural Workers Association.

In 1950 Alderston was sold in parts to the Secretary of State for Scotland for the National Health Service and the mansion house became a Nurses Home for Roodlands Hospital. A sister tutor was appointed and it became a Nurses Training School until 1972 when it was vacated. In 1958 the farms of Alderston were purchased from the Secretary of State by Alexander Hastie (39). Alderston House remained vacant until 1977 when it was sold with its grounds to the Lothian Regional Council and it accommodated three departments - Highways, Water and Drainage and Property Services. With the reorganisation of Councils in 1996 Alderston once again is subjected to change of use, the latest proposal being to use it as a training centre for East Lothian Council's 4000 employees

Alexandra Place

Alexandra Place, off Newton Port, was St John's Free Church which was built shortly after the 'disruption' in the Church of Scotland in 1842. St John's ceased to be used on completion of the new Free Church in Court Street (renamed Haddington West Church in 1932) and from 1890 St John's Free Church in Newton Port lay empty. The building was used as a store for the local brewery for a short time and there was even a suggestion that it could be used as the Fire Station for Haddington .

John Middlemass purchased the manse and church of St John's in 1892; he and his wife lived at Dale house and Mr Middlemass converted the manse into four flats in 1926. The name Alexandra Place was chosen to commemorate the well-loved Queen Alexandra who had died in 1925 when the conversion from a church building into flats was taking place.

There was national mourning for this gracious and stately lady who held a special place in the hearts of the people partly because of her charitable work and partly due to the sympathy she received as the neglected wife of Edward VII.

Princess Alexandra Caroline Marie Charlotte Louise Julia, was the eldest daughter of King Christian IX of Denmark, a royal household which was relatively poorer than others in Europe. She was born on 1st December 1844 and grew to become stately and beautiful. She was the second of a happy family of six children; a natural beauty, she had several suitors.

The suggestion that she would be a suitable wife for the Prince of Wales was made to Queen Victoria by her eldest daughter the Princess Royal who was Crown Princess of Prussia. At first, Queen Victoria and Prince Albert had reservations because of the long standing dispute between Denmark and Prussia over the duchies of Schleswig and Holstein, but after a visit to the Rhineland, when the Prince of Wales met Princess Alexandra with her parents, the Prince was immediately attracted to her Nordic beauty and fell in love with her almost at first sight and she became engaged to him on 9th September 1862. She was invited to Buckingham Palace 'on approval'. The Princess was terrified but she captivated the Queen who felt, at last, that her eldest son, 'Bertie', would give up his life of dissipation and settle down to happy married life.

They were married on 10th March 1863; it was a perfect match, or so it seemed until political differences arose between Denmark and Prussia. Prince Edward took the side of his newly-wedded wife against his mother - a year after their marriage war was declared between Denmark against Prussia and Austria over Schleswig-Holstein and the Queen, loyal to her husband's memory, supported the Prussians (Prince Albert had died of typhoid in 1861 and had passionately supported the Holstein cause).

Princess Alexandra had five children: Prince Albert Victor (1864-92, Duke of Clarence and Avondale), Prince George (1865-1936, later George V), Princess Louise (1867-1931, Princess Royal), Princess Victoria (1867-1935) and Princess Maud (1869-1938) who married Haakon VII of Norway. She adored her children and did everything in her power to keep them as childlike as possible. Her husband agreed wholeheartedly. He was determined that his children would be spared the rigid discipline to which he had been subjected by his father, Prince Albert. Their carefree life and their world of make-believe and eternal youth was a reflection of their gay, spontaneous, impractical and unpunctual mother, Princess Alexandra. She was a breath of fresh air in the Royal family but in the background there was the Queen. She did not approve.

Her sixth child, Prince John, lived only one day and in 1867, shortly before the birth of Princess Louise, she contracted rheumatic fever. She was left with a permanent limp in spite of which she enjoyed riding, skating and dancing. Sadly, she had inherited ostosclerosis and was afflicted with deafness which restricted her involvement in her husband's social life. She retreated to the country and took pleasure from horses and dogs and painting and photography.

Prince Edward soon returned to his wayward ways and Princess Alexandra's tolerance must have been stretched to its limit when her husband, whose weakness for beautiful women, led him into many indiscretions - actress Lily Langtree ("the Jersey Lily"), Parisienne Hortense Schneider, Princesse de Sagan, the Duchesse de Mouchy, the Hon. Mrs Keppel, La Goulue the star of Moulin

Rouge and many others. Princess Alexandra seemed to regard these mistresses with measured amusement referring to the rich American heiress, Miss Chamberlayne, as 'Chamberpots'. She was kind to Lily Langtree and to Mrs Keppel, whose company she found agreeable. Her two sons Eddie and George were educated together, mainly to help the backward Eddie. Their tutor, the Rev. John Dalton, was a young man who soon realised that the easy-going atmosphere of their family life worked against their progress. Tactfully, he suggested that the two boys should be sent to a naval training ship, the *Britannia*, to provide a change from ' the excitement of their parents' lives.' However, five years of travel and careful teaching did little to improve the apathetic, lethargic Eddie. At home his dissipated life led to his early death aged 28 years. Princess Alexandra was broken-hearted. Her darling boy was gone and the more intelligent George became heir presumptive.

When Queen Victoria died on 22nd January 1901 Princess Alexandra, aged fifty-seven, became Queen. She maintained an air of dignity, understanding and aloof tolerance; she remained steadfastly loyal to Edward VII throughout his pleasure-seeking life but her influence undoubtedly contributed to what became a successful nine-year reign during a time of social improvement (r.1901-1910). But there was undoubtedly a feeling of public sympathy for her as a neglected wife.

She took an interest in foreign affairs and travelled widely. She visited her relatives in Denmark each year and visited her sister in Russia and her brother in Greece several times. State visits to Russia and Germany in 1905 and an official visit to Portugal were very successful.

Queen Alexandra was noted for her charitable works especially for the nursing service and hospitals. After the death of her husband in 1910 she continued her charitable work and in 1912 Alexandra Day was instituted for the benefit of hospitals. She lived at Sandringham House which had been left to her under the terms of her husband's will for her lifetime. She lived there with her unmarried daughter Princess Victoria.

She suffered a heart attack on 19th November 1925 and died a day later. She lay in state at Westminster Abbey and was buried at Windsor.

Amisfield Park
Amisfield Place
Charteris's Dykes

A misfield Park was part of the estate of the Earl of Wemyss on which his magnificent mansion house, Amisfield House, was situated. It was built of red freestone from Garvald quarry for Francis Charteris about 1760. The wings were added in 1785 and it was demolished in 1923. Only photographs remain of what was the finest example in the country of the orthodox Palladian school. It was bought by Richard Baillie, the Haddington building contractor, who used the stone to build Vert Memorial Hospital and Prestonpans Secondary School. The park is the picturesque Haddington Golf Course which is surrounded by a stone wall known as **Charteris's Dykes**. Haddington Golf Club, instituted in 1865, was set out by the Town Council at Amisfield Park which was previously a military camp and a prisoner-of-war camp during the 1939-45 war.

The street named **Amisfield Park** is a cul-de-sac off Park Road which is part of the western boundary of the golf course. **Amisfield Place**, off Monkrigg Road, lies at the extreme south-east corner of Haddington.

The land belonged to a Cisterian Nunnery in the 12th century and in 1681 it became known as New Mills when a mill for the manufacture of fine woollen cloth became the principal industry of Haddington.

After Cromwell's victory over General David Leslie at the Battle of Dunbar in 1650, Cromwell established a wool factory at New Mills. After the Restoration in 1660 the Scottish Parliament granted immunity to an officer of the Cromwellian Parliamentary army, Colonel James Stanfield, to establish a company which prospered under the joint ownership of James Stanfield and Robert Blackwood of Edinburgh. They purchased the ecclesiastic land which surrounded the mill and Colonel Stanfield was the principal partner of the New Mill Company. Such was his success in manufacture and trade the Scottish Parliament and the Privy Council passed an Act to encourage trade and manufacture in Scotland and Colonel Stanfield was knighted by Charles II.

He became the Member of the Scottish Parliament for East Lothian and his success seemed assured when demand exceeded production. However, cheaper imports from England to supply General Dalzell's dragoons caused discontent among the 700 mill workers as did the importation of English weavers. The Privy Council agreed to burn imported cloth but dissolution was discussed among the shareholders and Stanfield proposed to sell his share of the company.

His financial difficulties were worsened by the spending excesses of his son, Philip; their relationship deteriorated into frustrated anger and the colonel disinherited his eldest son. Their quarrels were well known and talked about and when, in 1687, Colonel Stanfield's body was found in the River Tyne it was, at first, assumed that he had committed suicide but when it became known that his wife had prepared his burial before his death, suspicion was aroused. When his body was exhumed it was discovered that he had been strangled. His son Philip was accused of patricide and after a trial he was hanged in Edinburgh on 24th February 1688.

In those days of mystery and superstition it was believed that the body of the person murdered bleeds at the touch of the murderer. This was considered as evidence of guilt at the trial of Philip Stanfield.

Young Stanfield touch'd his father's corpse,
When rose a fearful wail;
For blood gushed from the winding sheet,
And every face grew pale.

James Miller

His head was displayed at the East Port (near the Tyne at the foot of Church Street) being the spot nearest to which the crime was committed. (2. p224).

The grave of Sir James Stanfield is at Morham Churchyard where his elaborately carved tombstone is near the church door. (30.p.132)

Twenty-five years later, in 1713, the land of New Mills was purchased by the infamous Colonel Francis Charteris. He probably paid for it with his winnings from gambling. He was well-known for cheating at the card table and had won the vast sum of £3000, it was said by the use of mirrors, in one sitting from the Duchess of Queensberry; the Duke was so furious that he tried to have an Act of Parliament passed to limit the amount which could be bet in games of chance; it came to nothing.

Born in 1675, Colonel Charteris was a grandson of Sir John Charteris of Amisfield in Dumfriesshire and appears as one of the rakes in Chancellor's *Lives of the Rakes* as a 'card-sharper, thief, and scoundrel generally' (20). He was thought to have had a liaison with the devil and was the subject of a satirical painting by William Hogarth in *The Harlot's Progress*.

He dismantled New Mills, disposed of the machinery and named the land Amisfield as a reminder of his Nithsdale home. His only daughter and sole heiress, Janet, married in secret James the second son of the 4th Earl of Wemyss in 1720 (16); the couple separated in 1732 because of her extravagances. The colonel died in 1732 at Stoneyhill leaving part of his vast fortune (£10,000) to his favourite grandson, Francis Charteris Wemyss, second son of the 4th Earl of Wemyss, on condition that he adopted the name Charteris. (15.Vol. III p.366)

The red sandstone mansion, of Grecian grandeur, 'the most important building of the orthodox Palladian school in Scotland' (26.p.76), was designed in 1755 by Isaac Ware (d.1766) for the Hon Francis Charteris Wemyss (1723-1808), de jure 7th Earl. He was known for his Jacobite sympathies as was his elder brother David, Lord Elcho who was ADC to Prince Charles Edward during the '45 Rebellion; the two brothers were attainted for their Jacobite activities.

The lands of Amisfield were used as a military camp during the Jacobite Rebellion. The day after the Hon Francis's marriage in September 1745 to Lady Catherine Gordon, (after whom 'Lady Kitty's Doocot' takes its name) 6th daughter of the Duke of Gordon, the bridal party, on its way to New Amisfield, was given warning of the 'enemy's' approach. It was a false alarm and not unexpected and much to his Lordship's amusement Sir John Cope's men made ready for battle. Cope extricated himself from embarrassment by thanking his men for their vigilance. (1.p.57)

On the death of his elder brother, David, Francis became Lord Elcho and was elected MP for the Haddington Burghs at the general election of 1780 and again in 1784 (2) in the Tory government of William Pitt the younger. He died at Amisfield in August 1808 aged eighty-five years. Robert Brown of Markle wrote of him,

> "a nobleman whose truly amiable manners endeared him to all who were honoured with his acquaintance, the whole tenor of whose active life seemed to be one continued series of kindness, friendship, and philanthropy" (14.p.246).

He was interred in the family aisle in St Mary's Church. He was succeeded by his grandson who had also inherited the Earldom of March; his only son, also Francis Charteris Wemyss, died six months before him aged forty-one years. The 1819 plan of Haddington and Nungate shows 'The Property of the Earl of Wemyss and March' on the east of the town.

In 1914 at the outbreak of the Great War the military again used Amisfield Park to accommodate wooden huts, the mansion being used for officers. This portended the end of the great mansion house which was deemed beyond repair after the war and was neglected. When Amisfield Mansion House was sadly demolished in 1923 its red sandstone was used for the construction of the new Vert Hospital, the Golf Club house at Longniddry (1929) and the school at Prestonpans.

The lands of Amisfield extending from Whittingehame Drive encompassing the Golf Course were sold by the present Earl of Wemyss in 1960 to the Town Council for the bargain price of £49,000. This allowed further expansion of Haddington and, in 1964, 189 houses plus 100 garages were built on part of Amisfield Mains at a cost of £750,000.

Artillery Park

The houses of Artillery Park, Craig Avenue, Traprain Terrace and the old section of Riverside Drive, 250 of them, were built in 1958 for the 'Glasgow overspill' - an agreement reached in 1957 between the authorities of Haddington and Glasgow. This was the first of its kind in Scotland to encourage families from Glasgow, where there existed a serious problem of overcrowding and housing shortage, to settle in Haddington. Provost William Crowe and Town Clerk John McVie were the negotiators for this successful arrangement and the Scottish Special Housing Association agreed to match Haddington's Town Council house for house. Accordingly 125 houses were built by the Town Council and a further 125 by the SSHA.

Artillery Park, between Dunbar Road and Traprain Terrace, north of the Tyne, takes its name from the fact that the park was used by the military during the period which followed the French Revolution (the Bastille fell in July 1789) - the authorities feared several uprisings especially when the French Revolutionaries offered their assistance to any Radicals in Europe who wanted to rid themselves of their tyrannical monarchies. The French had declared war on Britain on 1st February 1793 and by March 1798 an invasion seemed imminent; the possibility that the enemy could invade from the North Sea into East Lothian was considered to be a strong possibility.

The land around Artillery Park was used for army huts, 34 of which were used to accommodate 13 army officers and 288 non-commissioned officers. Workshops were built for smiths, farriers, saddlers and wheelers. Drills were a regular occurrence on the East Haugh. There was a signal station on East Garleton Hill and Templedean, Gourlaybank, Goatfield and Vetch Park had 104 huts for 74 officers and 1084 men with stables for 40 horses and a hospital.

Ba' Alley and the Old Bowling Green

B all Alley and the old Bowling green were created from moneys collected from the townsfolk of Haddington in response to a flood disaster at East Saltoun. The ford at East Saltoun had been washed away during the flood of 1660 and Haddington's Town Council in a spirit of good neighbourliness proposed to build a bridge to replace the old ford.

It took two years to collect sufficient money during which time there was a long dry spell. The proposed bridge now seemed unnecessary and so the money was used to create Ball Alley as an amenity for the people of Haddington. In 1657 the Council had proposed *"ane house at and wall about and laying out the ground of ane boulling grein in the Sands."* It became the first bowling green in Scotland when bowls were purchased and a greenkeeper appointed. However, twelve years passed before the green was ready and in 1670 a nineteen-years lease was granted to Robert Millar, the town's apothecary who, although given permission to erect a three-storey building, could not afford the upkeep of the bowling green which was abandoned.

In 1749 Robert Thomson and Provost George M'Call gained the lease of the "waste ground at the bridge" and the Old Bowling Green was born. It is clearly marked on the 1819 Plan of Haddington

Ba' Alley lies between St Mary's Parish Church and the Tyne where, on each Shrove Tuesday, a game of football was played between masters and scholars of the Grammar School. This contest started about 1799 and football was played there for many years.

Ba'Alley has been the venue for many events and celebrations over the decades: for example, in June 1900 Haddington celebrated the fall of Pretoria during the Boer War with a torchlight procession which culminated with a huge bonfire 15 feet in height and 60 feet in circumference.(1) Fun fairs were regular and popular events and Ba' Alley was the venue for the bonfires of Guy Fawkes nights.

Baird Terrace

Baird Terrace, between Hawthornbank Road and Aberlady Road, commemorates Major William and Lady Hersey Baird of Lennoxlove. This street was named during the 1940s when the houses were built.

At Lennoxlove the Bairds were well known in Haddington for their community service and generosity. The Major was Deputy Lieutenant of East Lothian County, a Councillor for eleven years, Chairman of the Territorial Army Association, Vice-President of the United East Lothian Agricultural Society, President of the East Lothian Antiquarian and Field Naturalists' Society, a member of the Haddington School Management Committee and an elder of Bolton Church. During the depression of the 1930s the Bairds welcomed unemployed men in the area to come to Lennoxlove and to cut up fallen trees for firewood.

William Arthur Baird was born on 20th March 1879. His father was Sir David Baird, 3rd Baronet of Newbyth, and his mother, the Hon. Ellen Stewart, was a daughter of the last Lord Blantyre. William Baird was their second son and he was educated at Winchester College. In 1900, aged 21 years, he inherited the estates of Lennoxlove and Erskine in Renfrewshire through his paternal grandfather, the last (the 12th) Lord Blantyre.

He took up residence at Erskine House and his great interest in agriculture, experimenting in quality breeding and in dairy farming led to his election as Vice-president of the Renfrewshire Agricultural Society. In politics he was an enthusiastic supporter of the Renfrewshire Unionist Association and in military matters he became a member of the Territorial Army Association in 1910, being appointed its chairman in 1920. Although not physically strong for service abroad he joined the Lothian and Borders Horse attaining the rank of major to serve at home during the 1914-18 war in command of 'A' Squadron.

In 1908 he married Lady Hersey Constance Evlyn Conyngham. Her title was Irish as the third daughter of the 4th Marquis of Conyngham She was born in Ireland on 24th September 1887. Her grandfather, the 3rd Marquis, was the Lord Chamberlain during the Whig government of Melbourne and he, with the Archbishop of Canterbury, had the duty of awakening the eighteen year-old Princess Victoria during the early hours of 20th June 1837 to give her the news of the death of her uncle, William IV.

For the first two years of their married life Major William and Lady Hersey lived at Erskine House in Renfrewshire. In 1910, Major Baird's mother, Lady Ellen Baird, died and Major Baird decided to sell Erskine House and to move to Lennoxlove where their two sons, David and Robert, and three daughters, Evelyn, Margaret and Hersey, were born. Major William and Lady Hersey carried out extensive restoration work, their architect being Sir Robert Stodart Lorimer who had completed the Thistle Chapel at St Giles Cathedral in Edinburgh as well as the Scottish National War Memorial at Edinburgh Castle.

The Major pursued his interest in stock-rearing and in particular, pig breeding becoming Vice-president of the United East Lothian Agricultural Society. From 1913 until 1922 he represented Bolton Parish Council on the Western Committee of East Lothian County Council and in 1929 he was elected County Councillor for Bolton and Saltoun. Simultaneously, he was Vice-Chairman of the Police Committee and a member of several other committees: Public Health, Property and Buildings, Valuation and General Purposes and the Road Board. He was also a member of the Haddington District Council and the Joint Public Assistance Committee. He was appointed a Justice of the Peace and Deputy Lieutenant of the County in 1918. He was therefore well known in the County not only for his enormous service to the County but for his care, concern and kindness for the poor.

In addition to his public service his interest in the history of East Lothian manifested itself in the foundation of the East Lothian Antiquarian and Field Naturalists' Society and having chaired a public meeting on 10th May 1924 he was invited to become the Society's first President. In 1927 he invited the members of the Society to visit Lennoxlove and he wrote his *Lethington (Lennoxlove) and its Owners* for publication in the 1929-30 edition of the Transactions of the Society.

The sudden death of Major Baird on 6th June 1933 at the comparatively young age of 54 and due to peritonitis was a shock to the whole community. He was buried in the Newbyth family burying-ground at Whitekirk Church cemetery.

Lady Hersey Baird continued his good work by giving devoted community service to East Lothian. From 1924 until 1930 she was East Lothian Branch President of the Scottish Central Council Branch of the British Red Cross. She was appointed a Justice of the Peace in 1934 and was a member of the County Council. Their second son, Robert, inherited Lennoxlove, David having inherited the baronetcy* and the estate at Newbyth. Lady Hersey moved firstly to Eventyr in Longniddry. She died aged 75 years on 6th August 1962 at Mount Charles in North Berwick and was buried beside her husband at Whitekirk Church cemetery. Robert Baird sold the lands and property of Lennoxlove in 1946 to Douglas-Hamilton, the 14th Duke of Hamilton.

A little of the background of the change of the name Lethington to Lennoxlove is interesting - the Will of the Duchess of Lennox (ref. Lennox Road) made provision for her nephew, Lord Blantyre, for the purchase of a mansion house in Scotland. Accordingly Lethington was acquired and a further provision of her Will required that its name be changed to **Lennoxlove** in memory of her love for her husband, the Duke of Lennox and Richmond (q.v.), who died in an accident when he fell from a ship in Denmark. She died on 22nd October 1702 and was buried at Westminster. The property was inherited by her nephew, the Master of Blantyre. The Masters of Blantyre owned Lennoxlove from 1702 for the next 250 years. On the death of the last Lord Blantyre (the 12th) in 1900 Lennoxlove was inherited by his second daughter, Ellen, who was married to Sir David Baird of Newbyth.

*The 1st Baronetcy of Newbyth was conferred on David Baird (1757-1829) by George III after a distinguished military career in India, Egypt, the Cape of Good Hope, the Siege of Copenhagen and at Corunna during the Peninsular War. He was promoted to General and knighted after the capture of Aboukir Bay in 1801 when Sir Ralph Abercrombie was killed and Baird captured 20,000 French soldiers. He was created 1st Baronet of Newbyth after the tactical retreat at Corunna in 1808 and he received the thanks of Parliament for the fourth time. But it was early in his military career that he captured the imagination of the nation when as a young captain he was captured at Seringapatam during the 2nd Mysore War. He was imprisoned in irons for three and a half years in a hell-hole and when his mother heard of his plight she was reputed to have remarked, "God help the man that's chained to oor Davie."

Bearford Place,
Hepburn Road
Monkmains Road,
Monkrigg Place and Road,
Seggarsdean Court, Crescent, Park, Place and Road

B **earford Place** off Seggarsdean Crescent takes its name from the farms East and West Bearford near Morham and owned by John Hepburn of Bearford (1770-1823) after whom **Hepburn Road**, between Princess Mary Road and Fortune Avenue, is named.

Several streets in this south-east extremity of Haddington take their names from surrounding farms: for example, **Monkmains Road**, between the Nungate and the Gifford Road, is named after Monkmains farm; **Monkrigg Road** after Monkrigg farm, about a mile south of Monkmains, also owned by John Hepburn and **Seggarsdean Crescent, Court, Park and Terrace** is named after Seggarsdean Farm, one mile east of Monkmains. [Lammermuir Crescent was originally named Sprotlands Crescent which was named from Sprotlands Farm].

Gray and Jamieson's *A Short History of Haddington* (1.p.44) makes mention of: "Lady Beirfoord's house" (renamed Maitlandfield) where a Captain Roger Legge made his residence during the occupancy of a detachment of General Monck's force in 1657. Cromwell had left for England after his victory on 3rd September 1650 at the battle of Dunbar and left Monck as his Scottish representative.

J ohn Hepburn was a relatively young man when he succeeded to the leases of the farms of Monkrigg and West and East Bearford. There was a 'Monkrigg Benevolent Fund' which disbursed £5 annually to each of the old and poor people of the parish for over sixty years in the 19th century. The benefactor was James More who had inherited the estates of Monkrigg following a lawsuit.(1.p.127).

John Hepburn was born at the manse of Athelstansford in 1770. He was educated in Edinburgh at the 'Tounis College' - the University - when it consisted 'of nothing else than a mass of ruined buildings of very ancient construction' (15.Vol.III p.20).

Hepburn distinguished himself as a student and after leaving the university he lived in London and travelled extensively through Europe. He was greatly influenced by the ideals of the Revolutionaries in France.

He returned to Haddington in 1800 having inherited the farm leases. He decided to live at Bearford where the rent was ten shillings per Scotch acre. Having studied new innovations of farming, he treated the land with a liberal dose of lime and increased production for several years. He inherited another farm at Sydserf in the parish of North Berwick which added to his considerable wealth, estimated at £30,000 (about £3 million today). He had the old castle at Bearford demolished and built his farmhouse with a water mill and the mile-long lead from Morham Burn to Shuit-her-tae Mill. On the latter he spent about £2000 and in its day this mill was 'the best and most powerful in the county' (14.p.390).

Hepburn continued to use modern farming methods and his farms prospered to such an extent that they became models for others to follow. In fact, he wrote many articles for the Agricultural Society of Saltoun and won several of the Society's medals. He became a recognised authority in farming methods in East Lothian.

His interests were not confined to farming: in politics he courted dangerously with Republican sympathisers. During his visits abroad he had met several revolutionaries in Paris, including the feared Robespierre who was Public Accuser at that time. In addition he met the audacious Danton who voted for the death of Louis XVI and was himself guillotined. He met with the vitriolic and powerful Maran who had to hide in the sewers of Paris to escape his enemies. Hepburn's vindication of Robespierre was published in the London Review in 1796 and on his return from France he expressed the view,

> "in a short time there will be liberty, fraternity, and equality in this country - servants will be equal to their masters, and Lord Wemyss and all other aristocrats will be no better than common men, and their lands will be divided among the citizens." (2. p.393).

This was an incautious statement during this time of the Dundas-Pitt 'reign of terror' when several of Hepburn's friends such as

Thomas Muir, Thomas Palmer, William Skirving, Maurice Margarot and Joseph Gerald (whose names are inscribed on the Political Martyrs' Monument in the Old Calton Burying Ground in Edinburgh) had been tried and sentenced, by the feared Lord Braxfield, to many years of transportation to Botany Bay. Hepburn was watched but no action was taken against him. Martine in his *Reminiscences* (14) describes Hepburn as: 'a gentleman of the most honourable feelings. Kind, hospitable, and facile to a fault, possessed of abilities of mind far above the average, sober, and never extravagant in person or habits, he yet ran through a large fortune, and died at the age of fifty-three in penury and distress.' (14. p.393).

For many years John Hepburn had been an 'easy touch' to dozens of scroungers who had taken his hospitality and borrowed large sums of money from him. The debts were never repaid; 'his property and effects having been devoured by ravenous wolves - wrongly called friends.' Even his servants stole from him knowing that they would never be challenged by their trusting master.

Finally, in 1823, forced to clear out of his fine house at Bearford, he moved to Edinburgh to take up a post as editor of a magazine but the stress due to his debts and the enormous upheaval in moving to Edinburgh caused his death before he could embark upon his new career.

Brown Street

B rown Street, off the south side of Market Street at its eastern end, leads into the High Street; it was known as Strumpet Lane around 1531. A further reference to this name is dated 1764 when one William Thompson was ordered to rebuild his house there (2.p.227). When the 'Old Post House' was renamed 'The George', Strumpet Lane was changed to George Inn Wynd and finally to Brown Street (14.p.46). It is thought to have been named from a little general store known as 'Brown's Shop'.

John Brown Court

J ohn Brown Court is the converted Burgher Church built in 1806 behind the manse which is reached from the north side of Market Street. John Brown Court was named in 1989 after the famous minister, the Reverend John Brown who died over 200 years ago in 1787. A plaque on the manse wall is inscribed:

'John Brown DD lived in this house for 30 years and here wrote his "Self-interpreting Bible". He died here in 1787 and was buried in Haddington. Original manuscripts of his works can be seen in the public library Newton Port.'

A Burne-Jones stained glass memorial window is dedicated to him in the south aisle of the nave in St Mary's Parish Church.

The story of John Brown is one of a 'lad o' pairts' so greatly admired in Scotland. John Brown was a humble herd boy in the Parish of Abernethy where he attended the local school for a mere two years in the first half of the eighteenth century. He was born in the small village of Carpow in 1722 and his father, a poor weaver, insisted that his son be sent to school to learn the basics of reading, writing and arithmetic. His reading skills would have been gained from *The A B C with the Shorter Catechism* and as far as numeracy was concerned he would have learned from *How to know the numbers from one up to a thousand* at the end of *The Lord's Prayer, Creed, Graces*. After his meagre schooling he became a shepherd boy.

There was no thought that the boy should enter the ministry, not for the want of Christian sincerity but from the economic impossibility of such an apparently unattainable ambition. However young John Brown, unknown to his father, studied Latin for one month. This was followed by the study of philosophy and divinity supervised by the local minister, the Rev. Ebeneezer Erskine. During his long treks in the hills he put his mind to the further study of Latin and Greek, always returning to the minister for help with a difficult passage.

Such studies by a country lad were so unusual as to arouse the suspicions of the superstitious local community who remembered the black days of witch burning and devil worship. John Brown's learning and sparkling intelligence frightened them and, as was so often the case, their fear turned into threats of violence. His exceptional learning was attributed to Satan; he was forced to undergo an inquisition - it is a remarkable coincidence that many years later his malicious inquisitor was excommunicated on the day that John Brown was licensed to preach the Gospel (22).

John Brown had to clear out of his village; there was no sense in alienating the villagers because of something they did not understand. He became a wandering packman. He had been orphaned by the age of eleven years, but to quote his eighth son, Samuel Brown: 'he used to aver in his hyperbolical way that he had never missed his parents, for when his father and mother had forsaken him the Lord had taken him up.' (27. p.3).

In 1745, the year of the Jacobite Rebellion, we find him in Edinburgh during the month of Bonnie Prince Charlie's occupation of the city and John Brown, disgusted by the barbarity of the Jacobite Highlanders and fearful of a return to Catholicism, joined the garrison forces in Edinburgh Castle. Soon after the butchery at Culloden he returned to the wanderings of a packman but he was not content, the acquisition of wealth held no interest for him; he became a teacher and started his own school in 1747 near Kinross. Its success was due not only to his sincerity but to the fact that being self-taught he, more than most, understood the learning difficulties of his pupils; eight of them entered the ministry.

His own studies were remarkable, in one evening after school he memorised fifteen chapters of the book of Genesis. He rarely required more than four hours sleep; his work schedule was prodigious. In addition to his studies of Latin, Greek and Hebrew he learned several oriental languages and during school vacations he attended classes in philosophy and divinity under the Rev. Ebeneezer Erskine and James Fisher. He easily satisfied the Presbytery of Edinburgh and gained his licence to preach the Gospel.

In 1751, on completion of his probationary period, he was offered two calls - one from Haddington and the other from Stow. He chose the Burgher Church of Haddington partly because this congregation had already received several disappointments but also because this congregation was the smaller and would allow him time to continue his studies. He remained in Haddington for the rest of his life but to compensate for Stow's disappointment he preached there for several Sundays until a new minister arrived.

The 'Breach' of 1747 had brought about the 'Burghers' and 'Anti-Burghers'. The latter considered it unlawful to take the Burgess Oath swearing allegiance to King George and renunciation of the 'Old Pretender'. The Anti-Burghers however, were more concerned that by swearing the oath they would be committing themselves to acceptance, 'to their life's end', of a 'mutilated form, a corrupted shadow' of the reformed religion (22). As far as the lawfulness or otherwise of the oath, John Brown had his doubts; he believed that the dispute merely split the Church unnecessarily and he preached forbearance but he remained with the Burgher Synod.

When John Brown arrived in Haddington to take up his new charge one member of the congregation expressed his opposition. John Martine in his 'Reminiscences' relates the conversation:

"Why do you think of leaving us?" mildly inquired Mr Brown.
"Because I don't think you a good preacher," said the sturdy oppositionist.
"That is quite my own opinion," admitted the minister, "but the great majority of the congregation think the

reverse, and it would not do for you and me to set up
our opinions against theirs. I have given in, you see,
and I would suggest you might do so too."

"Weel, weel," said the grumbler, quite reconciled by
Mr Brown's frank confession, "I think I'll just follow
your example, sir." (14.p.73).

Courtesy of Eric Groome

John Brown was Professor of Divinity to the Associate Burgher
Synod for twenty-five years. This was a 'labour of love'; it was
an unpaid post in which he taught students in a five-year course
for entry to the ministry of the Secession. During his ministry he
took four services each Sunday and regularly visited members
of his poor congregation. He found time to write his famous
Self-Interpreting Bible, the two volumes of which were published
in 1778 for family worship after church. A copy of his Bible is
displayed on his pulpit in St Mary's Church.

His stipend was £50 per year and his publications earned him
little money but were testimony to his great scholarship. His other,
perhaps less well-known, works were equally scholarly and
included his *Dictionary of the Holy Bible*, in two volumes, *A
History of the Churches of Scotland and England, from the
earliest period* in two volumes and many others.

His influence reached the young poet Robert Fergusson (1750-74), so admired by Robert Burns, who was said to have burned several of his unpublished works and took to a study of the Bible after his meeting with this sincere minister. John Brown was also respected for his work in natural sciences and for his knowledge of Oriental and European languages including Arabic, Syriac, Persian, Ethiopic, French, Spanish, Italian, Dutch and German. A man of great intellect, his preaching was powerful and scholarly and yet his message was clearly understood by the humblest of his congregation. A strong voice in support of religious freedom, he raised questions about the alliance of the church with the state. A staunch Calvinist, he corresponded with and befriended the Countess of Huntingdon in her stand against Arminianism (the Arminians were against rigid Calvinism and were suspected of trying to re-introduce Catholicism).

John Brown's first wife was Janet Thomson, daughter of a Musselburgh merchant. They had eighteen years of happy marriage and several children but only two sons, John and Ebeneezer survived. Both entered the Secession ministry. In 1773, two years after the death of his first wife he married Violet Croumbie of Stenton; they had nine children.

John Brown never retired, he dedicated his life to the church and to his adoring congregation. Early in 1787 the effects of his punishing work load had taken their toll; he was exhausted. He preached his last sermon on 25th January. His weakened state was obvious to his congregation and as he preached his farewell message they sensed that this was to be his last service; they cried openly. After thirty-six years as minister he died on 19th June 1787 and he was buried in St Mary's Parish Churchyard,

Haddington. Many admirers from far off places and the whole population of Haddington attended. His tombstone is inscribed:

To the Memory of
MR. JOHN BROWN
Thirty-six years Minister of the Gospel
At Haddington
and Twenty-five Years PROFESSOR OF DIVINITY
under the Associate Synod
After maintaining an eminent Character for
PIETY, CHARITY, LEARNING, AND DILIGENCE
he died
Rejoicing in the hope of the Glory of God
And admiring the riches of Divine Grace to him as a sinner,
The 19th June, A.D. 1787,
AGED 65 YEARS

Four of his sons entered the ministry: Rev. John Brown of Longridge, Rev. Ebeneezer Brown of Inverkeithing, Rev. Dr. Thomas Brown of Dalkeith and Rev. George Brown of North Berwick. His eighth son, Samuel Brown, was the last Provost of Haddington under the old self-perpetuating Council with its trade bailies and councillors and he was the first to be elected under the Reformed system in 1833. He founded the Haddington School of Art and started the first of the East Lothian 'Itinerating Libraries'.

As a final tribute to Haddington's great and scholarly minister the great philosopher and historian David Hume, on hearing one of Brown's sermons, was heard to remark,

"that old man speaks as if Christ stood at his elbow."

BURLEY'S WALLS or BURLIEGH'S WA'S

B urley's Walls, known locally as Birlie's Wa's, is a narrow passage off Brown Street. The derivation of the name Burley is unknown. A local version refers to an old worthy called Burley who frequented the area around Brown Street to join his companions for the purpose of liquid refreshment; he was known to imbibe heavily in alcoholic beverage. When he was sufficiently *non compos mentis* children took great joy in 'birlin' him aboot' until he steadied himself against a nearby wall - hence 'Birlies Wa's'. The verb: to birl meaning to spin or to whirl round, also to birle meaning to ply with drink or to carouse.

A more credible version is: the name *Burley* is a corruption of the name Burleigh and that the word wall refers to the old Scottish meaning: *a well or a natural spring of water which forms a pool or stream.*(11) During the 17th century well-diggers, or 'wall-houkers' were in demand in Haddington and elsewhere and one such travelling team of well-diggers possibly from Yorkshire (where Burleigh is a not uncommon name) could have been led by their captain, Edward Right Esq., at the behest of the Magistrates, to "repair and mend with all due haste and speed" the wells in the vicinity of Brown Street (Council Minutes of 26th November 1660). Another minute dated 20th December 1660 refers to:

> *"Counsall Tresorer's Account: sum paid to Edward Right Esq., for mending of (2) 'Burlies Walls, if being mindful in all respects 36 hours of work and time at the cost of £0005 00 00."*

A margin note makes reference to: *"the fastening of the (entangled) chain and capping of (2) Burlies Waals"*

It was not until 1869 that a water company was established in Haddington. There were public wells in the High Street and in Hardgate and several private wells existed until 1874 when, for an outlay of £5000, a copious supply of pure spring water was obtained from the reservoir at Chesters on the estate of the Earl of Wemyss.

The Butts

Access to The Butts may be gained from either the High Street via Ross's Close or from Sidegate via Langriggs. This Sheltered Housing scheme by the Bield Housing Association Ltd was built from 1979 and named in 1981.

It is thought that the name The Butts is derived from the 'bow buttis' or the archery butts which existed at the Sands during the 16th century. There may well have been archery butts in the vicinity of The Butts.

James I (r.1406-1437) had been imprisoned at the English Court for 18 years and had observed the excellence of English archery. On his return to Scotland in April 1424 (a ransom of £40,000 having been paid by the Scots) he had become anxious about the apparent neglect of archery among Scotsmen; he ridiculed their awkwardness in handling their bows in his humorous poem of Christ's Kirk. He therefore made a law in his first parliament of 1424:

> *"That all men busk (prepare) thame to be archares*
> *fra the be 12 years of age, and that at ilk ten punds*
> *worth of land thair be made bow markes, and specialle*
> *near paroche kirks, quhairn upon haylie dayis men may*
> *cum, and at the leist schute thyrse about, and have usage*
> *of archarie; and quhasa usis not archerie, the laird of*
> *the land sall rais of him a wedder, and giff the laird*
> *raisis not the said pane, the king's shireff, or his*
> *ministers, sall rais it to the king."*

Archery therefore assumed great importance and was well-practised at The Butts of Haddington before and after James's law.

However, a much simpler explanation of the derivation of the name Butts relates to the buttresses of the old Haddington Wall, part of which still exists in the vicinity of The Butts.

Calder's Lawn

A 1990 addition to the streets of Haddington was Calder's Lawn; it is more of a driveway than a street, being the entrance to the Council's car park, off Newton Port. The land which forms this driveway was acquired from Robin Calder who lived nearby at Dale House (originally the manse for the old church at Alexandra Place).

Calder's Lawn therefore is named after the Calder family of rugby fame. Robin Calder was an unpretentious man who seemed surprised that a street should bear the family name. The Calder family and their four rugby-playing sons became famous, not only in Haddington but throughout Scotland and the UK, when sons Jim and Finlay Calder were 'capped' for Scotland.

Robin Calder's maternal grandparents, Mr and Mrs John Middlemass who farmed at Northrig and West Bearford, preferred to live at Haddington and purchased the old manse and the church, now Alexandra Place, in 1892. The property was only about fifty years old at that time and had been vacated when most of the congregation had voted to form a Free Church to be free of the shackles of Patronage in the church (this was in 1843 shortly after the 'disruption'). It was Robin Calder's maternal grandfather who converted the church into four flats in 1926; the rent was eight shillings per week. His father, Robert Calder, married Miss May Middlemass and after the death of her mother they came to live at Dale House

Robin Calder was born on 23rd June 1923. His parents had farmed in Dumfriesshire but moved back to Haddington when Robin was two years old. He was educated at Knox Primary School and at the Royal High School in Edinburgh where he was a contemporary of solicitor John McVie, then the High School captain, who became Haddington's Town Clerk.

In 1939 Robin Calder left school to work for John Swan & Sons at £40 per year. He learned the profession of the auctioneer from the bottom - he started by chasing cattle and sheep up alleyways to their pens, he helped keep sales records and progressed to be allowed to sell livestock. He was 'called up' in 1942 and posted to the Scots Guards. His initial training was at

Caterham in Surrey. "We weren't allowed out for four months - until we were considered fit to be seen outside", such were the standards expected of Guardsmen. Then to Pirbright for 'action training' followed by further training at Wiltshire, Nottinghamshire, Yorkshire and Kent.

He served at the invasion of France carrying out reconnaissance in light tanks. On one such reconnaissance his tank was attacked by German anti-tank weapons; a shell cut through the steel side of his tank and shot through the other side; not one of his men received a scratch. He attained the rank of Sergeant Tank Commander and, with this armoured division of the Scots Guards, he crossed the Rhine and the Elbe to await the retreating German army from the Russian front; "these German soldiers were very relieved to be captured by the British" said Robin Calder.

In 1947, demobilisation meant his return to John Swan & Sons and he took up auctioneering again, working in Haddington, the Borders and as far north as Caithness with occasional trips to the Orkneys.

His favourite recreation was sport. He played cricket and rugby for Haddington and was captain of the local team. His love of the game was to be instilled in the hearts of his four rugby-playing sons.

Robin Calder married Elizabeth Hamilton, a daughter of Gavin Hamilton, a farmer at Adniston at Macmerry, and her mother, also Elizabeth, was an accomplished singer who was well-known for her concerts in the area. Robin and Elizabeth Calder had four sons: Gavin who is a farm manager in the Borders, Jim who works for Ernst Young Accountants and Finlay and John who work for a grain exporting company, Glencore Grain UK of Montrose. Robin Calder died on 13th March 1995.

The Calder brothers had rugby in their blood and as small boys they practised every move and learned the skill of the game from their father whom they followed into the Haddington Rugby Club. On their arrival at Daniel Stewart's and Melville College in Edinburgh their first choice of sport was rugby. They played for their school every Saturday morning and again for Haddington Rugby Club in the afternoons. Soon they were selected for the school's first team and later for the Former Pupils' team - brilliant careers were launched.

Jim Calder, the elder of the twins, was born on 20th August 1957 and achieved his boyhood ambition at the age of twenty-three when he was selected to play for Scotland against France in Paris. He was 'capped' no fewer than 27 times and in 1983 he toured with the British Lions. But his never-to-be-forgotten great day was his match-winning try to win the 'Grand Slam' for Scotland against the French in 1984. That day he was the hero of all Scotland - the 'Grand Slam' meant defeat at the hands of the Scots for every competing team - the English, the Welsh, the Irish and the French and Jim Calder of Haddington had done it.

The brothers were never selected for Scotland at the same time; Finlay Calder's international career seemed to start when his twin brother Jim's ended. Finlay was first selected as a Scottish internationalist in 1986. Again, this was cause for great celebration in the Calder household and at Haddington Rugby Club where 46 years before the club produced its very first international in the famous Andrew 'Jock' Wemyss (1893-1974), one of the founders. This was a goal for which Finlay had striven all his young life. He was to be capped for Scotland no fewer than 34 times and ultimately to captain Scotland's team in 1989 in which year he was chosen captain of the British Lions.

The year 1990 was the most dramatic of all. Scotland versus England for the 'Grand Slam', the Championship, the triple crown and the Calcutta Cup to be decided on 17th March. It was the talk of all Scotland and England and no doubt every ex-patriot Scot abroad. England seemed invincible; there were no discernible weaknesses, England was favourite. This was to be Scotland's greatest ever triumph and Finlay Calder had the privilege of contributing his best on that momentous day.

Finlay Calder is a grain exporter in Leith and describes his recreation as "work". He lives in the Borders with wife Elizabeth and their family, David and Hazel. He was made an Officer of the Order of the British Empire (OBE) for his services to rugby in 1990. He was recalled to play in the World Cup in 1991.

In Haddington, the Royal Bank of Scotland paid an unusual tribute to the Calder brothers in January 1991 when the bank commissioned two paintings commemorating their triumphs in Scotland's 'Grand Slams' of 1984 and 1990. The first was entitled "The Turning Point" and the other "Underdog Rampant". Matching prints were presented to the Calder family and were proudly displayed at Dale House in Calder's Lawn.

Caponflat Crescent,
Hawthornbank Road

Caponflat Crescent, off Hospital Road, takes its name from the fact that Franciscan monks owned an acre in the "Capoun Flatt" shortly after 1560. (1 p.27).

Caponflat House which is shown on the 1892 plan of Haddington adopted this ancient name, changing it from Hawthornbank House. **Hawthornbank Road**, which runs between Hospital Road and Davidson Terrace is named from this earlier name of the house.

John Wood's 1819 Survey Plan of Haddington and Nungate shows Robert Vetch as the owner of the land in the north-west part of the town and in the vicinity of Vetch Park. In addition, the land between Aberlady Road and Hospital Road which was the 'Property of Robert Vetch Esqre.'

Caponflat House was the residence of Robert Vetch (ref. **Vetch Park**). The change of name from Hawthornbank to Caponflat must have occurred between 1854 and 1892. The 1819 Plan of Haddington and Nungate and the 1854 plan shows 'Hawthornbank' whereas the 1892 plan shows 'Caponflat.'

The Vetch family lived at Hawthornbank House from about the middle of the 18th century. Robert Vetch had three sons and six daughters The twin sons, George and James, had distinguished military careers. No record exists of the third son who may have died early in life.

George Anderson Vetch (1789-1873) served in the 54th Regiment of Native Infantry for 27 years in India where he distinguished himself as a soldier-peace-keeper. He returned home to his estate at Caponflat with the rank of Lieutenant-Colonel in 1859. He proved his talent as a writer and poet and he led the recruitment drive of Haddington men into the Volunteer movement with stirring speeches in the Assembly Rooms when the threat of an invasion by the French seemed imminent.

James Vetch was born on 13th May 1789 and served in Portugal during the Peninsular War. In peace time he became a surveyor, being the first to triangulate Orkney and Shetland and the Western Isles. In Mexico (1824) he was the manager of a silver mine, on returning home he became a railway engineer (1836) and was appointed as consulting engineer to the Admiralty in 1846. He published many learned papers and was a member of several learned societies. His election to Fellowship of the Royal Society (FRS) took place about the same time as that of another great academician, Haddington born Professor George Harley FRS (1829-1896), and was testimony to his internationally recognised academic excellence. James Vetch died in London on 7th December 1869.

The house and grounds of Caponflat were sold by Miss Vetch to the Town Council but a later relative, Henry Vetch (1857-1936), fifth son of Lieutenant-Colonel George Anderson Vetch, re-purchased the property in 1916 and gifted part of the land for the building of the Vert Memorial Hospital. (ref. **Vert Hospital**).

Caponflat House fell into disrepair and was finally demolished during the 1930s for the housing developments of firstly Baird Terrace followed by Davidson Terrace, Hawthornbank Road and later Caponflat Crescent, Hopetoun Drive, Beechwood Road and Hope park Crescent.

Carlyle Court,
Carlyle Gardens

Carlyle Court is a new development off Market Street and Carlyle Gardens, off Florabank Road, in Herdmanflatt was built in 1933 and is named after Thomas Carlyle (1795-1881), the Scottish writer whose influence on English literature astounded his contemporaries; he exposed hypocrisy and sham; he was suspicious of mass movements, even democracy, and he believed strongly in the individual and in strong leadership. He admired Schiller and Goethe and popularised German literature in Britain.

He is commemorated in Haddington not only for his literary genius but because he married the beautiful and intelligent Jane Welsh, daughter of Dr Welsh, a well-respected Haddington surgeon whose house is now the Jane Welsh Museum in Lodge Street and was referred to by Carlyle as: "At home was opulence without waste, elegance, good sense, silent practical affection and manly wisdom, from threshold to rooftree." (4)

Thomas Carlyle was the second son of a stonemason of Ecclefechan in Dumfriesshire and was educated at Ecclefechan School, Annan Academy and at the University of Edinburgh. He did not enjoy the latter and left after four years without a degree. Although he studied the arts he excelled in geometry and his first job, in 1814, was as a teacher of mathematics at Annan and two years later he taught at Kirkcaldy. Teaching pleased him even less than his course at the University and he decided to take up tutoring which he found to be fairly lucrative. It was at about this time that he translated a French geometry book and decided to study law. His poor health made his life miserable; he suffered continuously from indigestion (probably gastric ulcers) but this did not stop him from writing many articles for the *Edinburgh Encyclopaedia*.

His life changed dramatically when he was introduced to Jane Baillie Welsh (1801-66) by her tutor Edward Irving who was a churchman and the first teacher of the 'Mathematical School' - part of the Grammar School of Haddington. She was a bright and vivacious girl who was greatly admired in Edinburgh and

Haddington. She was born at the family home in Lodge Street; her father, the local and well-beloved doctor, was Dr John Welsh and her mother, a kind and capricious lady, was Grace Welsh of Crawford in Lanarkshire; they arrived at Haddington in 1800. Dr Welsh's illustrious antecedents were thought to include John Knox and William Wallace.

Carlyle, in love, threw caution to the winds and defied convention, presumably to impress her, but she was not to be hurried and it was some years before Jane Welsh eventually agreed to marry him on 17th October 1826. In celebration, Carlyle gave a generous donation towards the building of the Knox Institute in Haddington.

At first they lived in Edinburgh at No.21 Comely Bank for eighteen months during which time he wrote his translations from Tieck, Musaus and Richter (four volumes) and an article on Jean Paul Richter for the *Edinburgh Review*. For the next six years the Carlyles lived in her father's ancestral house 'Craigenputtock' on the Solway Moors. In this solitude he wrote *A History of German Literature*, several articles on Burns, Samuel Johnson, Goethe, Voltaire and others. But it was his famous Sartor Resartus (the Tailor Retailored) - his philosophy of existence which caused an uproar when it was published. These volumes were the results of dedicated research during which he taught himself foreign languages in order to study documents and books in their original tongue.

Jane, writing from Craigenputtock to her cousin, Eliza Stodart of George Square, Edinburgh, describes her thoughts:

"The solitude is not so irksome as one might think. If we are cut off from good society, we are also delivered from bad; the roads are less pleasant to walk on than the pavement of Princes Street, but we have horses to ride, and, instead of shopping and making calls, I have bread to bake and chickens to hatch. I read and work, and talk with my husband and never weary. Letters from Germany and all parts of the earth reach us here just as before. It is so strange to see 'Craigenputtock' written in Goethe's hand."

Carlyle was attracted back to London in 1834, his previous visit having been during his tutoring days, ten years before, when he published his *Life of Schiller*. They settled in No.5 Cheyne

Row, Chelsea where he wrote many essays and biographies including his largest work which took twelve years to complete - the *Life of Frederick the Great*. Then followed his famous histories of the *French Revolution* which gave him well-deserved recognition as a literary genius.

He delivered several paid lectures on German literature, the history of literature and many others which were duly published and such was his reputation, he earned the sobriquet, "the Sage of Chelsea". The Carlyle residence was the centre of London's literati. Jane Welsh was a most brilliant, attractive and accomplished hostess and when she died suddenly, only three weeks after his Rectorial address to the students of the University of Edinburgh, Carlyle was heart-broken. His sadness worsened into remorse when he discovered from his wife's journals and letters that she had suffered badly due to his neglect of her wishes during a period of their married life. He discovered too late that her brilliant writing: *The Letters and Memorials of Jane Welsh Carlyle* made her one of the cleverest critics of her day. She was buried beside her father at St Mary's Church in Haddington.

Carlyle's brother John, who was a doctor, came to live with him in Chelsea but Carlyle was ascerbic and another relative replaced him, but again only for a short period. His niece, Mary Carlyle Aitken, was persuaded to move from her house at No. 30 Newbattle Terrace in Edinburgh to Chelsea. She ignored the irascible reputation ascribed to her uncle. Instead, she thought of him as kind and considerate. Carlyle, however, described himself as a "dyspeptic polar bear." She became his housekeeper, nurse and amanuensis for the next twelve years during which she was an indispensable assistant in his revision of the 34-volume Library Edition of his works. He continued writing on British democracy in his article, Shooting Niagara published in Macmillan's Magazine in 1867. He received many honours but he refused to accept Prime Minister Disraeli's offer of a baronetcy.

In the summer of 1879, during one of his annual visits to Dumfriesshire, his brother John lay dying and Carlyle delayed his return to London. His niece, Mary, married her cousin in August of that summer and Carlyle, who had himself suffered ill health, was sufficiently well to allow his enjoyment of the happy occasion. A year later Mary and her husband, having set up home with Carlyle in London, had a baby boy which they named Thomas after his eminent great-uncle. The old man, now visibly weaker, never-the-less took a keen interest in his great-nephew. He visited Haddington for the last time in 1880 to kneel by his wife's grave at St Mary's Parish Church.

Carlyle died on 5th February 1881, aged eighty-six, surrounded by mementoes of his wife Jane. His dying wish was to be buried near his family in Ecclefechan, even though Westminster was offered.

His favourite water-colour, by Helen Allingham in 1879, portrays him reading from his armchair; the oval portrait of Oliver Cromwell in the background is a reminder of another of his great works, *The Life and Letters of Oliver Cromwell*. The painting is exhibited in the Scottish National Portrait Gallery in Queen Street, Edinburgh.

Church Street

Church Street, at the east end of Haddington, off Sidegate leads to the Sands and to the Nungate Bridge and undoubtedly takes its name from the existence of the Franciscan monastery which supposedly stood on the site of the present day Elm House (2 p.176). McWilliam (26) places the Franciscan Friars' Church on the site of Holy Trinity Church.

It was richly endowed and so magnificent that it came to be known as "Lucerna Laudoniae" or the "Lamp of Lothian." This name was given to it because of its bright lights which could be seen from afar by lonely travellers at night. The monastery was almost destroyed in 1355 when Edward III invaded Scotland during the so-called 'third war of Scotland' but it was restored to its former glory and re-endowed with 15 altars. However, John Major (1469-1550), the distinguished theologian and historian of East Lothian, expressed his disapproval against the holy fathers who indulged in such an ostentatious edifice.

In 1804 the Town Council decided, in the interests of road widening, to demolish St Ann's Chapel which was another ecclesiastical institution in Church Street and from which **St Ann's Place** takes its name.

The Episcopal Church, Holy Trinity, in Church Street was built in 1769-70, the 6th (or de jure 8th) Earl of Wemyss subscribing to half the cost of building. The eastern apse was built in 1930 and the wall surrounding the church was built from stones taken from the old Town Wall of 1597.

The two-storey block opposite the church is a 1960 restoration of the mid-18th century old Burgh School with its red sandstone quoins and its central chimney gable into local authority houses (Nos. 14-16). Its lower whitewashed neighbour with two chimney gables has the popular Haddington Day Centre incorporated at ground floor level. Elm House at the far end of Church street was built in 1785. Picturesque **St Anne's Gate**, off the south side of Church Street, is entered through a wide arch and has a relief panel of the Haddington goat above; the restoration was undertaken by architect John A W Grant in 1955.

County Buildings

The foundation stone of the County Buildings in Court Street was laid on 27th May 1833 by Sir Gordon Sinclair Stevenson, Baronet. This Anglo-Gothic edifice was designed by William Burn (1789-1870), the well-known architect whose reputation was already established from his Jacobean addition to Lauriston Castle, John Watson's School, Edinburgh Academy, St John's in Princes Street etc.

The Town House was, by 1831, too small for the judiciary and an Act of Parliament of 6th June 1832 permitted that the sum of £5250 could be raised in the burgh at a rate not exceeding three pence in the pound of valuation of houses and lands. The sum included an amount to allow the purchase of 'eligible properties'. (2.p.229)

Miller in his *Lamp of Lothian* (2.p.229) explained the choice of site in King Street, (the former name of Court Street), for the proposed building:

'The site chosen was that of the remains of one of the oldest buildings in the burgh, which appeared to have been of considerable extent, and to which tradition assigned the importance of a palace. The ruins removed consisted of a vault, and part of an arched passage communicating with it. The pillars of the arches were of Saxon order. In the fountain-stone of the new

buildings is deposited a bottle, hermetically sealed, containing several current coins of the realm, printed extracts of the proceedings of the county in reference to the erection of the building, a copy of the Act of Parliament, and Miller's East Lothian Register.'
The latter document contains a drawing of the old palace.

William Burn specified that the stone for the facade should be obtained from Culello quarry in Fife and the remaining stone from the local Jerusalem quarry.

A committee was appointed to control and manage the erection of the building which cost a little over £3000 plus £960 for the purchase of property. The Committee members were: The Marquis of Tweeddale, Lord-Lieutenant; Sir John Gordon Sinclair; Sir David Kinloch; David Anderson of St Germains; James Hamilton of Bangour; and Robert Riddell, sheriff-substitute.

Immediately in front of the County Buildings there is an impressive crown-topped monument commemorating the committee's chairman; it is inscribed:

Erected by Public Subscription
AD 1881
In Grateful Remembrance of
The Public Services in War and in Peace of
George, VIIIth Marquis of Tweeddale FM,KT,GCB.
Lord Lieutenant of Haddingtonshire
Born February 1st 1787 died October 16th 1876

Extensions to the County Building were added to the west along Court Street in 1931 by Dick Peddie & Walker Todd and the Court House itself was extended to the south by Peter Whitson in 1956.

Court Street

A ccording to the 1819 Plan of Haddington and Nungate, the street which is now Court Street was part of the old High Street. The latter stretched from the George Hotel to the Ferguson Monument. However, according to Gray and Jamieson (1.p.139) Court Street was originally named King Street, no doubt as an allusion to the fact that the palace of Alexander II was situated on the site of the Sheriff Court. The name was changed to Court Street in 1833 after the foundation stone of the new Court House was laid by Sir Gordon Sinclair Stevenson, Baronet on 27th May of that year.

The Court House was designed by the Edinburgh born architect, William Burn (1789-1870). He chose an Anglo-Gothic (Tudor) style for his design.

In addition to the County Buildings in Court Street there is the Corn Exchange which was designed by Francis Farquharson in 1853. It was opened on 29th September 1854 by Provost George More. This was the regular venue for the Friday markets of local farmers; it is now a well-used community hall.

The most recent building in Court Street is the Fire Station by Reiach and Hall and built in 1964. The Post Office, by William T. Oldrieve (1853-1922) was built in 1908 and the Police Station is pre-1819. There are several 18th and early 19th century stately town mansions such as No.32, the Royal Bank of Scotland which was the home of seed merchant and Provost William Dods who was a friend of Jane Welsh Carlyle. It was in this 19th century mansion that the body of Jane Welsh Carlyle, brought from London by her husband Thomas Carlyle, lay prior to her funeral at St Mary's Parish Church on 2nd April 1866. No. 44, the Bank of Scotland, was built c1850 as the British Linen Bank and is adorned with decorative panels, urns and sphinx.

Hilton Lodge Nursing Home, formerly Craig Lodge (as shown on the 1819 Plan of Haddington and the Nungate) in red brick, is set back and has an attractive walled garden in front. The original building was a two-storey villa and became the residence of Francis Farquharson, the Haddington builder and architect who added the present red brick frontage about 1850 (ref. Hilton Lodge).

The West Church (formerly the Free Church), built in 1890 in red sandstone, obtained its land from John Farquharson of Hilton Lodge (eldest son of Francis Farquharson above) for the sum of £500 in 1889.

Craig Avenue

Craig Avenue runs between Artillery Park and Traprain Terrace just north of the Tyne. It is named after Provost Hugh Craig who farmed Harperdean off Aberlady Road.

Hugh Craig was born on 8th March 1887 at Littlehill Farm in Cadder between Bishopbriggs and Lenzie. In 1891 the Craig family moved to Westerhill Farm so that young Hugh could attend Lenzie Academy. In 1903 they moved south to Surrey; their new home was Well Farm (now a listed building) in Banstead.

Having failed to obtain a farm tenancy in Kent, Hugh Craig decided to try his luck in Canada and at the age of twenty-six, in 1913, he worked his way across that vast country. He had left his future wife, Martha Thomson, behind with the intention of asking her to join him when he had his own farm. Meantime negotiations for a farm in East Lothian were progressing; his mother journeyed from Surrey to Harperdean in Haddington and the deal was clinched by cable to Canada. Hugh rushed home to Britain arriving by boat at Liverpool where he was met by his beloved Martha. They were married in Liverpool on 3rd March 1914 and before travelling to Scotland the young couple spent some time with Hugh's mother at Banstead. His father had died shortly after their move to Surrey.

Life at Harperdean was tough at first but Martha, the daughter of an Ayrshire born East Lothian farmer, was made of strong stuff and soon made Harperdean a home of which to be proud. The farm had been neglected and it took many years to bring it into a sound condition of mixed arable and animal production.

Their children, two girls and a boy were born there and Hugh Craig became an elder of St Mary's Parish Church. He held broad ecumenical views and promoted friendship and co-operation between various denominations. In this respect he was ahead of his time as inter-denominational relationships were often strained in the '50s. He was a keen curler and was selected to play for the Scottish team when they toured Canada. As a father, he loved his family. His daughter Helen recalled their pony 'Robin' with the letter 'C' branded on his neck to indicate that he had been 'cast' from the army; this was due to the fact that Robin had a tendency to shy. On one occasion he bolted in Haddington complete with his light cart. Its wheels soon fell off and a few soldiers, billeted in Haddington, tried to stop the runaway but to no avail. It fairly flew along Market Street into Court Street and finally Robin, no doubt tired out, came to a halt near the railway station - amazingly, no-one was hurt.

Courtesy of Mrs Helen Miller (daughter of Hugh Craig)

The happy life of the Craig family was devastated in 1946 when their only son, James Hubert Craig, a Flying Officer in the Royal Air Force, was killed in Burma on 26th March 1946. He had just completed a mercy mission delivering food to the starving Burmese. On his way to Calcutta his aircraft developed engine trouble and he turned back.. The aircraft rapidly lost height and crashed on the airstrip from which they had taken off. All but four of its occupants were killed. The dead were buried in the War Graves Cemetery in Rangoon - seventeen young men were buried that day.

Hugh Craig and his family were numbed with grief and Hugh decided to give up farming no longer able to give it his high standard of dedication. The family moved out of Harperdean and bought 'The Elms'. Hugh Craig effectively retired but his expertise was soon required; he became involved in cattle grading for the Ministry of Food and being an energetic man he found himself embroiled in local government.

He was elected Councillor, then Bailie and finally, in 1959, first citizen of the Royal Burgh of Haddington - Provost. It was a proud day when he was host to the young Queen Elizabeth II during her visit to the town in 1959.

Provost Hugh Craig died on 22nd September 1967 and was buried at St Mary's Church graveyard where his son James is commemorated.

Davidson Terrace

Davidson Terrace runs between Hospital Road and Aberlady Road on what was the 'property of Robert Vetch' (Plan of Haddington and Nungate, 1819). The old section of Davidson Terrace, which consists of semi-detached cottages, was built in 1938, the year in which the Council decided to name it after one of their most respected leading citizens, Provost William Davidson who died that year. The new section of Davidson Terrace was built after December 1950 when the land was disponed to the Scottish Special Housing Association Ltd and eighteen months later to East Lothian Housing Association.

William Davidson was the first of three Provosts of Haddington to come from the West Mill of Haddington; the others were Alexander Aitchison, a wool-buyer and manager of the tweedmill, and Robert Fortune (ref. Fortune Avenue), three times Provost who was responsible for examining, passing and invoicing of all tweed to many parts of the world.

William Davidson was born in 1863 at Hawick. He arrived in Haddington with his uncle, Adam Paterson, the founder of the West Mill. His schooling was meagre and he started work in Paterson's West Mill at the age of twelve. His boyhood was spent in the Nungate and each day he walked through the Churchyard of St Mary's Parish Church on his way to the mill. One morning early his eye caught a movement as he passed by the then ruined part of the church. He stopped to investigate and there he saw an old man kneeling by a grave. The year was 1880, the grave was that of Jane Welsh Carlyle who had died in 1866 and the old man was the eighty-five year-old literary genius Thomas Carlyle, the 'Sage of Chelsea.' William Davidson was a self-taught and well-read youth. He had read Carlyle's famous *Sartor Resartus* (the tailor retailored) and in awe and respect he crept away unnoticed by the great man.

After his marriage he lived in one of the cottages near the Maltings. Sadly his marriage failed, a subject he never discussed, except on one occasion when he was heard to remark "never marry a rich women because she will wake you every night to remind you!" His family consisted of two sons and one daughter.

One of his sons became the 2nd Engineer aboard the SS *Berngaria* and the other a lumber jack in Canada.

At Paterson's Tweedmill he worked in the scouring house of the West Mill and spent most of his leisure hours reading, although as a youth he was a keen athlete and competed in the pole vault, the high jump and the 440 yards race. But William Davidson was no ordinary mill worker, he was an accomplished handloom woollen pattern weaver *par excellence*. On receiving designs from the design office he completed the initial instruction from which he created his variations on the original theme. He alone was responsible for passing all new orders which were started up in the 40 power looms and his well-known initials on weavers' work tickets was always a welcome "get weaving" sign.

Courtesy of William Taylor of Gifford

The Chairman of the Adam Paterson Board of Directors, Mr Andrew Jamieson Blake, and his son, Douglas Jamieson Blake, were far-sighted and enlightened employers, who encouraged their employees to become interested in local affairs. It was this policy which gave the Royal Burgh of Haddington three Provosts, all employees of the tweedmill. William Davidson was the first to become a local Councillor, being elected in 1925, and Mr Blake was generous and understanding in giving time off work for Council duties - this at a time when many employers paid men off for short absences due to illness.

William Davidson was an ideal ambassador for the working man; he had a soft spot for the underdog and no poor man wanted a friend who knew William Davidson. He was a rough diamond but with emphasis on the word diamond. His logic was impeccable, his speech forceful but humorous, his intelligence sparkled and his heart was in the right place. A self-educated man, he was an avaricious reader. One of his prime interests, a subject he never tired to talk about, was the French Revolution. The cause of the French peasants and the works of Paine's *Rights of Man* caught his imagination. It is possible that his grandparents would have related in graphic detail the trials of the political martyrs in Edinburgh in 1794 during the Pit-Dundas 'reign of terror' when men were sentenced to death and given long sentences of transportation for what was described as sedition but in reality they preached only reform.

William Davidson lived and worked in Haddington almost all of his life. He became interested in local politics and was elected to the Town Council in 1925. A popular and dedicated Councillor, he worked selfless hours as Convenor of the Housing Committee for the improvement of housing in Haddington during the 1920s and 30s. After the 1914-18 War the town's population had expanded quickly and housing was not only deplorable but exceedingly scarce. The Council embarked upon an ambitious housing plan. Many an old Haddingtonian today can recall the crowds which gathered outside the Town House to inspect the lists of new housing allocations. Some were pleased and relieved to see their names on the list whilst others, disappointed, had to await the next allocation.

William Davidson was elected Bailie in 1930 and finally Provost in 1933. He was justly proud to represent the Royal Burgh of Haddington at the Convention of Royal Burghs in Edinburgh and as a representative of the Town Council on East Lothian County Council.

The crowning event of his Provostship, during his second term of office, was his invitation to attend the coronation of George VI at Westminster on 12th May 1937. He wrote to his friend an ex-apprentice at the mill, William Taylor of Gifford who represented the mill in London, to ask him to try to arrange accommodation other than an hotel which seemed too pretentious. Accommodation was almost an impossibility but William Taylor, who lived at the Caledonian Christian Club, asked the club secretary, Miss A.M.Robertson, for help. She in turn asked two friends, elderly ladies in Bloomsbury, if they could accommodate the Provost of Haddington for a few days. They were delighted to have as their guest this Scottish celebrity of the coronation. Lieutenant-Colonel Douglas J Blake, now Managing-Director of the mill in Haddington but based in London, was as kindly as his father; he arranged to have his chauffeur-driven Daimler take Provost Davidson accompanied by the two ladies from Bloomsbury to and from Westminster.

Once seated in Westminster Abbey Provost Davidson was surprised and delighted to find a few daintily prepared sandwiches in the hidden pocket of his new robes. He had arrived early and witnessed the arrival of the Lords and Ladies of the Court amid the buzz of conversation which was immediately silenced for the dignified arrival of the regal Queen Mary.

This was indeed a proud day for William Davidson but more thrills were to come: the BBC decided that they would like to interview the Provost of the ancient and Royal Burgh of Haddington on the *In Town Tonight* programme. His interview was an astounding success. He recalled his youthful encounter, fifty-seven years before, with the great Thomas Carlyle at St Mary's Parish Church and so captivated his listeners; back home in Haddington the huge mail from devotees of Carlyle astonished him.

Although he spent most of his time on Town Council business he loved to quote the poems of Robert Burns and he became President of the Haddington Burns Club in 1928 proposing the 'Immortal Memory' on 14 occasions. Davidson was keenly interested in the history of the town and he was instrumental in the placing of plaques on buildings to denote their historical significance. He was a founder member of the Literary Society, an original member of the East Lothian Antiquarian and Field Naturalists' Society and Vice-President of the Haddington Branch of the League of Nations Union.

There was a hut in Neilson Park named after him and a plaque affixed to Vert Memorial Hospital, commemorating the opening of the hospital on 24th April 1930, bore his name as Chairman of the Cottage Hospital Committee and for which he organised fund raising activities. Sadly, the plaque was lost in 1995 during the refurbishment of the building into flats.

He became ill during the funeral ceremony of an old friend; he did not recover and died at the age of seventy-five on 16th August 1938. His funeral cortege was accompanied through the town by the whole Council.

Dobson's or "Dobie's" Well,
Dobsons Place, View,
Chalybeate,
Long Cram

Dobie's Well, on the Pencaitland Road (the old coal road) near Clerkington Acredales probably takes its name from a local landowner. It is situated in the garden of a house which has come to be referred to as 'Dobie's Well House'.

In days long past, many a Haddingtonian was refreshed after a walk in the Lammermuirs or from Pencaitland at Dobie's Well which was 'fed from the coal measures which crop out from on the Letham lands' (14). The well was fenced by pointed iron railings on one of which was suspended an iron cup attached by a chain.

Sadly, the water supply was cut off during the construction of the new houses at Acredales which were planned in 1978 and completed by 1985 - a Wimpey Construction UK scheme. Martine (14) describes the water as 'slightly chalybeate, cool, pure, and pleasant to drink'. He tells the story of Letham born Andrew Shiells, a soldier of the 42nd Regiment who was badly wounded at the Battle of Corunna (1809). Forlorn and untended, hungry and thirsty he was heard to cry out, "Oh! I wad gie a' I hae for a drink of Dobie's Well."

The modern houses nearby form **Dobsons Place** and **Dobsons View** which were named in 1980. **Wellside**, off the Pencaitland Road, is also appropriately named after the well. **Chalybeate**, off **Long Cram**, is part of the same housing estate and takes its name from the cool waters of Dobson's Well which were believed to have curative powers. In fact several old maps dated 1854, 1892 and 1906 show Dobson's Well with the word Chalybeate added, meaning - iron water. **Long Cram** which was named in 1980 takes its name from a length of the River Tyne nearby.

Robert Ferguson of Raith Memorial

The imposing figure of Sir Robert Ferguson, standing on a 45ft (13.7m) high pillar at the corner of Knox Place and Station Road, is a splendid memorial to a Radical Member of Parliament for East Lothian. The site chosen was originally occupied by the West Port tollhouse and the memorial is a smaller version of that to the 1st Viscount Melville, Henry Dundas, which stands in the centre of St Andrew Square in Edinburgh - being designed by the same sculptor, Robert Forrest (1791-1852) at a cost of £650.

The base of the memorial is inscribed as follows:

In Memory of Robert Ferguson of Raith M.P. Lord Lieutenant of Fife FRSD, FRSE &c &c. A kind landlord and liberal dispenser of wealth. A generous patron of literature, science and art. An enlightened supporter of his country. This monument is erected by the tenantry of East Lothian and many friends of all classes who united in admiring his public virtues and to whom he was endeared by every quality which flows from the goodness of heart. AD MDCCCXLIII.

However, not everyone in East Lothian agreed that such an imposing monument was deserved. One dissenter, writing to the editor of the Haddingtonshire Courier and referring to "this meaningless monument", commented:

"He was not a Haddington man; his connection with the county was brief and sketchy; his public contribution called for no undying commemoration. It is rather silly, come to think of it, that in the county town of Knox, Rennie, Meikle, Jane Welsh, Balfour, and other famous men and women with some claim to our remembrance, the most eye-catching memorial (and the finest site) should be reserved for a nobody."

An interesting description of site chosen for his monument is given in the Register of Sasines, 20th February 1879:

'The 3rd or eastmost Lot of the Wester Gallowgreen Part of Haddington situated to the westward of the West Port of Haddington and bounded on the south by the Turnpike Road to Edinburgh and on the east by the Avenue to Hawthornbank House also the Wester Lot of the Easter Gallowgreen Park adjoining to the Easter Lot of Wester park....'

R obert Ferguson of Raith in Kirkcaldy was born in 1767. He was the eldest son of William Ferguson of Raith in Fifeshire and Jane, daughter of Ronald Craufurd of Restalrig (sister of Margaret, Countess of Dumfries). Educated in Edinburgh and trained for the law, he was admitted to the Faculty of Advocates in 1791.

About this time he toured Europe, an activity which occupied many young aristocrats of his day; the purpose being to broaden their minds, if not their education, through travel. It seems that Ferguson took his tour very seriously becoming a member of the

Institute of France. The events in France appealed to Ferguson, indeed the activities of the Revolutionaries were considered by many, including Charles James Fox (1749-1806) 'the greatest debater the world ever saw', to be 'the greatest and best event that has happened in the world' - he was referring to the fall of the Bastille in 1789 followed by the sweeping powers adopted by the National Assembly in ridding the country of feudal rights, disestablishing the Church and taking power in the name of democracy and the rights of man. These were exciting times for young radicals such as Ferguson.

His interests were wide as was evident from his membership of the Geological Society of London, his Fellowship of the Royal Society of Edinburgh and his presidency of several scientific societies.

In 1835 he married Mary Nisbet (formerly Countess of Elgin) the heiress of William Hamilton Nisbet of Dirleton, MP for East Lothian in 1779. She was governess to Princess Charlotte, daughter of the Prince of Wales and his estranged wife, Princess Caroline of Brunswick. The prince and princess loathed each other and Mary Nisbet acted as go-between on many occasions.

Following the passing of the 1832 Reform Act, which gave the vote to the middle classes, Robert Ferguson of Raith was the first to be elected in 1835 for the burgh of Haddington under the new law. The Whigs who supported the abolition of slavery, Roman Catholic Emancipation and who championed Parliamentary Reform were anxious to win the parliamentary seat of East Lothian against the Tories. Ferguson's majority of 34 over the Tory, John Thomas Hope younger of Luffness, was a slender one; the electorate of 188 was small and exceeded the number of guests, which totalled 300, at the celebration dinner held on 6th February 1835 at the Assembly Room, Haddington.

Ferguson had been MP for the Kirkcaldy Burghs and was one of the supporters of the Reform Bill through its difficult passage through Parliament. This was a period of rapturous and nation-wide celebration; Prime Minister Earl Grey had, after three attempts, steered the Reform Bill through Parliament and his arrival in September 1835 in Haddington was greeted with the ringing of the town bells and a display of banners of various trades. Robert Ferguson was among the first to heartily welcome Earl Grey.

In 1837 Ferguson, now aged seventy, lost in his bid for a second term as MP for East Lothian to Lord Ramsay (later Marquess of Dalhousie). George Hope of Fentonbarns commented that the Tories went to extreme lengths to ensure that Ferguson would lose this election when they were alleged to have kidnapped some of his supporters - one was firstly taken to Garvald and then abandoned at Traprain Law and another was dumped as far away as possible in the Pentland Hills.

Sir Robert Ferguson died, aged seventy-three, on 3rd December 1840 in London and three years afterwards the Whigs of East Lothian organised the subscription for his monument which was unveiled on 2nd June 1843.

The Ferguson name continued in Parliament through his only son, Colonel Robert Ferguson, who was MP for Kirkcaldy in 1841 until 1862.

Fortune Avenue

Fortune Avenue, off Newton Port, is named after Robert Leslie Fortune, Provost of Haddington for almost ten years from 1947. During his thirty-five years on the Town Council of the Royal Burgh of Haddington he must have become the most well-known face in the town. His 'surgeries' were held in the street - to quote his only son, George Fortune; "it took him hours to get home, he met and chatted to so many people on the way, always about council business".

Courtesy of Mr George P.L. Fortune (son of Provost R. Fortune)

Robert Fortune was born in Haddington on 18th December 1895, his father George Fortune was a drayman in Haddington Brewery and his mother, Helen Leslie who came from the north of Scotland, was a cook. Young Robert attended the Knox Institute until the age of twelve when he was given a job at Adam Paterson & Son's Tweedmill at West Mill where he worked as a warehouseman until he retired in 1966 at the age of seventy-one.

His long service for the Town Council started through his involvement with the tenants association in the 1930s. He stood as an 'independent' - neither a socialist nor a conservative; he was a 'working-man's man' whose concern for fairness and for the best solution, irrespective of party politics, was paramount. His strength was not physical but vocal; he could hold the floor and captivate his audiences effortlessly and without reference to a note. He held all the important posts - councillor, treasurer, bailie and finally Provost. His service knew no bounds, his time was never measured, his concern for the well-being of his fellow man never diminished.

During the disastrous flood of 1948 when so many were made homeless Robert Fortune addressed dozens of meetings and lost no opportunity in raising money to help those who had suffered. Again, to quote his son, "he fought to the death for something he believed in especially on behalf of others".

In 1922 he married Christina Scott Burns, a Haddington girl who, in a sense, was the opposite in temperament of her husband; she was a happy-go-lucky wife and mother and provided a perfect balance in the Fortune household at No.9 Station Road. Their only son George had a very happy childhood and an excellent relationship with his father. They shared an interest in many sports and enjoyed each others company. Mrs Fortune died in 1954 and George, now married, brought his wife to live with and care for his father.

Robert Fortune was a member of the Haddington Co-operative Board and when it merged with the Tranent Board to become the East Lothian Co-operative Board he was elected to its membership; his service on the two boards totalled over thirty years. He was appointed a Justice of the Peace and after thirty-five years of dedicated service to the Town Council he was made a Freeman of the Royal Burgh and given a civic dinner during which he was presented with a magnificent silver casket on 15th March 1964.

He died aged eighty-one on 11th November 1977 being survived by Mr and Mrs George Fortune and his grandson George. Their sadness and sense of loss was shared by all the people of Haddington. His funeral was attended by his family, their friends, councillors, bailies and ex-Provosts of Haddington.

Gifford Road,
Giffordgate

Gifford Road appears on the 1819 Plan of Haddington and Nungate as the 'Road to Gifford'. It runs parallel with Giffordgate which with Gifford Road take its name from the ancient Norman family of Gifford of Yester. Giffordgate, across the Nungate Bridge, was itself a village, as was the Nungate, outside the Haddington boundary.

The lands of Giffordgate belonged to Hugh de Giffard of Norman origin an ancestor of whom was Count de Longueville. The Count was a kinsman of William the Conqueror (1027-87); his aunt was the great-grandmother of the king, and Hugh de Giffard was the first to settle in Scotland having been given grants of land in East Lothian from David I (1124-53).

His son, also Hugh, was rich and powerful during the reign of William the Lyon (1143-1214). He was one of fifteen Regents following the 'safe-keeping' of Haddington-born Alexander II (1198-1249) and his Queen in 1244.

Hugh de Giffard (original spelling) owned the old barony of Yester and built Yester Castle as well as its mysterious vaulted cavern which came to be called Goblin Hall and was said to have been built in one night by Moor servants. Sir Walter Scott added to the romance in his *Marmion* in which there is reference to "Hobgoblin Hall.":

'A vaulted hall under the ancient castle of Gifford or Yester (for it bears either name indifferently,) the construction of which has from a very remote period been ascribed to magic.'

The Statistical Account of the Parish of Garvald and Baro gives the following account of the present state of this castle and apartment:-

"Upon a peninsula, formed by the water of Hopes on the east, and a large rivulet on the west, stands the ancient castle of Yester."

Sir David Dalrymple, in his Annals, relates that 'Hugh Gifford de Yester died in 1267; that in his castle there was a capricious cavern, formed by magical art, and called in the country Bo-Hall, i.e. Hobgoblin Hall.'

A Clerk could tell what years have flown
Since Alexander fill'd our throne,
(Third monarch of that warlike name,)
And eke the time when ere he came
To seek Sir Hugo, then our lord;
A braver never drew a sword;
A wiser never, at the hour
Of midnight, spoke the word of power:
The same, whom ancient records call
The founder of the Goblin Hall.
I would, Sir Knight, your longer stay
Gave you that cavern to survey.
Of lofty roof, and ample size,
Beneath the castle deep it lies:
To hew the living rock profound,
The floor to pave, the arch to round,
There never toil'd a mortal arm,
It all was wrought by word and charm:
And I have heard my grandsire say,
That the wild clamour and affray
Of those dread artisans of hell,
Who labour'd under Hugo's spell,
Sounded as loud as ocean's war,
Among the caverns of Dunbar.

Scott

Hugh de Gifford's son, William de Gifford, was one of the guardians of Alexander III (1241-86) and a Regent who was appointed through the Treaty of Roxburgh in 1255. He died in 1267 and was succeeded by his son, also William, who was to become a powerful force for the independence of Scotland. When Stirling Castle was captured by the 'Hammer of the Scots,' Edward I, in 1304, William de Gifford was captured and held prisoner for the next six years in Corfe Castle in England.

His son, Sir John Gifford, became owner of the lands of Morham through his marriage to the heiress of Sir Thomas de

Morham. Their son Sir Hugh de Gifford was the last of the Gifford line. He died in 1409 and his lands were inherited by his four daughters the eldest of whom, Jean, married Sir William Hay the Sheriff of Peebles, an ancestor of the Marquis of Tweeddale, who thus acquired the barony of Yester. In 1350, Hugh Gifford of Yester gave land in the village of Giffordgate (which explains the derivation of the name) for the upkeep of the Nungate Bridge. (1.p145).

Giffordgate is generally believed to be the birthplace of John Knox (c.1505-1572). There is some evidence for this from his signature in 1554: 'John Knox of Giffordgate' on a document signed on his arrival in Geneva. The literary genius, Thomas Carlyle, husband of Jane Welsh, after his last visit to the grave of his beloved wife in St Mary's Parish Church, wrote to his friend, Colonel Davidson, asking him to plant a tree to mark the position of the Knox family home in Giffordgate, Knox's supposed birthplace. This request was carried out in 1881.

However, reference must be made to the Morham claim: Mary Stenhouse in her, *A History of Morham Parish* states:

"Mainshill farm also has the doubtful honour of being the birthplace of John Knox. The foundations of the building where his people lived still obstruct ploughing and have been known for generations as the 'Knox Stones'. Haddington and Gifford both claim Knox as their son, but most of the land south of Haddington was in the possession of the Gifford family and Morham parish lay within the ecclesiastical area of Bothans Kirk. There was no village of Gifford until one hundred and fifty years after Knox's birth in 1505. His father, William Knox, was the third generation of the family to live at Mainshill. His mother was a Sinclair of Northrig and her sister was married to George Ker of Samuelston. The Knox family bought Knox's Croft in Giffordgate, Haddington on the eighteenth of February 1598 and moved there to live, that was about twenty-six years after the reformer's death. There are supposed to be nine gravestones of the Knox family in Morham, three are still to be seen in reasonable condition for their age." (32 p.12)

Gimmersmills,
Bermaline Mill

Gimmersmills, on the north side of the Tyne just over the Victoria Bridge, had the only double undershot water wheel in East Lothian and was originally built by the monks of Haddington as far back as the 14th century. Nearby, tenants were under obligation (thirled) to grind the corn. Around the year 1460 the nuns of Haddington complained to Pope Pius II that their entitlement of a tithe (one tenth of the produce) from 'Gimmersmill' had been refused. On learning of this the Magistrates of Haddington promptly paid up. A court of "schillinghill" of the mills of Haddington was held twice each year and had powers to fine any who evaded the thirlage (duty on the corn).

During the Siege of Haddington of 1548-49 the besiegers, having requisitioned French cannon, had them placed at Gimmersmills and fired indiscriminately into the town. Shortly after the Siege a deed in favour of Alexander Forrest of Haddington was signed and witnessed on behalf of the Prioress and Convent granting a 19-year lease of 'Gymmersmylnes' with a few acres of the Nungate.

Grey and Jamieson (1.p.29) make reference to a seal dated 4th September 1569 at Nunraw, appended to which is the *Precept of Clare Constat by Isabel Hepburn, Prioress of the Abbey of Haddington* giving legal possession of Gimmersmills and certain lands in Nungate to David Forrest as the son and heir of John Forrest, Provost of Haddington. David Forrest was host to George Wishart (c.1513-1546), the reformer and martyr who preached at St Mary's and when reformer John Knox of Giffordgate (or Morham?) returned to Scotland in 1556 from Geneva with his two sons he renewed his friendship with David Forrest of Gimmersmills, declaring him to be *"ane man that long hes professed the trueth and upoun whom many in that tyme depended."*

Another charter of James VI during his visit to Haddington when he was rescued from the Tyne in 1605-6 granted the corn mills of Gimmersmills, the mansion with the haugh and a number of acres to David Forrest, burgess of Haddington and his wife Isabell Sympsone.

According to Martine (14) the mills were gifted by the Bishop of St Andrews to the Forrest family who were devoted choristers of St Mary's Church. Martine makes no reference to the year of this gift and the earliest record of ownership by the Forrest family is contained in the Register of Seisins (Sasines) Haddington 1781-1868 and is dated 13 January 1786:

'Dr George Forrest of Gimmersmills as heir to David Forrest of Gimmersmills his father seised, December 29, 1785 in Gimmersmills with Mansion House, Mylecroft, Milneland, parts of Broadcroft etc.'

The Forrest family retained ownership of Gimmersmills until 1795 when it passed to a relative, Dr Alexander Maitland.

In 1848 Gimmersmills was owned by the Provost of Haddington, George More, who opened the new Corn Exchange in 1854. His house, situated at the end of an old wooden bridge which connected the mill with Hardgate, was eventually sold (by Frank Rayner) and demolished to make way for a cinema. The Ideal Garage was built on the site of the bombed cabinetmaker's shop and house which was owned by Mr Robert Pringle during the 1939 -45 war.

In 1900 a new mill was built - the **Bermaline Mill** of red rock-faced sandstone which was famed for many years for its Bermaline flour and bread. Since 1972 Messrs. Bruce and Guy Turner have managed the mill for the production of pure malt for the baking, biscuit and brewing industries.

Gourlaybank

Gourlaybank lies adjacent to the Dunbar Road. The houses of Gourlaybank were built in 1958 on the property of 'the late David Gourlay' (shown on the 1819 Plan). The housing development was designed to encourage some expansion of the town which at that time had a population of just over 4500. This was the first Co-operative Housing Scheme of forty houses of shared ownership under the Adam Housing Society whose first chairman was Major Broun-Lindsay,.

Gourlaybank takes its name from the Gourlay Trust which in turn commemorates the name of David Gourlay whose house and distillery were near the Bell Inn Close in the High Street, now Carlyle Court. The Blue Bell and Post House, known as the 'Bell Inn' now demolished, was reached through the arch at Carlyle Court and was an 18th century staging post with several dozen stables; in 1764 it was the White Hart Inn.

In 1801, David Gourlay left a legacy of £1290 for the 'industrious poor' of Haddington, the interest from his legacy with rent from land at Gourlaybank were used to alleviate their condition. Martine (14) in his Reminiscences gives us a description of David Gourlay thus:

> *'A well-known eccentric man. ....By all accounts he made excellent small still whisky, for which there was a great demand. He was silly in keeping lots of cats, and had mounds and avenues of flowers and shrubs in his garden for their playing among and around. Menie Coach was his maid, and had to feed and attend them regularly....... He used to give frequent supper parties, and make very strong toddy in a large bowl. On his guests complaining of its strength, he would soon remedy that, but the more liquor he ran from the kettle, the drink was always the stronger (he had put whisky in the kettle). His delight was in making his company very happy. He was of the family of the Gourlays of Kincraig in Forfarshire, an old respectable family. He died in 1801, and bequeathed the interest of £1290 and the rent of the field of Gourlay Bank, in aid of the industrious poor of*

Haddington, and under charge of the parochial ministers of the parish, and at their own disposal, without count or reckoning.'

One of David Gourlay's servants was found guilty of stealing his master's whisky on 15th September 1785. The unfortunate tippler was one of the last to be 'put into the juggs for an hour, upon Friday, September 30th, with a label on his breast, in large letters, "infamous thief of his master's property," and that upon Friday, October 7th, he should be pilloried again in the same manner; to be continued in the Tolbooth of Haddington till Thursday, 13th October, (being Haddington fair-day) and then to be whipped through the town, and within 48 hours after to depart from the county and never to return...' (2.p.221).

Miller in his *Lamp of Lothian* makes reference to a tombstone in the west end of Haddington churchyard, erected to the memory of Miss Gourlay, a sister of David Gourlay, with the following inscription:-

'Here lies one, there is not room to say what;
Think what a woman should be; she was that.'

Regarding which, the Rev. Robert Scott, minister of the second charge of Haddington, impromptu, opinionatively and rather impudently wrote:-

'Every woman should be both wife and mother,
But Miss Gourlay was neither one nor t'other.' (14.p.15,16).

Gowl Close

The word 'Gowl' means a narrow pass, usually between hills. It also refers to a gust or howl of wind (11). This is probably the origin of the name of **Gowl Close** which runs down to the Tyne by the side of Victoria Terrace, opposite the Ideal Garage (formerly the site of Pringle the cabinetmaker which was destroyed by the direct hit of a German bomb during the 1939-45 World War).

Another school of thought relating to the name 'Gowl' refers to the fact that the Franciscan friars of the 12th century used this route passing the Haddington Wall to their Friary. Their heads were covered by their cowls or cools (close-fitting caps). Gray and Jamieson (1) makes reference to a Franciscan called Friar Gowl, one of the friars of the old Friary which was called the 'Lamp of Lothian' on the site of the present Episcopalian Church in Church Street. Friar Gowl used this pathway to the Friary.

Martine (14.p.63) describes Gowl Close as: ...a *place of great antiquity. In the Haddington war and Siege time it was often the scene of many a hot fray betwixt the French and English on their way along the Tyne to the Sands. There was once a gate in it which no doubt was often forced by opposing bands.*

Gowl Close receives a mention in *A Short History of Haddington* (1): the infamous 4th Earl of Bothwell, hunted by the Earl of Arran and Lord James Stuart (who became the 'Good Regent') with 200 horsemen, made his escape from Bothwell Castle (Cockburn of Sandybed's house) nearby down a "lane called the Gowl" to the Tyne. The year was 1559 and Bothwell, as hereditary Sheriff of Haddington, had attacked Cockburn of Ormiston's men and relieved them of £3000 on its way to the Lords of Congregation against Catholic Mary of Guise, the Queen Regent.

Haddington House

Haddington House is the oldest and most quaint example of 17th century architecture in Haddington; it was built by Alexander Maitland; one of the Lauderdale Maitlands. The engraved initials 'A.M. and K.C. 1680' on the lintel above the entrance give us not only the date of his marriage but his initials and those of his wife - AM.KC - Alexander Maitland and Katherine Cunningham. However, Haddington House is even older than 1680; its rear view shows its L-shape with its octagonal stair-turret which, according to McWilliam (2.p.243) indicate 'a somewhat earlier c17 house.'

This lovely old house was saved from demolition by the Earl of Wemyss on his return to Scotland in 1948. The East Lothian Antiquarian and Field Naturalists' Society intended to use it for a museum but it became the Lamp of Lothian Collegiate Centre and the library of the Society. It was restored in 1969 by restoration architect, W. Schomberg Scott.

The early owner of Haddington House, Alexander Maitland, was made a Burgess of Haddington in 1673, possibly in recognition of giving 'many favours' to the town. As well as serving in the Town Council, he was acting-Provost in 1689 and a Commissioner of the Convention of the Royal Burghs. In 1688 it was Maitland who brought the message from the Duke of

Hamilton to the Town Council informing the Council that no magistrates should be elected in the meantime (1.p.144) - the whole country was in turmoil when king James II (VII of Scotland) clashed with the English Parliament and the Scottish Covenanters refused to recognise him as king.

A later illustrious owner of Haddington House was Justice James Wilkie (1733-1825) who lived there until his death at the age of ninety-two. He had two beautiful daughters and at noon each day Wilkie had his carriage and two black horses, *Captain* and *Admiral*, brought from his stables on the opposite side of Sidegate for his daughters who duly entered their carriage to be taken for a short ride through the town (14. p.52,53)

The porch at the entrance to the house was added in 1680 and attracts immediate attention; its curved roof is supported on stone pillars, its eight steps with a stone balustrade lead to the canopied entrance doorway with a broad moulded architrave. The garden wall was built by French prisoners during the Napoleonic war of 1793-1815. Haddington House Garden, St Mary's Pleasance, has been laid out in the manner of a 17th century walled garden of herbs and trees, the herbs being described in terms of their curative powers. A special feature is the alley of hornbeams which leads to the Laburnum Walk.

The sunken garden at the entrance has been designed to replicate that which would have been seen in the 17th Century. The whole creation is that of the Haddington Garden Trust.

The house and garden were bought by the Antiquarian Society in 1950. At that time two brothers, Harry and Fred Faunt, had rented the ground for the production of fruit for Fred's fruit shop in Wilson's Close, off Court Street. It was agreed that the brothers should retain their right to use the garden for their lifetimes. Harry Faunt was a tenant of one of the properties of Haddington House. Eventually, the brothers retired and the garden was carefully developed to its present immaculate and interesting state.

Haldane Avenue

Haldane Avenue is a small section of the A1 between Alderston Road and Ab.erlady Road; its houses were built in the 1930s by Richard Baillie & Sons. The name Haldane Avenue was chosen to commemorate the brilliant East Lothian MP, Richard Burdon,1st Viscount Haldane, the eminent Liberal statesman, philosopher and lawyer who died during the construction of this section of the A1.

He was a member of a distinguished Scottish family of intellectuals - his sister, Elizabeth, an author who managed the Royal Infirmary of Edinburgh and was the first woman to be appointed a Justice of the Peace in Scotland; his brother John, a Professor of Genetics, was an eminent biologist, a Fellow of the Royal Society and a Darwin Medalist of the Royal Society.

Viscount Haldane represented East Lothian after the three East Lothian Burghs were combined following Gladstone's 1884 Reform Bill which was supported by all Liberals. It gave the vote to rural labourers and Haldane surprised the 'establishment' of East Lothian by ousting Lord Elcho by 1528 votes from what was thought to be a safe Conservative seat. He held it for over 25 years and attained high office in government - Secretary of State for War (1905-12), Lord Chancellor (1912-15) and Minister of Labour (1925).

He was born in 1856 and educated at the Universities of Edinburgh and Gottingen. He was called to the bar in 1879 and entered parliament the same year.

It was Haldane, in 1899, who was the brain behind the proposed teaching universities in London to be followed by Manchester and Liverpool. He supported the war against the Boers (1899-1902) even when the conduct of the war, especially Kitchener's concentration camps, caused a split amongst Liberals.

As Secretary of State for War, Haldane overcame the anti-militaristic suspicions of his party which wanted an army on the cheap. The army seemed directionless and Haldane appointed men of ability on his Army Council - Haig, Nicholson, French, Ewart and Grierson - and by army order he formed a general staff and created an expeditionary army of six infantry divisions and one cavalry division. Against considerable opposition he amalgamated the Yeomanry and the Volunteers into a Territorial Force consisting of fourteen divisions and fourteen cavalry brigades. Haldane therefore deserves the credit for the formation of the Territorial Army.

He was convinced that Britain had to be master of the seas and that a professional striking force was essential. Haldane undoubtedly deserves full credit for Britain's ability to send four highly trained infantry divisions and one cavalry division to the front in 1914 - these were the men who were dubbed contemptible by the Kaiser and became known as the 'Old Contemptibles.'

For the excellence of his service to the nation he was raised to a viscountcy in 1912 and appointed Lord Chancellor. His elevation to the House of Lords with the departure of James Bryce to the ambassadorship in America weakened the front bench at a time of vulnerability for Premier Asquith; Lloyd George and Churchill leading the younger generation were not dependable - this was Liberalism in its last stage.

Haldane was much more than a politician: he was a statesman and a philosopher of merit. Such was his reputation he was invited to give the Gifford* Lectures at the University of St Andrews between 1902 and 1904 and he published three philosophical treatises.

The 1914-18 War was going badly, Lloyd George feared calamitous defeat, our armaments were sorely deficient, retreat seemed to be the order of the day in France, the disaster of the Dardanelles, 300,000 casualties in 1914 alone - the sequence of disastrous defeats brought down Asquith's government. The new coalition government was useless and lasted less than two years. Admiral Lord Fisher had resigned, refusing to send more ships to the Dardanelles. Haldane was not included in the Cabinet and Churchill was demoted.

No longer Lord Chancellor in 1915 Haldane was awarded the Order of Merit (OM), a most coveted and special distinction awarded to those supreme in the arts and literature. It is the sole gift of the Sovereign and in the twenty-six year reign of George V, from whom Haldane received his award, only two awards were given.

In 1924 he was again in the Cabinet, as Minister of Labour, under Prime Minister Stanley Baldwin but he went over to Labour with some support while Churchill with the majority went over to Conservatism. The Liberals now had only 40 seats and Haldane died in 1928.

* The Gifford lectureships were endowed by Lord Gifford (1820-87), who was an Edinburgh born Scottish Judge. He endowed lectureships at Edinburgh, Glasgow and St Andrews for undogmatic studies in natural theology.

High Street

T he **High Street** of Haddington was known as 'Crocegait' during the reign of Alexander II (1214-49). His palace was situated near the west end of Crocegait, now Court Street. *Croce* is the old Scots word for a market cross or market-place.

One side of the High Street was almost completely destroyed by fire on 18th May 1598 and about that time Haddington's weekly markets, which were held in the High Street, were arguably the greatest in Scotland, the main commodity being grain although dairy products were sold near the Cross. The High Street fleshmarket was transferred to Newton Port in 1757 and to the Hardgate in 1804.

The shape of the High Street has changed little over the past 200 years or so. The wooden buildings and thatched roofs have gone and the old outside stairs and bow windows have been removed. The 1819 Plan of Haddington and Nungate shows the High Street stretching from the West port Toll near the present Ferguson Monument to the Sidegate at its eastern end. Of course, the interiors of the buildings have been altered many times but the frontages have largely maintained their 18th century appearance.

On the north side of the High Street there are several interesting wynds: from west to east, the first is **Jail Wynd** which takes its name from the old prison in the adjacent Town House built in

1748. On the wall at no.52 High Street there is a plaque commemorating the birthplace of Samuel Smiles, doctor and author of Self Help in 1859.

Secondly, **Broad Wynd** was known variously as Wheat and Pease Market in 1800, and Mark Lane in the Valuation Roll of 1978 (an abbreviation of Market Lane). Broad Wynd was also called Pirie's Wynd, probably named after George Pirie, the wright who with Robert Reid, a mason, built the Town House in 1742. The large house adjacent was called Pirie's Building which became the Heather Inn. Its next name was Neilson's Wynd after a local draper.

Thirdly **Britannia Wynd**, also renamed in 1981, was previously Commercial Lane from the Commercial Hotel (now the Mercat Hotel). Fourthly **Cross Lane**, previously Fishmarket Wynd, opposite which is Haddington's Mercat Cross.

Finally, **Brown Street** which takes its name from a local trader of bygone days; it was previously known as Strumpet Lane then George Inn Wynd, being adjacent to the George Hotel. The 18th century houses of **Kilpair Street**, off Brown Street, runs parallel with the High Street. The name Kilpair is thought to be derived from 'Caleperys' an early reference to which is dated 1426 (1.p.81) indicating in turn that a central island of buildings, called Middle Raw, existed then.

On the south side of the High Street walking east from Lodge Street, **Carlyle Court**, named after the celebrated man of letters and husband of Jane Welsh Carlyle, Ecclefechan born Thomas Carlyle (1795-1881), was the entry to the Blue Bell and Post House. This was a reputable inn and changing station for local and London stage coaches during the middle of the 18th century when it was known as the White Hart Inn. The change of name was made in 1764 when one James Fairbairn took over ownership. The Blue Bell vied with The George for just over 90 years.

Ross's Close, opposite Britannia Wynd, was the business premises of a cheery and successful plumber, Thomas M. Ross (1860-1937), a councillor and Provost of Haddington for 31 years.

At no.5 High Street, the Carlyle Cafe was the printing shop of George Miller father of Dunbar born James Miller (1792-1865) best known for his authorship of *Lamp of Lothian or The History of Haddington* (1844). This shop became a tobacconist shop owned by the father of another famous son of Haddington, the internationally famous artist and teacher Sir William Gillies (1898-1973) who was born in the house above the shop on the wall of which a plaque commorates this event.

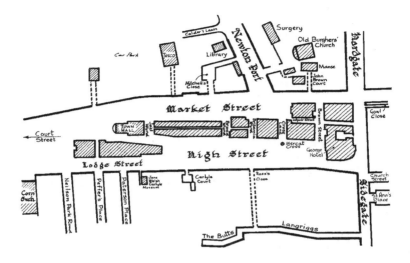

Hilton Lodge (formerly Craig Lodge), Hilton Court

Hilton Lodge, originally Craig Lodge, on the north side of Court Street is set back from the street to give it a beautifully kept town garden.

The land was owned by John Dudgeon as shown on the 1819 Wood's Plan of Haddington and Nungate which shows the villa as Craig Lodge. This was a stone built two-storey house. Its name was changed in the 1850s when the Haddington builder and architect Francis Farquharson bought the property. It is likely that he added the present red brick frontage with the bay windows and sandstone corners. Its magnificent wrought-iron gates which led to steps and a pathway as wide as the gates were removed during the 1939-45 war.

The Register of Sasines (SS518) gives records of Hilton Lodge from the year 1872 and contains a brief description of the property as: 'The villa now called Hilton Lodge formerly Craig Lodge consisting of stable, pig house and porter's lodge with gardens on north side of High Street*.'

In May 1852 Francis Farquharson bought 'a piece of ground sometime a barn and barn yard near the West Port' (Scottish Record Office). The Farquharson family gravestone in St Mary's Churchyard is inscribed:

In Memory of
FRANCIS FARQUHARSON
Builder and Architect, Haddington
who died 16th December 1878 aged 74
and of JESSIE RICHARDSON his wife
who died 16th August 1888
ROBERT
their youngest son who died 5th September
CATHERINE
their daughter who died 28th April 1919
JOHN FARQUHARSON
Builder and Architect, Haddington
Their eldest son who died 18th January 1933 aged 87

When Francis Farquharson died in 1878 his trustees transferred the property to his eldest son John Farquharson in a disposition dated 9th October 1880.

In February 1889 John Farquharson sold part of the grounds of Hilton Lodge (98ft along the south boundary x 55ft along north boundary to 100ft from centre of Court Street) to the Trustees of the Free Church of Scotland under the pastoral care of the Rev. James Matthews for the sum of £500. The West Church was built soon afterwards in 1890; the path behind was part of the old Town Wall and was known locally as the "Black Paling" footpath which stretched from Hope Park to the south side of Victoria Road (1.p.84); it formed the boundary of the Auction Mart

The mansion is listed by Historic Scotland as of 'special architectural or historic interest' and is within the conservation area of the Burgh of Haddington. When John Farquharson became owner of Hilton Lodge he made provision for his sister Catherine to live there for her lifetime. She died in 1919 and part of the house was purchased by the Education Department of the County Council of East Lothian in 1920 for use as offices. The County Library had two rooms upstairs with outside access. When the offices became surplus to their requirements, on completion of the extension of County Buildings, the whole building and land was sold on 17th May 1934 for the sum of £1200 to Lieutenant-Colonel William Farquhar McLean MC, MD of The Hollies, Station Road.

Dr William Farquhar McLean was a well-known figure in Haddington. During the Great War of 1914-18 he performed hundreds of operations at the front in France, often at the risk of his own life and was heard to remark that he had learned more about surgery in the trenches than anywhere else. He rose to the rank of Lieutenant-Colonel and was awarded the Military Cross for gallantry. He was 'Mentioned-in-Despatches' three times for conspicuous devotion to duty in 1917 when he co-ordinated the evacuation of the wounded from advance dressing stations.

He was a big, red-faced, jovial man and a crack shot who won many trophies both as a member and president of the Haddington's Miniature Rifle Club at The Butts. He was a member of 'Scottish Twenty' and the 'King's Hundred' at Bisley and won both the Daily Graphic and The Times Cups.

His daughter Mary became a doctor, graduating with her elder brother James in 1949. James had returned to Haddington from the RAF to study medicine at Edinburgh. Mary's twin brother Ian became a dentist and James assisted his father until his father's death in 1951.

James, followed in his father's footsteps in his presidency of the Rifle Club. He was an accomplished singer being a member of the choirs of St Mary's Church and of Dunbar Parish Church. There is a touching story of him attending a dying patient: an old shepherd in the Lammermuir Hills who, realising that little could be done for him, asked Doctor James if he would sing "All in an April Evening." This he did with gentle simplicity and beauty and the old shepherd died happily.

According to the Register of Sasines Hilton Lodge was disponed on 15th September 1964 "by the Trustees of William Farquhar McLean with the consent of beneficiaries to James Douglas Farquhar McLean MB, ChB." Dr James McLean lived at Hilton Lodge until he retired in 1983; he now lives on Isle of Seil (reached by bridge across the Atlantic). He continues to sing and has maintained his interest in technical things. Dr Mary now lives at West Linton. The McLeans lived at Hilton Lodge for a total of almost fifty years, father and son having served the community of the Royal Burgh of Haddington for thirty-two years apiece.

In December 1983 Dr James McLean sold the property with the half acre of ground and the buildings at 3 Hope Park to Hilton Lodge Limited to be used as a Nursing Home giving 'tender loving care' to elderly people. Approval for this change of use was given in October 1983.

In November 1988 the firm of William Elder & Sons Limited, the Agricultural Engineers, sold their land adjacent to Hilton Lodge to Hilton Lodge Limited, who in turn sold it to Cala Homes (Lothian) Limited for the construction of four flats and eight sheltered houses named in 1988 - **Hilton Court**. This little enclave of Haddington's west end has been carefully and tastefully designed to merge old an new in harmony.

* The High Street of Haddington extended from the West Port Toll at the Ferguson Monument to Sidegate.

Hope Park,
Hope Park Crescent, Hopetoun Drive,
Hopetoun Mews,
Hopetoun Monument

At the beginning of the 18th century the Earl of Haddington sold his patronage and property in East Lothian to Charles, 1st Earl of Hopetoun; this explains the Hopetoun connection with Haddington. Another connection with East Lothian occurred through the 2nd Earl's purchase of the estates, mines, the distillery, the brewery and the mill of John Cockburn, the 'Improving Laird' of Ormiston in 1747. Cockburn's ambitious schemes for Ormiston had over-reached his finances and he sold out to the only buyer, the 2nd Earl of Hopetoun, for the bargain price of £12,000.

Hope Park, which leads to its continuation of Aberlady Road, **Hope Park Crescent**, off **Hopetoun Drive**, between Hawthornbank Road and Aberlady Road and **Hopetoun Mews**, off Lydgait, are all named after Sir John Hope, 4th Earl of Hopetoun.

The **Hopetoun Monument**, on Byres Hill, 560 feet above sea level in the Garletons, is a well-known landmark for Haddingtonians. The monument is three inches less than one hundred feet; its height was restricted in order to avoid the tax payable on buildings of over one hundred feet. It was erected in 1824 and is inscribed:

This Monument was erected to the Memory
of
the Great and Good
John - Fourth Earl of Hopetoun
by
His affectionate and grateful tenantry
in East Lothian
MDCCCXXIV

The land on which the monument was erected (its foundation stone being laid on 3rd May 1824) belonged to the Hope family until 1960 when it was purchased by Sir James Miller, Lord Provost of Edinburgh and Lord Mayor of London. In 1977 Sir James, learning that East Lothian District Council expressed a desire to own the site, gifted the land and the monument to the Council for the enjoyment of the people.

Sir John Hope is best remembered for his heroism at Corunna during the Peninsular War (1808-14). His family can be traced back to John de Hope who came to Scotland from France with Magdalen de Valois, daughter of Francis I who married James V to become Queen in 1537.

John de Hope's son was a member of the newly-formed Protestant General Assembly in 1560 during the turmoil and struggle of John Knox to advance the Reformation. Hope's grandson was appointed Lord Advocate by Charles I to become Sir Thomas Hope and his son became Master of the Mint. He was elevated to the Bench as Lord Hope of Hopetoun - the first of the family to use the name 'Hopetoun'. He married the heiress, Anne Foulis, which brought the rich lead mines of Leadhills to the Hope family and financed the purchase of the shale mines at Bathgate in 1657.

Charles Hope (1681-1742) was elevated to the peerage as lst Earl of Hopetoun and became a Privy Councillor in 1702. He married Lady Henrietta Johnstone, the sister of the 2nd Marquess of Annandale. He was a strong supporter of the Union of the English and Scottish Parliaments in 1707 and was Lord Lieutenant of Linlithgow in 1715. In 1699 he commissioned Sir William Bruce to build Hopetoun House near South Queensferry but it was considerably altered by John, the 2nd Earl of Hopetoun. William Adam's extensions were carried out from 1721 and the interior was designed by the Adam brothers, Robert and John, in 1767.

The 3rd Earl of Hopetoun married Lady Elizabeth Carnegie, the heiress of Annandale and succeeded to the Annandale estates through this marriage.

The 4th Earl of Hopetoun, Sir John Hope was a brave soldier and a distinguished general who served in Egypt at the battle of Alexandria to drive out the French in 1802. Hope distinguished himself in 1808 at Corunna in Spain when he took command. Sir John Moore, the great Glasgow General had defeated the French in a brave last stand against the numerically superior enemy but Moore was killed at the moment of victory. Sir David Baird of Newbyth now took command but he was severely injured and had to leave it to Hope to carry out the extremely difficult task of evacuating the remnants of the British Army.

John Hope was born on 17th August 1765 at Hopetoun House; his father, also John Hope the 2nd Earl, married three times and it was by his second wife, Jane Oliphant, that John was born. He succeeded to the title as 4th Earl of Hopetoun in 1816 on the death of his step-brother James, the 3rd Earl.

He was educated by tutors at Hopetoun House and during his tour of Europe he was accompanied by his brother and Dr John Gillies who became Historiographer Royal. John Hope started his army career at the age of eighteen as a cornet (sub-Lieutenant) in the l0th Light Dragoons. He rose steadily through the ranks to attain the rank of Lieutenant-Colonel of the 25th Foot within nine years and he was returned as MP for Linlithgowshire during this period.

At the start of the war with France in 1793 he was stationed at Plymouth for two years and in 1795 he sailed to the West Indies in charge of ten companies but he was invalided home from Grenada. He returned a year later as Adjutant-General under Sir Ralph Abercrombie who commended him several times for bravery under fire at the destruction of the French and Spanish West Indies.

His army service included North Holland (1799), the Mediterranean (1800) and Egypt (1801) where he was badly wounded at the Battle of Aboukir on 21st March when his commander, General Abercrombie, was tragically killed by a stray bullet. Hope had commanded two of the most distinguished regiments of the British Army - the 28th Foot and the 42nd Highlanders and he had been deputed to arrange the surrender of the French. But the year 1801 was disastrous for him; not only did he suffer from his severe wounds but his wife, Elizabeth Hope-Vere died.

In 1803 he was promoted to Major-General in command of a brigade stationed in eastern England to defend against threatened invasion. That year he married Louisa Dorothea, daughter of Sir John Wedderburn and they had eleven children.

Hope had been appointed Lieutenant-General of Portsmouth in 1805 but he was anxious to join the expedition to Hanover and he resigned his appointment to do so. The great victory of Trafalgar was followed by Napoleon's victory over the Austro-Russian army at Austerlitz and in despotic style he gave each of his brothers a Kingdom: Joseph - King of Naples; Louis - King of Holland; Jerome - King of Westphalia.

In 1808 Hope, now a Lieutenant-General, was sent to Sweden and then to Portugal under Sir John Moore. In Portugal Hope commanded a division and linked up with Moore at Salamanca, but the odds were too great against them and they were forced to retreat over 250 miles of snow-covered hills and mountains to Corunna where Sir John Moore was killed at the point of victory. During the embarkation to England, Hope rode through every street in Corunna to ensure the safety of his men; this act of stubborn bravery earned him the thanks of Parliament and a Knighthood of the Order of the Bath from George III.

Hope was appointed Commander of the forces in Ireland in 1812 and a year later he succeeded Sir Thomas Graham (later Lord Lyndoch) in the Peninsular army to command a division under Wellington at the battles of Nivelle and Nive where he was wounded. Wellington described him:

> 'I have long entertained the highest opinion of Sir John Hope......but every day more convinces me of his worth. We shall lose him if he continues to expose himself as he did during the last three days. Indeed his escape was wonderful. His coat and hat were shot through in many places, besides the wound in his leg. He places himself among the sharpshooters, without sheltering himself as they do....he is the ablest man in the Peninsular army.' (3).

In February 1814 Hope blockaded Bayonne with stubborn skill until the end of the war. He had his horse shot from under him and, wounded again, he was captured but soon released. After Wellington's magnificent victory at Waterloo, which marked the total and final defeat of Napoleon, Hope was raised to the peerage as Baron Niddry of Niddry Castle in Linlithgowshire.

In 1816 he succeeded his half brother as the 4th Earl of Hopetoun and he became a full general in 1819. He was appointed Colonel of the 42nd Highlanders, Lord Lieutenant of Linlithgowshire, a governor of the Royal Bank of Scotland and as Captain of the Royal Company of Archers, the King's Bodyguard, he attended George IV during his visit to Scotland in 1822. He entertained the King in royal style at Hopetoun House to celebrate the first visit of a reigning monarch since Charles II's visit in 1651.

He died during a visit to Paris ten days after his fifty-eighth birthday on 27th August 1823. He was mourned not only for his integrity, his strong common-sense but as a courageous soldier who was well-liked both in the army and as a civilian. He was succeeded by his eldest of nine sons. His wife, Lady Louisa, died at Leamington on 16th July 1836.

Jane Welsh Carlyle Museum

The **Jane Welsh Carlyle Museum** in Lodge Street commemorates the life and times of the accomplished and beautiful daughter of Dr John Welsh in whose perfectly restored house the present museum is situated. It was saved from conversion into business premises by the Lamp of Lothian Trust with a generous grant from the Scottish Tourist Board.

It is a matter of some speculation whether or not such a museum might have existed at all had she not married the greatest literary figure of his day - Thomas Carlyle (1795-1881). The aspirations and achievements of women were discouraged, diminished and denigrated in her day and for that reason she might not have been remembered. However it is recorded that her father was a forward-thinking man who encouraged his only daughter's aspirations in literature and mathematics.

Jane Welsh was born on 14th July 1801, the only daughter of Dr John Welsh who arrived in Haddington with his young wife, Grace in 1800. Dr Welsh earned deserved gratitude and respect in Haddington for almost twenty years but he died aged only forty-four from the dreaded disease, typhus, in 1819.

Jane was incredibly bright in childhood; at school she was the 'dux' of St Anne's Street School, ahead of both the boys and girls. Her childhood days were full of fun - there was the dare of the boys to walk the parapet of the Nungate Bridge. Alone, she crawled across the parapet to gain confidence and afterwards she walked falteringly, then finally she ran across, not to be bettered by the boys with whom she skated on the ice under the bridge. Then there was the lovely domestic incident (recalled by Mrs Margaret Oliphant (1828-97), the Scottish novelist); Dr Welsh, having dined and settled comfortably in the luxury of his armchair, heard a small voice from under the table, that of the six-year old Jane who proceeded to recite a few sentences in Latin which she had learned from her friend William Dods (who became Provost of Haddington in 1825 and 1829 and a well-known seedsman). She then appeared from her hiding place to plead, "I want to learn Latin, please let me be a boy." Her father readily agreed but her mother was doubtful about such precociousness in a girl.

Edward Irving, the first teacher in the Mathematical School in Haddington, was her tutor. He was an excellent young teacher, aged only eighteen, who attracted children and made learning enjoyable. In this bright little girl, Jane Welsh, he found mercurial intelligence and a love of life, full of fun and charm. That she became the 'The Flower of Haddington' to be wooed by several aspiring suitors was not surprising; that she turned them away disappointed, tongue-tied and embarrassed seemed almost to be expected.

Courtesy of The Scottish National Portrait Gallery

In 1818, aged seventeen, she was sent to Miss Hall's finishing School in Leith. Edward Irving, who by now had left Haddington and was teaching in Kirkcaldy, was encouraged by Jane's early infatuation to form a romantic friendship with his former pupil but he was engaged to another. However, when Irving introduced Jane, now nineteen years of age, to the somewhat forbidding twenty-six year old Thomas Carlyle it was clear that Carlyle was in love at first sight. Her beauty was matched by her scholarly intellect and she recognised a kindred spirit, a free and enquiring mind, a scholar of talent - at last, she was impressed. This was the start of their five-year courtship. The somewhat unkempt and awkward Carlyle was given little encouragement by Mrs Welsh whose ambitions for her daughter included the more presentable and successful George Rennie son of the great civil engineer John Rennie of Phantassie.

Jane married Thomas Carlyle in 1826 and they took up residence at Comely Bank in Edinburgh. After eighteen months they moved to Craigenputtock, near the Solway Firth, the birthplace of Jane's father. Carlyle wrote most of his best works during these six years including his Sartor Resartus. Jane, in a letter to her cousin, Eliza Stoddart of George Square, Edinburgh, wrote:

> 'The solitude is not so irksome as one might think. If we are cut off from good society, we are also delivered from bad; the roads are less pleasant to walk on than the pavement of Princes Street, but we have horses to ride, and, instead of shopping and making calls, I have bread to bake and chickens to hatch. I read and work, and talk with my husband and never weary. Letters from Germany and all parts of the earth reach us here as before. It is so strange to see 'Craigenputtock' written in Goethe's hand.'(4)

The Carlyles left their idyllic life in Dumfriesshire in 1834. Thomas Carlyle had published some of his best works and was in great demand by the literati of not only London but of Europe. They moved to No.5 Cheyne Row in Chelsea the rent of which was £35 per year. This was a complete change for Jane. Her husband took on a monumental workload and she suffered long periods of loneliness which brought nervousness and hypochondria. However, their home was a magnet to the literary set - James Henry Leigh Hunt, the essayist and poet who lived a few doors away, Charles Dickens, Lord Tennyson, William Makepeace Thackeray and many other admirers were welcomed by Jane who was an impeccable hostess - vivacious, attractive, witty and welcoming. Her husband became known as 'the sage of Chelsea' and was hailed as the literary genius of the age. The Haddington born Lord Mayor of London, Sir Peter Laurie, knowing that Jane was a Haddingtonian, invited the Carlyles to dinner but the 'sage' found it not to his taste describing the event as "very sumptuous, very cockneyish - strange and inadmirable to me."

When Thomas Carlyle was elected Rector of the University of Edinburgh in March 1866, he and Jane worked themselves into a state of anxious frenzy over his forthcoming address to the students. He detested public speaking and travelled to Edinburgh three weeks before the event to be feted and admired but his anxiety only worsened. He need not have worried, the students were held spellbound for ninety minutes and afterwards he telegraphed Jane with the words: 'A perfect triumph.' The students had erupted in spontaneous applause.

Jane was overjoyed and only two days before he was due to come home, while taking her pet dog for a ride in her carriage, she stopped to let the dog have a walk. No sooner had the dog touched the ground than it was struck by a passing carriage and slightly injured. Jane, thinking that the her pet had been killed, was so shocked she suffered a heart attack and died in her carriage. Thomas Carlyle was in Dumfries when he received the numbing news of his wife's death. Heartbroken, he hurried to London. His grief was almost beyond endurance when he read her memoirs; he had no idea of her loneliness and boredom and the beauty and perfection of her written language astounded him, again he no idea of her exceptional talent which he found in an unfinished novel, now lost forever.

Jane had expressed the wish to be buried beside her father at St Mary's Parish Church in Haddington. Accordingly, Thomas Carlyle had her body brought north to be met by William Dods, her childhood friend who had readily agreed to have the coffin brought to his spacious house at No.32 Court Street (now the Royal Bank of Scotland).

That night the dejected figure of Thomas Carlyle walked slowly through the dark streets of Haddington until he came to the entrance of Dr Welsh's House. Entering the garden he looked up at the window of the very room in which he had first met Jane, '1821 on a Summer evening after Sunset - five and forty years ago. The beautifullest young creature I had ever beheld'. The great man cried tears of grief.

Next day, 26th April 1866, the funeral at St Mary's Church was attended by a few close friends. Jane was buried beside her father and Carlyle composed the inscription for her gravestone:

Here likewise now rests
JANE WELSH CARLYLE,
spouse of Thomas Carlyle, Chelsea, London.
She was born at Haddington, 14th July 1801; only child
of the above John Welsh, and of Grace Welsh, Caplegill,
Dumfriesshire, his wife. In her bright existence she
had more sorrows than are common; but also a soft
invincibility, a clearness of discernment, and a noble
loyalty of heart, which are rare. For forty years she
was the true and ever-loving helpmate of her husband;
and by act and word, unweariedly forwarded him, as
none else could, in all of worthy that he did or attempted.
She died at London, 21st April 1866; suddenly snatched
away from him, and the light of his life as if gone out.

Kings Meadow Primary School

K ings Meadow Primary School in its green field site opposite Neilson Park takes its name from King Alexander II who was the only surviving son of William the Lion and Queen Ermengarde. He was born at Haddington in the palace which stood on the ground on which the County Buildings now stand. The palace was in a completely ruined state and, according to James Miller's Lamp of Lothian (2 p.229):

'The ruins removed (in 1832) consisted of a vault, and part of an arched passage communicating with it. The pillars of the arches were of the Saxon order.'

A drawing of the palace, by Adam Neill, was printed in the East Lothian Register of 1834.

The name King's Meadow Primary School was originally suggested by Admiral Reid of Letham House when he was a member of the School Board. The school was opened in 1970 by Mr J B Miller, the County Convenor, at a cost of £247,000. It was the latest in modern design and the land on which it stood was undoubtedly the meadow on which the boy prince had played before he became king in 1214. Sadly, the school was destroyed by fire and rebuilt in 1994/5.

I t was here that Alexander II was born, in the year 1198, much to the great relief and joy of his parents when their son arrived. His father, William the Lion, thought that he may have to name his daughter as his successor despite the objections of the Scottish magnates who preferred a nephew. Alexander succeeded his father at the age of sixteen. He spent most of his boyhood in Haddington and the King's meadow south of the palace where the primary school now stands was his playground.

Alexander succeeded to the Scottish throne in 1214, the year of the death of his father, William the Lion. Alexander's coronation took place at the centre of Scottish monarchy at Scone. His main preoccupation was in giving protection to English nobles against King John who, in 1216, invaded Dunbar and Haddington which he wantonly burned down. Alexander gathered his army at the Esk forcing John to retreat to Berwick which was sacked unmercifully. Alexander followed him as far as

Richmond. His Highlanders pillaged and burned as they went, equalling John's ferocity. Alexander's enmity with King John resulted in his excommunication from the Church of Rome. However, the ban was lifted after two years and the liberties of the Scottish Church were restored.

He was, however, a good and wise ruler and when Henry III acceded to the English throne he signed a peace treaty in 1217 and he married Henry's eldest sister, Princess Joan (daughter of King John), in 1221. They had no children and the princess died in 1238. His choice of second wife, Mary, a daughter of Baron Couci, a very rich French noble, and the birth, in 1241, of an heir to the throne who would succeed him as Alexander III at the age of eight, annoyed Henry who marched on Scotland in 1244 to demand Alexander's homage. It was Alexander's wisdom and clever negotiation which ensured peace without resorting to arms.

Alexander II now sought to gain the Hebrides from Norway but on his way north he became ill and died of a fever at Kerrera near Oban in 1249, aged fifty-one.

In 1251 Alexander III (1241-1286), having become king at the age of eight, married Henry III's eldest daughter, Princess Margaret, (1240-75). He was a mere ten year-old and he spent most of his reign repelling the Norwegian invasion.

Knox Academy,
Knox Statue, Knox Court,
Knox Place

Knox Academy owes its existence to the proposal in 1870 that a memorial to the great Scottish Reformer John Knox be erected in the form of an educational establishment and nine years afterwards the Knox Institute was opened. It was designed by John Starforth in Gothic style with a central tower in a niche of which is a statue of Knox in his Geneva gown by D.W. Stevenson (1842-1904). It was the gift of the Misses Trail of Aberlady.

The Knox Institute was formally opened in January 1880 by Arthur James Balfour, 1st Earl of Balfour of Whittingehame House who became Prime Minister in 1902-06. The first rector was J.C.Graham MA, a classics master from Merchiston Castle School in Edinburgh.

The Institute, now **Knox Court** in Knox Place, was converted internally in 1985 into flats for Sheltered Housing. The new school, in Rosehall, was opened in 1938 and named Knox Academy in 1948; its first rector was James Black. It was extended in 1959 and today there are approximately 800 pupils.

Knox Place is a small section of the Haddington - Pencaitland Road between Meadow Park and Victoria Road.

The Public Library in Newton Port was the Knox Church in 1852 when the 'Auld Lichts' joined the Free Church.(1)

The great preacher and leader of the Reformation, John Knox, was born near Haddington about 1505. The site of the actual house, in Giffordgate, in which he was thought to have been born, was marked by the planting of an oak tree by Colonel Davidson at the request of Thomas Carlyle after his last visit to the grave of his beloved wife, Jane Welsh Carlyle, in 1880. However, Knox's actual birthplace is disputed, the most likely being Mainshill Farm at Morham, a small village three miles south-east of Haddington.

John Knox attended the Grammar School of Haddington and the University of Glasgow (1521-22) and was ordained as a priest in 1529. He remained in the Catholic Church for fifteen years during which the writings of Martin Luther, the German religious reformer, had become so popular to be a threat to the Catholic Church and an Act of Parliament was passed to forbid their importation. From 1530 religious persecution was rife; the first martyr in Knox's time was Patrick Hamilton, a twenty-three year-old aristocrat who was burned at the stake in St Andrews. Other martyrs followed a similar fate and only served to arouse passion for the cause of the Reformation.

John Knox was inspired by George Wishart, the Scottish reformer, who translated the Swiss Confession of Faith and who after preaching the Lutheran doctrine at St Mary's Collegiate Church in Haddington, was arrested by Cardinal Beaton's men at Ormiston and burned on 1st March 1546 at St Andrews.

Knox, completely disenchanted with the cruelty and corruption of the Church of Rome, surrendered his Orders in 1544 when Cardinal Beaton had advised the 'ill-beloved' James V with his second wife Mary of Guise to wage war against Henry VIII. The disastrous battle of Solway Moss in 1542 left James V totally depressed; he died within a month, leaving his one week old daughter, to become Mary Queen of Scots.

Henry VIII now enforced a treaty of marriage in which his son, Edward, would marry Mary when she reached ten years of age. The 'rough wooing' followed Cardinal Beaton's advice and refusal to allow the marriage. Henry's attempt at Union with Scotland was ruined with his claim of sovereignty, the burning of Edinburgh and Holyrood and the murder of Cardinal Beaton in 1546 - only two months after Wishart's martyrdom.

John Knox was now in a precarious position as a devotee of Wishart and a known enemy of Cardinal Beaton (who had tried to have Knox assassinated). Knox had to flee with his pupils; they took refuge in the castle of St Andrews with Beaton's murderers and although Knox was not involved, he was now implicated.

Henry had ordered Regent Arran to allow the use of the Bible in the Scots tongue. The Bible, which included the New Testament, was soon widely available and this new religious awakening delighted the Reformers. The Scottish Catholic nobles sought assistance from the French and Knox was taken prisoner when a French fleet laid siege to the castle of St Andrews in 1547. With his fellow Reformers he was chained, confined to the galley and taken to Rouen then to Nantes. Meanwhile Henry VIII had died (1547) and his son Edward VI, now twelve years old, interceded on Knox's behalf. Knox was set free in February 1549. However, Henry's "rough wooing" was pursued by Protector Somerset to try to force an agreement. The Scots had been thoroughly defeated at the Battle of Pinkie Hill near Musselburgh in September 1547 and an English garrison was stationed at Haddington. The French were pleased to be requested to drive the English out of Haddington (the Siege of Haddington, 1548-49) to keep open the wedge between England and Scotland and, by prior agreement, young Queen Mary was sent to France to marry the Dauphin. The French King talked of Scotland as a French dependency; the Scots had made a bad deal with the French and Knox dare not return to Scotland.

He remained in England to be appointed one of King Edward's Chaplains in Ordinary by the Privy Council but the ways of the English Court displeased Knox and no one escaped his stern reproof. He made enemies, one of whom was the Duke of Northumberland who cunningly arranged that Knox should be offered the Bishopric of Rochester in order to curtail his influence; Knox declined it, risking criticism and accusations of treachery but he knew that Edward VI favoured him. However, Edward died on 6th July 1553, aged only fifteen; Knox shed tears of grief and cleared out of London on the day that Mary I, a staunch Catholic, was proclaimed Queen.

Young Mary, still in France, was now twelve years of age and her mother, Mary of Guise, argued that she should now govern Scotland in her own right. The Earl of Arran was persuaded (or bribed) to resign as Regent and young Mary's choice of Regent was of course her own mother.

Mary of Guise, as Queen Regent, took immediate control and the French influence in Scotland increased to the point of their mastery. Again Knox's position was precarious, this time in England. Within six months Protestants were penalised as heretics as 'bloody Mary' (Mary I of England) exerted repressive and vindictive authority. Knox refused to leave the country, he continued preaching in peril of his life but after his marriage to Marjery Bowes he was persuaded to leave for Dieppe in January 1554 and afterwards he travelled to Geneva where he and Calvin became friends. Knox's two sons were born there and after two happy years he returned with his family to Scotland.

The Protestant nobles formed the 'Lords of the Congregation' and in 1558 with several learned nobles of his 'Congregation' Knox made a new translation of the Bible into English - this was the 'Geneva' Bible named from the place it was originally written. The unrelenting cruelties of Mary I provoked Knox to write *The First Blast of the Trumpet against the Monstrous Regiment of Women*. This caused much controversy particularly in Court circles because the word 'regiment' meant 'government' and not women in general. Mistakenly, it branded Knox a misogynist.

Knox left Geneva for the last time in 1559. He was given the freedom of that city where he was greatly respected. Mary I had died in 1558 and Protestant Elizabeth I was Queen. However, on his arrival in Scotland he found open hostility from Mary of Guise, the Queen Regent. Knox was proclaimed an outlaw and a rebel; ministers were put on trial for administering the Sacrament and the Protestant nobility were threatened. After a riot in Perth and the burning of monasteries Knox was told that he would be shot if he attempted to preach. He ignored the advice of his friends and proceeded to denounce the Papacy in the Cathedral of St Andrews where he gained strong support from the Provost, the Bailies and the inhabitants. They agreed to set up the Reformed worship and to strip the Church of all its Catholic images.

Knox's influence had spread rapidly and he was called to a meeting of nobles, barons and borough representatives in Edinburgh. It was agreed to suspend the authority of the Queen Regent until a meeting of a free Parliament. She sought reinforcements from the French who attacked the fortifications of Leith. The Reformers, under the Earl of Arran, repelled the French from Fife and for the first time in the history of Scotland, English troops were asked for their support. In March 1560 they blockaded Leith and starved the French to surrender. However, Mary of Guise died suddenly and in July the Treaty of Edinburgh was signed between Queen Elizabeth and the French agreeing to their withdrawal, an amnesty for the supporters of the late Queen Regent and a free Parliament in Scotland.

In December 1560 young Mary's French husband died and she, avoiding Queen Elizabeth's interception of her ships, landed at Leith on 19th August 1561. She was eighteen years old, tall, comely and beautiful. She had many offers of marriage but asked only to be left in peace to practise her religion. She promised not to interfere with the new Scottish Protestantism. However, one of Knox's early rows with her was over the land revenues of the Catholic Clergy, one third of which was shared between the Crown and the Kirk. Knox, dissatisfied, claimed all of it saying "two parts freely given to the Devil and the third divided between God and the Devil." It soon became apparent that a great gulf separated her from the Reformers but Knox counselled against using armed forces to prevent the service of Mass even though he was vehemently against it.

Protestantism was now formally established as the religion of Scotland. Knox with four ministers was commissioned by the Privy Council to plan the ecclesiastical government - *The First Book of Discipline*. It averred that a school for every parish be erected and that all monies should support the Universities and the Churches. The nobles were unhappy with the new proposals of financing. They had enjoyed the rich revenues of the Papish clergy. Neither the *First* nor the *Second Book of Discipline*, compiled twenty years later, received legislative sanction.

The first meeting of the General Assembly of the Church of Scotland was held on 20th December 1560 in Edinburgh with forty members of which six were ministers. Knox was minister of the only Reformed Church in Edinburgh and he took Mary under his special charge. She, on the other hand, had sympathy with the Catholic Princes of Europe who advocated universal extermination of Protestants. Knox corrected and criticised her behaviour and public policy. Their arguments often reduced her to tears of frustration; she was no match for his dialectic.

The Scottish Parliament met in May 1563, the first since Mary had returned, to ratify the Treaty of Edinburgh of 1560, but Mary had prepared well and the self interest of the Protestant leaders allowed it to be shelved. Knox angrily severed his old friendship with the Earl of Moray. Queen Mary was delighted, but in his next sermon Knox preached against the deep ingratitude among the Lords for their deliverance from bondage. This incurred the fury of the Queen especially when Knox predicted serious consequences if she married a Papist. He had offended both sides and she declared as treasonable a letter he had written supporting two Protestants who had been indicted for rioting. Knox was put on trial. He was begged to acknowledge a fault and throw himself on the Queen's mercy. Knox would hear none of it. After long argument the Lords voted that they could find no offence. The Queen and her 'flatterers' were enraged and commanded a second vote. The nobility, highly offended, spoke out and absolved Knox again.

In 1564 Knox having lost his wife three years before, married Margaret Stewart the sixteen year old daughter of Lord Ochiltree. Knox was now accused of ambitions to the throne; the Ochiltrees were of royal blood.

At the meeting of Parliament in December 1564 the Queen's impending marriage with her cousin Henry, Lord Darnley, was the main subject of discussion. The nobility would give their consent on condition that she agreed to the legality of the Protestant religion in Scotland but again she procrastinated and married Darnley in June 1565.

She proclaimed Darnley King without even consulting the Estates of the Realm. He was vain and vindictive, overbearing and odious. He found fault in one of Knox's sermons and demanded his arrest for an imaginary insult. Knox was ordered to stop preaching but he replied simply that commands to speak or to abstain could be made only by the Church. The Queen and Darnley renewed their efforts to encourage Catholicism and restored Catholic ecclesiastics to Parliament but they fled after the murder of Rizzio by Darnley. Knox had retired to Ayrshire to write his *History of the Reformation in Scotland.*

In 1567 Knox was given leave of absence by the General Assembly to visit his two sons in England. During this time Darnley, who had completely lost Mary's respect, was murdered. The Earl of Bothwell, now in the Queen's favour, was strongly suspected. His trial was a farce. He was found guiltless in his absence and after a pretended abduction he took the Queen to Dunbar Castle and they were married on 15th May 1567. The marriage was condemned as scandalous and several lords joined against Bothwell who fled to the Orkneys after his defeat at Carberry Hill in June. Mary was imprisoned in Lochleven Castle and compelled to sign a deed of abdication.

Knox, having returned to Edinburgh, preached the sermon at the coronation of James VI and advocated that Mary should answer to the crimes of murder and adultery but eventually he agreed to her detention. The Earl of Moray was invested with the Regency, James VI being one year old. Immediate improvements took place, Moray worked for peace; he summoned Parliament and ratified all the Acts of 1560. Protestantism was finally established and Knox, whose health was now suspect, wished to retire. Moray, however, had enemies - the family feud with the Argylls and the jealous Hamiltons. Moray had to crush two revolts and his victory at Langside compelled Mary, who had escaped from her prison at Lochleven, to flee to England.

Moray was assassinated by the treacherous Hamilton of Bothwellhaugh (a nephew of the Archbishop of St Andrews) whose life had been spared after the Battle of Langside. There was national mourning. Hamilton fled to perpetual banishment and Knox, overwhelmed with grief, preached the funeral sermon.

The 'Good Regent's' body was interred in the south aisle of St Giles.

In his grief Knox had a stroke which affected his speech and in a letter of March 1570 to Sir William Douglas of Lochleven he wrote that he would soon take his 'good-night of the world', but there was to be no rest for him. Leith was under attack from the Queen's forces. Protestants were harassed and assaulted and Knox was now accused of complicity in Darnley's murder. He travelled to St Andrews in slow stages and easily defended his conduct discrediting his accusers, Robert and Archibald Hamilton, in the process. The latter was hanged for his part in Darnley's murder after Dumbarton Castle was taken by the Regent's forces on 2nd April 1571. In September the Queen's forces took Stirling Castle and killed Regent Lennox. The Earl of Mar succeeded to the Regency and conscientiously tried to restore peace.

Although Knox was weakening he could still electrify his audiences. On 6th August 1572 he wrote a touching farewell to the General Assembly. By November he was dying; he asked to hear the evening prayers after which Dr Preston asked him if he had heard. Knox replied, 'would to God that you and all men had heard them as I have heard them; I praise God for that heavenly sound.' He gently raised his hand and died peacefully. The day was 24th November 1572, he was sixty-seven. He was interred in the Churchyard of St Giles on 26th November; his burial place is at car park No 44. The newly-elected Regent Morton summed up his character: "here lies one who never feared the face of man."

Lady Kitty's Doocot and Garden

Lady Kitty's Doocot is immediately opposite the southern end of the Nungate Bridge. It dates from 1771 when Lady Catherine Charteris Wemyss, the wife of Francis, de jure 7th Earl of Wemyss, petitioned the Town Council to have the gateway of St Mary's Parish Church moved eastwards so that the wall surrounding her 'Garden' could be built. It was probably about this time that the old buildings were demolished and removed, the site having been used for archery, bowling and executions. On the Sands nearby the Battle of the Sands in 1548 took place during the 'Siege' when the English occupied Haddington against the French who had arrived from Edinburgh to assist the Scots. English bullets were said to have ricocheted off the walls of St Catherine's Chapel the grounds of which became **Lady Kitty's Garden**.

Archery was practised on the Sands during the brief reign of Mary Queen of Scots (1561-1567) and this was said to have been the site of the first bowling green in Scotland in 1657 when the Burgh Treasurer was authorised to 'purchase bowls and to engage a greenkeeper' (1.p.124).

Lady Kitty took over ownership of the common, the Sands, when she claimed payment of debts incurred by Lewis Gordon Esq., a road surveyor. At the north end of Lady Kitty's Garden there was a house in what was then known as Friars Croft; it was probably built by Alexander Maitland (of Haddington House). In 1920 Lady Kitty's Garden was acquired by the Parish Council as an extension to the church grounds.

Lady 'Kitty' was the 6th daughter of Alexander, the 2nd Duke of Gordon (1678-1728) an ardent Jacobite who commanded reinforcements for the 'Old Pretender' in 1715. Her mother was Henrietta, daughter of the Earl of Peterborough and Monmouth. Catherine was born c1720 at Edinburgh.

On 13th September 1745, three days before the 'Young Pretender' entered Edinburgh, she married Francis Wemyss, second son of the 5th Earl of Wemyss and Janet, the only daughter of the infamous Colonel Francis Charteris. The wedding took place at the enlarged old house of Preston Hall (by William Adam in 1738) and was attended by the groom's elder brother, David, on his way to join Prince Charles Edward.

After the wedding ceremony the young couple were driven to Amisfield when the wedding party received an urgent message that the Jacobites were about to attack. This could well have been true but was in fact a practical joke at the expense of Sir John Cope who immediately called out his men in readiness. He covered his embarrassment by thanking his men for their speedy reaction to his command.

They were an exceedingly rich young couple. As the favoured grandson, Francis Wemyss had inherited his grandfather's (the infamous Colonel Charteris's) ill-begotten fortune including the estates of Amisfield in 1731/2. With her husband, Lady Kitty spent many happy hours in the planning of their new mansion house, Amisfield, which was designed for them by Isaac Ware in 1755. During the planning stage she gave birth to her only son, Francis Charteris Wemyss on 31st January 1748. The new Amisfield House, became the magnificent red sandstone mansion of Grecian grandeur, the finest example of the Palladian school in the country (sadly, it was demolished in 1923).

To the delight of Lady Catherine, Francis bought the Elcho estate in 1750 from his father, the 5th Earl, for the sum of £8,500.

It consisted of the old nunnery and Elcho Castle overlooking the River Tay, 4 miles from Perth. The old Earl had amassed huge debts due to the spendthrift ways of his wife Janet (daughter of the infamous colonel) and his son's expenditure in support of the '45 Rising.

A happy event for the family was the marriage of their son, also Francis Charteris Wemyss, on 18th July 1771 to Susan, 2nd daughter of Anthony Tracy-Keck and Susan, daughter of the 4th Duke of Hamilton. As a wedding present Lady Kitty agreed that the young couple should be given Amisfield while she and her husband moved to Gosford.

In 1780 and in 1784 her husband was elected MP for the Haddington Burgh in the Tory Government of William Pitt the Younger and some of their time had to be spent in London. She longed to return to Gosford and in 1784 Francis bought the old Gosford House and estate and again Lady Kitty took a great interest in planning their new house to be designed by the great Scottish architect Robert Adam. Sadly, she did not live to see its completion. She died suddenly on 21st January 1786 (her husband died 22 years later in 1808, aged 85 years).

Lennoxlove

The original name of the estate of Lennoxlove was Lethington which lies 1.5 km south of Haddington. The first house was built by the Giffords (de Gyffard) of Yester (ref. Gifford Road, Giffordgate) who sold it to the Maitland family early in the 14th century.

It became the seat of the illustrious Maitland family from 1345 when the old L-shaped keep was built replacing a much older structure. Above the entrance are the arms of the 1st Lord Thirlestane, John Maitland, and his wife, Janet Fleming. Almost three hundred years passed until John Maitland, the 2nd Earl of Lauderdale, built the long east wing during the 1630s and the tower at the south-east end is dated 1644.

Another early Maitland was Sir Richard (1496-1586), although blind he was a lawyer and a poet of note. He became a Lord of Session in 1551 and Lord Privy Seal in 1562. His son, William Maitland (1528-73), was the illustrious 'Secretary Lethington' and was Secretary of State in 1558 to Mary of Guise, the Queen Regent and mother of Mary Queen of Scots. He was a loyal supporter of and Secretary to Mary Queen of Scots during her short reign and after her flight to England. With Kirkcaldy of Grange William Maitland held Edinburgh Castle against Regent Morton and the Protestants. However, they were eventually trapped in the Castle; Kirkcaldy was executed and Maitland died in prison. His brother, John Maitland of Thirlestane, was Chancellor to James VI for ten years from 1585.

Yet another famous Maitland was John who was born at Lethington in 1616. He succeeded his father as the 2nd Earl of Lauderdale and was a staunch Royalist during the Interregnum (from 1649, when Charles I was executed, to 1660 when Charles II was restored to the throne). Charles II trusted him completely and elevated him to a dukedom in 1672. As the virtual master of Scotland he was detested by the Covenanters especially after the battle of Bothwell Bridge in 1679. His dukedom died with him in 1682.

The Duke of Lauderdale left Lethington to his step-son, Lord Huntingtower. He was the son of his wife, the Countess of Dysart, by her former marriage. Huntingtower sold the house to Lord Teviot who in turn sold it to the Trustees of the Duchess of Richmond and Lennox.

In 1702 after the death of the Duchess of Lennox, 'La Belle Stuart', the widow of the Duke of Richmond and Lennox (ref. **Lennox Road**), her Trustees bought Lethington for her nephew, the Master of Blantyre, as directed in her Will. Her husband died in 1672 when he fell from a boat in Denmark and she lived at the Court of Charles II as a lady of the bedchamber for the next thirty years; she was a favourite of the Queen, Catherine of Braganza. On 22nd December 1673 the king granted her the Lennox estates and for an annuity of £1000 she resigned her estate of Aubigny to the crown.

Sadly, her beauty was marred from the effects of smallpox and the King, in sympathy and to cheer her, presented her with a magnificent inlaid tortoise shell writing cabinet which can be seen at Lennoxlove today. She had no children and left her estate to her cousin, Alexander Stewart, Lord Blantyre. Her Will contained a provision that the name of Lethington should be changed to **Lennoxlove** in memory of her love for her husband. She died on 22nd October 1702 and was buried at Westminster. Her full-length portrait by Sir Peter Lely with another of her husband in his Garter robes hang at Lennoxlove.

The Masters of Blantyre owned Lennoxlove for the next 250 years. A portrait of the 10th Lord Blantyre, by Sir Henry Raeburn, Limner to George III, hangs at Lennoxlove as a reminder of the Blantyre family connection. On the death of the last Lord Blantyre (the 12th) in 1900 Lennoxlove was inherited by his second daughter, Ellen, who was married to Sir David Baird of Newbyth. Extensive restoration work and several alterations were carried out by their son, Major William Baird and his wife Lady Hersey Baird, both well-known and well-loved in Haddington. Their architect was the eminent Sir Robert Stodart Lorimer (1864-1929), the designer of the Thistle Chapel in St Giles Cathedral, The Scottish National War Memorial at Edinburgh Castle and many others.

In 1946, their son Robert Baird sold Lennoxlove to Douglas-Hamilton, the 14th Duke of Hamilton. This Duke, born in 1903, made his name as the chief pilot and the first man to fly over

Mount Everest in 1932. During the war in 1941 Rudolph Hess, Hitler's deputy, flew alone from Germany to Scotland in an attempt to negotiate an Anglo-German peace with the Duke of Hamilton. He was MP for East Renfrew for ten years from 1930 and Lord High Commissioner of the Church of Scotland between 1953 and 1955 and again, for the fourth time, in 1958. He was Lord Steward of the Royal Household. He died at Lennoxlove in 1973.

The present Duke, Angus Alan Douglas Douglas-Hamilton, born in 1938, lives at Lennoxlove and seems to have inherited his father's love of speed and flying. He holds the diesel speed record over two miles at 129.89 mph. He loves motorbykes and has a collection of them in the old kitchen of Lennoxlove. As the Premier Peer in Scotland he is Keeper of the Palace of Holyroodhouse. He was an RAF pilot, a flying instructor and Test Pilot. He is a member of the Royal Company of Archers (the Queen's Bodyguard in Scotland) and has published a learned history, *Mary R*.

Happily, Lennoxlove is open to the public three afternoons per week. Exhibits include the death mask of Mary Queen of Scots, her sapphire ring from Lord John Hamilton and the silver casket in which the incriminating 'casket letters' (probably forgeries) were found.

There are many portraits by Van Dyck, Janssens and several by Sir Henry Raeburn with 18th century armorial porcelain. In the 'Petit Point Room', used as a boudoir by Lady Hersey Baird, several pieces of 'La Belle Stuart's' furniture with her inlaid tortoiseshell writing cabinet (a present from Charles II) are on display. The staircase, the China Hall, the Blue room, the Yellow Room, the Ante Room and the Great Hall are full of interesting exhibits; it is a rare treat of history. The gardens are extensive and an avenue of trees - the 'Politicians Walk' - reminds us that 'Secretary Maitland' strolled with the political greats of his day deeply immersed in the affairs of State in total privacy.

Lennox Road
Lennoxlove

Lennox Road, previously Amisfield Road, was renamed in 1955 when the six five-apartment houses were built. It lies on the east side of Haddington off Whittingehame Drive and joins Ford Road to Giffordgate.

It is named after Charles Stuart, Duke of Richmond and Lennox who was drowned in 1673 aged 33 years near Elsinore in Denmark seven years after his marriage to Francis Teresa Stuart - 'La Belle Stuart', daughter of the Hon. Walter Stuart.

Lennox's titles were numerous: Duke of Richmond, Earl of March, Duke and Earl of Lennox, Earl of Darnley and Seigneur d'Aubigny. His father was Lord George Stuart, 9th Seigneur d' Aubigny and his mother was Katherine, daughter of the 2nd Earl of Suffolk.

He was born in London on 7th March 1639 and was three years old when his Royalist father and his uncle were killed at the start of the Civil War as faithful supporters of Charles I. At the age of six he was created Baron Stuart of Newbury and Earl of Lichfield, titles which would have been those of his uncle. When his cousin died in 1660 he succeeded to his title, Duke of Richmond.

He supported Charles II in the Royalist rising of August 1659 and was appointed Gentleman of the Bedchamber in 1661. That year his first wife Elizabeth, the widow of the Viscount Mansfield, died in childbirth. He married his second wife, Margaret, widow of William Lewis of Bletchington, in 1662; she died in 1666.

At Court he fell deeply in love with Lady Francis Theresa Stuart. She was a maid of honour to Queen Catherine of Braganza in the court of Charles II but the king had designs to make her one of his mistresses; he adored beautiful women having eight mistresses and fourteen illegitimate children. The king so admired her beauty he had her figure modelled by Bothier for Britannia which adorns British coinage (although Oman in his *The Coinage of England* dismissed this as 'fanciful legend'). She became known as 'La Belle Stuart'. However, the king's romantic attentions meant nothing to her; she was in love with the Duke of Richmond and Lennox and, realising that the king would disapprove, the couple eloped in 1666. The king, not a little annoyed, banned them from court. The young couple lived abroad but she was a favourite of the queen and was soon allowed to return to court.

The Duke was appointed ambassador to the court of Denmark but he came to an unfortunate and sudden end when, as a guest of a visiting British frigate at Elsinore, he fell overboard to his death on 12th December 1672. The Duke's embalmed body was sent back to London in a new ship painted in black with black sails provided by the King of Denmark. He was buried on 20th September 1673 in the chapel of Henry VII at Westminster. His honours became extinct, his nearest male heir being Charles II.

They had been married only seven years and the Duchess continued to live at the court of Charles II as a lady of the Bedchamber for the next thirty years. On 22nd December 1673 the king granted her the Lennox estates and for an annuity of £1000 she resigned her estate of Aubigny to the crown. Sadly, her beauty was marred from the effects of smallpox and the King, in sympathy and to cheer her, presented her with a magnificent inlaid tortoise shell writing cabinet which can be seen at Lennoxlove. She had no children and left her estate to her cousin, Alexander Stewart, Lord Blantyre. Her Will contained a provision that the name of Lethington should be changed to **Lennoxlove** in memory of her love for her husband the Duke of Lennox. She died on 22nd October 1702 and was buried at Westminster.

Lennox Milne Court

L ennox Milne Court, off Poldrate on the way to the Waterloo Bridge, was named in 1980 to commemorate a famous and well-loved Scottish actress, Lennox Milne. The naming of this lovely little court was the proposal of the Dowager Duchess of Hamilton, a good friend and admirer of Lennox Milne. Also, at the instigation of the Dowager Duchess, a plaque in the beautiful garden of Haddington House was erected in her memory shortly after her death in 1980. This was entirely appropriate because Lennox Milne gave unstintingly of her time and great talents to the administration of the 'Lamp of Lothian Collegiate Trust' and as its Organiser she was the energy behind the opening of the newly-restored Haddington House in 1969.

Lennox Milne was born on 9th May 1909. She was educated at the University of Edinburgh where she graduated Master of Arts in 1932. She studied music to qualify as a Licentiate of the Royal Academy of Music and she trained for the stage with Ann Turner-Robertson at the Royal Academy of Dramatic Art in London.

She became a school teacher and this experience gave her a clear insight into the needs and learning processes of children. It seemed a natural progression for her when she was appointed the producer of the BBC Schools Department in Scotland during the 1939-45 war.

Shortly after the war she met the talented author Moray McLaren who became the BBC's first Programme Director for Scotland. He had agreed to stand in for John Laurie for one night in his own play at Perth Repertory Theatre. The experience, although not entirely novel, was nightmarish for him. It was on this stage and in that play that he met his future wife, Lennox Milne. Their marriage in 1946 was the start of a wonderful twenty-six year partnership of theatre and authorship.

During her acting career between 1946 and 1949 she played many leading roles as a member of the Citizens' Theatre Company in Glasgow. In 1948 her portrayal of Veritie in Tyrone Guthrie's play *The Thrie Estaites* was so successful it was repeated many times.

With actor, director and commentator Tom Fleming she was a co-director of the Edinburgh Gateway Company having co-founded the Company in 1953. This happy association was to last for twelve years during the last five of which she was Director of Productions. Fleming and she played several major roles together in such as: *The Flouers O' Edinburgh, A Singular Grace* and many others. On one memorable occasion her husband, while taking his stage call as author of *One Traveller Returns*, kissed his wife's hand in congratulation and respect for her impeccable performance as Sister Chisholm.

Another husband/wife success occured in 1955 when she played the lead in her husband's award-winning play *Heather on Fire*. He had written it for her and he won the Charles Henry Foyle New Play Award - a £100 prize. Her vast contribution to her profession was given Royal recognition in 1956 when she was honoured with the award of the OBE - Officer of the Order of the British Empire. In 1959 her solo performance at Stratford, Ontario in Kemp's *The Heart is Highland* was again received with acclaim.

Between her engagements she loved to travel with her wanderlust husband; in an article *Actress Wife Spotlights her Husband* written for the Edinburgh Evening Despatch of 6th March 1954 she wrote:

> I have 'sat in boats paralysed with cold, cowered in motor cars starved and miserable, slept on river banks, waded in icy Shetland estuaries, and still the man will fish, hour after hour, without food, soaked to the skinÖÖI find myself on a small Icelandic cargo-boat making for the Arctic Ocean or standing in the Palais des Papes in Avignon or sitting in the Tivoli Gardens at Copenhagen, while the Scottish man of letters tears round the scenic railway yelling like a schoolboy.'

In 1967 she received an invitation from Broadway in New York. This was further recognition of her now international stature as an actress of the highest merit. Her portrayal of the Headmistress, Miss Marcia Blaine, in the stage version of *The Prime of Miss Jean Brodie* earned her another award for her performance; it was a sell-out. Her magical portrayal of eccentric comedy characters had again endeared her to her public.

Much to the great benefit of Haddington she settled with her husband at Pegh-de-Loan in Station Avenue. She was soon to become a well-known and popular figure in the Royal Burgh. At the formation of the 'Lamp of Lothian Trust' in 1969 in Haddington the Duchess of Hamilton, the prime mover of the Trust, was looking for someone who could give inspired leadership to its development and administration; the wise choice was Lennox Milne who had by now retired from the stage. She became 'Lamp Organiser' and was responsible for the opening of the newly restored Haddington House.

Two years later, on the bicentenary of the birth of Sir Walter Scott, she wrote and produced the *Young Scott*, which was performed in the Corn Exchange of Haddington with school children from all over East Lothian. It was acclaimed in the National press as, 'the most animated of all the Scottish Bicentenary programmes.' At the first meeting of the Haddington Literary Society at the Bridge Centre the first speaker was Lennox Milne. In the words of artist and author Doris Ann Goodchild who witnessed her speech, 'her face and eyes were so alight, she was a flame of interest.'

She threw herself into work for the Edinburgh International Festival of 1971. She with Tom Fleming and Richard Todd performed *A Singular Grace* - a bicentenary tribute to Sir Walter Scott. At the Gateway Theatre, in the learned Robert Kemp's *The Other Dear Charmer* she played Miss Nimmo (it was of course at Miss Nimmo's house at a tea party she introduced Robert Burns (Tom Fleming) to Mrs McLehose - Clarinda (Iris Russell).) Such was Lennox Milne's superb acting ability she appeared in eight of the first ten Festivals (41).

The Dowager Duchess of Hamilton came to admire and to befriend Lennox Milne. She was an ideal companion to accompany the Dowager Duchess on a tour of Europe in 1971 after the death of her husband, Moray McLaren, that year. Lennox Milne was essentially a reserved and private person but she had a magnetic quality which 'moved and delighted a public who came under the spell of a personality of great strength, power and originality.' She inspired an enormous confidence in a quiet almost self-effacing manner.

In 1971 she retired as Organiser but continued to serve the 'Lamp' as arts adviser and committee member. She was appointed to the Lamp's Board of Trustees in 1980 but by now she had become ill, suffering from cancer and in a few months she died.

On 20th June 1980 Lennox Milne McLaren OBE, MA, LRAM, ELOC died. Hers was a full and excitingly active life. She bore the dreaded cancer with bravery. 'It ought never to have happened so soon; she was too great a loss.' said Pamela Roberts, her colleague and successor. One sentence contained in her obituary and composed by the Dowager Duchess of Hamilton sums up the sense of loss felt by all who knew her, "In whatever success we may have achieved or to which we may aspire, her influence remains a potent factor."

Lodge Street

L odge Street was so called from the fact that the Masonic
Lodge, St John's of Kilwinning, was established there, its
charter having been granted from the Grand Lodge of Scotland
in 1599. The former name of this little street was 'Yarmouth
Roads' being difficult to negotiate in darkness - its only light
being 'a solitary peeping oil lamp' (14 p.21).

The building next to the Masonic Lodge was the School for Girls
attended, in 1811, by Jane Welsh who was taught by Edward
Irving (4. p.19). A Parish School was proposed by the heritors
(Parish landholders) in 1822 but it was not until 1826 that the
proposal of the landward heritors came into being and it was
built in Lodge Street. It was called The Landward Public School
under the control of the new School Board in 1872 with the
passing of the Education (Scotland) Act of that year.

Also in Lodge Street is the 18th century classical Carlyle House,
'a tiny five-bay palace'(26.p.241) with its rusticated arched
entrance above which are giant Corinthian pilasters. Behind this
'palace' is a house of 'opulence without waste, elegance, good
sense, silent practical affection and manly wisdom, from
threshold to rooftree' (Thomas Carlyle) - the Jane Welsh Carlyle
Museum. This was the residence of Dr and Mrs Welsh and their
delightful daughter, Jane Welsh who was born in this house on
14th July 1801. The Welsh family lived there from 1799 until
Dr Welsh died in 1819. Thomas Carlyle was a frequent visitor
during his courtship of Jane.

Lydgait,
Lydgait Gardens

Lydgait links Aberlady Road to the junction of Victoria Park, Vetch Park and Florabank Road. Lydgait Gardens is a cul-de-sac off Lydgait.

Miller (2) gives a 1558 reference to a common gait, called Lydgait,

> '.....as lying betwixt the common lone passing from the town of Haddington to Aberlady, and the east lone, called Barmy Lone, as being alluterlie (completely) telit doune and destroyed by the possessors, etc. In 1601, April 24th, the Lydgait is noticed as lying on the north side of the town, "betwixt Harmaneflat and the Buttis passing fra the zairdis heidis.'

A simple derivation of the name Lydgait may be a 'sheltered walk', Lyd or Lithe, according to the Scots Dictionary, meaning 'calm, sheltered or snug' and gait meaning a 'way of walking.'

The 1819 Plan of Haddington and Nungate shows Lydgait as 'Lead Lau' being thought to have been named from the fact that lead was transported along this road to Longniddry.

There is a brief mention of Lydgait in Grey and Jamieson's *A Short History of Haddington* which refers to the existence of 'cavalry barracks erected in Hope Park situated between Lydgait and the footpath now known as 'Blackpaling Road.' Haddington had become a garrison town in June 1803. There was fear of an invasion from Napoleon's army after renewed aggression in Europe when Napoleon seized Hanover and prepared to invade Britain.

Maitlandfield House
(formerly Bearford's House)

Maitlandfield House, now Maitlandfield House Hotel, stands at the end of the Sidegate at the corner of Mill Wynd. The original house was named Bearford's House an early reference to which is given by Gray and Jamieson (1.p.44) - in May 1657 a detachment of General Monk's army occupied Haddington and its commander, Captain Roger Legge, took up 'his abode in "Lady Bearfoord's House."'

Bearford's House was one of many properties of Francis Charteris, Earl of Wemyss and was transferred to the ownership of Lieutenant Thomas Maitland in April 1754. The house was probably remodelled about this time and renamed Maitlandfield.

In 1794 Thomas Maitland made over the property to his son Charles who served with distinction in the Indian army and became Colonel of the East Lothian Yeomanry and Cavalry in 1797. In 1820, in command of the Yeomanry, he set out to quell the 'Radicals' in Glasgow but on reaching Airdrie they returned to Haddington having been informed that rebellion was over.

Martine in his *Reminiscences* (14.pps.129-130) recalled the colonel's sister, Miss Mary Maitland, who 'had an old Scotch aristocratic pride about her.' Shopkeepers of the town being commonly referred to as 'esquires,' Miss Maitland was heard to exclaim, 'Gude save us, folk canna spit owre the window noo for fear o' spitting on an "esquire"!'

The 1819 Plan of Haddington confirms that Maitlandfield was the residence of Colonel Maitland. He was elected MP for Haddingtonshire in 1774 when he successfully opposed Sir David Kinloch of Gilmerton. In 1825 Maitlandfield was inherited by Thomas Maitland, the heir of Charles Maitland of Maitlandfield and Pogbie.

The Howden family took ownership of Maitlandfield during the 1840s. The Howdens were goldsmiths in Edinburgh from about the middle of the 18th century. Deacon Francis Howden was treasurer of the Incorporation of Goldsmiths of the City of Edinburgh in 1790 and was elected deacon in 1811. As treasurer he gave competent and conservative service to the Incorporation objecting on occasions to unnecessary expenditures on such as - the lavish dinner to be given in honour of the visit of George IV in 1822, twenty guineas for the victims of 'The Great Fire of Edinburgh' of 1824 and money for the new High School at Calton Hill.

Thomas and Agnes Howden became the new owners; she owned 4 acres of arable land at North Shott, near the village of St Laurence. Thomas Howden died in 1868 and his son Dr Thomas Howden MD inherited the property; he was Provost of the Burgh in 1877. In 1901 the property was inherited by his son, Robert Howden MB, CM, a ship's doctor with a Master's Certificate who died on 27th June 1907 aged 43 years. He was an elder of St Mary's Parish Church for 17 years and left Maitlandfield to his son Thomas. The last of the Howden family to own Maitlandfield was David Thomas Howden who lived in St Andrews; he sold the house in October 1942 to George Paterson & Sons of Haddington for the sum of £1400.

The Rayner family were the next residents of Maitlandfield. Frank Rayner, the Assistant County Treasurer and Collector, sold his house which stood at the end of the old wooden bridge over the Tyne. The Rayners lived at Maitlandfield during the 1940s. Frank senior played double bass in the orchestra for the Haddington Operatic Society. His family were teachers: Willie taught Art, Frank junior taught English and his daughter, Peggy, gave private tuition in music.

During World War II Maitlandfield was used by the Ministry of Food as offices and in 1952 it was taken over by the British Transport Commission. To enable the widening of Mill Wynd 330 sq.yds. of the Maitlandfield garden was acquired by the County Council of East Lothian in 1952 and five years later the mansion was sold to Production Efficiency Ltd for £1700 who in turn sold it to Matthew Dickson Carlaw, the Burgh Chamberlain of Haddington. He sold the ground floor area to Stanley Frank Godek, a shopkeeper of Haddington in 1958.

Mr and Mrs Godek took over the whole property in 1961 including the cottage which stood at the Mill Wynd corner of the garden. Paterson's Sawmill stood at the opposite side of the garden. Mr and Mrs Godek with their two sons made several changes to Maitlandfield: they transformed the little cottage into a laundrette and altered part of the interior to form six flatlets for newly-weds who were waiting for Council houses; their average stay was about two years. The Godeks converted the mansion into an hotel. The three rooms at the rear were knocked into one to form a large dining/function room and in 1967 an extension at the south end of the building was added to form new kitchens and a cocktail lounge. The cottage, having been transformed into a workshop for Mr Godek who built cycles and motor-bikes there, had to be demolished and part of garden was lost, again for road widening.

In 1968 Maitlandfield was now sold to Anthony and Cecily Morga who took over the hotel complete with its clients. The Morgas gave up the business in 1987 and sold it to Ivor Reid Craig who carried out a complete refurbishment adding a spacious L-shaped conservatory over-looking the garden and the ancient and picturesque St Mary's Parish Church. In the cocktail bar and dining rooms of the Maitlandfield House Hotel a link with the past has been created in the 'Restaurant of Sixteen Kings' which reminds us that Haddington was the fourth largest town in Scotland during the 15th century and that two of the sixteen kings were born in the town. The naming of its 'Bearford Bar' is a reminder of the original name of the house - Bearford's House in 1657.

The hotel was purchased in 1988 by Peaston & Co Ltd who leased it to Ivor Craig. In 1989 the new owners were Rollo & Sons of Cockenzie who sold it to Kirkton Investments Ltd in December 1990.

Market Street

Market Street was originally described as Tolbooth Gait (1.p.83) presumably because it lay immediately east of the Tolbooth where the Fish market was situated. It became known as Fishmarket Street and was shortened to Market Street. (1.p.92). Fishmarket Wynd was named from the fact that it led from Fishmarket Street to the High Street. However, Market Street only came into existence as an identifiable street when buildings were first erected in the open area of the High Street - this was before 1426 when Caleperys (now Kilpair Street) was first mentioned. (1. p.81)

Market Street was a cul-de-sac but by 1800 it opened via Tolbooth Wynd to Hardgate and the 1819 Plan shows Market Street as 'Back Street' for the obvious reason that it lay at the back of the High Street.

A Saturday market was sanctioned by James V about 1530 and in 1633 Charles I granted an additional market to be held on Wednesdays. The markets were held mainly in the High Street although Newton Port was used for the Flesh Market, the High Street having become over-crowded. During the 18th and early 19th century Market Street was a hive of activity with farmers and grain merchants gathering with their families for the annual fairs, Hiring Fridays (usually in February), shopping at stalls, exchanging gossip and finding work as agricultural servants. The last of Hiring Fridays took place as recently as 1925.

Market Street today is a busy thoroughfare; it has character in its irregular shape being constricted at both ends and lined with late 18th and early 19th century three- and four-storey buildings. At its east end it is quaintly constricted by the 19th century Pheasant Hotel (No.71) where the street continues into Hardgate passing the five bays of the Palladian palace front of Nos.7 and 8 Market Street. This building dates back to about 1760; its rusticated ground level has a pedimented centre with giant Ionic pilasters above. The three-storey block of Nos. 60-62 has a pedimented doorway and scrolled skewputts but the oldest building in Market Street is adjacent to Cross Lane and is the crow-stepped gable of No.78 High Street.

M'Call's Park

M'Call's Park, on which the old Knox Institute was built (now Knox Court), is named after Alexander M'Call who was Provost of Haddington from 1723 and 1728.

He was the Postmaster of Haddington when the Post Office was in the Sidegate (until 1817 or 1818). His house, at the foot of Sidegate Lane, was a superb example of baronial design with its tower and spiral staircase. It was built early in the 17th century and was characterised by Martine in his *Reminiscences* as 'one of the few specimens of the old style left in the Burgh.' (14)

The M'Call family consisted of a son and a daughter. The son, also Alexander, was law agent for the Town Council and, as a Writer to the Signet, he was the solicitor of his close friend Sir Walter Scott. The daughter, Janet, married Hay Donaldson who became the Town Clerk of Haddington. They lived firstly at the old house in Sidegate Lane and later at Sunnybank (1819 plan) which became Tenterfield (1854 plan). Sadly, the old house at Sidegate was demolished during the road widening activities of the 1950s.

M'Call owned the swamp land of M'Call's Park in a corner of which stood an old wooden house. It was built in 1803 and was the last of the huts which formed the Haddington barracks being demolished in 1813. The park was 'obtained by the burgh in Provost Martine's time in 1813 in exchange for the "Lots" which lay alongside the post road from Governor Houston of Clerkington - acre for acre - a good bargain for the town.' (14. p.6). The area is shown as 'Town's Property' on John Wood's 1819 Plan which also shows the Rosehall Toll at its western extremity and a Powder Magazine at the east end of the park.

Alexander M'Call was succeeded as postmaster shortly after his death by John Martine in 1781 (14. p.228-9).

Neilson Park
Neilson Park Road

B road Wynd, between Market Street and High Street, was variously called Pirie's Wynd then **Neilson's Wynd** - Pirie and Neilson were local High Street traders (1 p.82).

Neilson Park Road, off Lodge Street, leads to **Neilson Park**, each of which were named in recognition of the legacy of George Neilson whose Clothier shop was situated adjacent to Neilson's Wynd near his tenement in the High Street.

He died on 14th November 1897 and in the Trust Disposition and Settlement of his estate George Neilson directed his Trustees to use the money for 'any deserving object of public beneficence in the town of Haddington or the surrounding district.' Accordingly, the trustees decided to purchase a park and recreation ground. The piece of ground chosen was known as Mylne's Park which is shown on the 1819 Plan as 'Geo. Mill Esqrs. Property.'

It was not until June 1910 that Neilson's Park was to be formally opened by Lord Wemyss but the death of Edward VII on 6th May delayed the event. A further delay occurred because of an accident suffered by his Lordship. However the Trustees 'placing reliance on the common-sense of the public have informally given admittance to the park, and this privilege has been popularly appreciated.' (Haddingtonshire Courier - 31st June 1910). The original ornamental gate and iron palings were made by John Nisbet, a blacksmith in Lodge Street. The artistry of his work was of 'exceptional character, scroll-work, Scottish thistles, curves and iron lettering combining to give a splendid effect.' Twenty tons of iron was used for 20,000 railings all of which were removed during the 1939-45 war.

In 1912 only one of the original Trustees was still alive and he transferred the Park and securities amounting to £5,500 to newly appointed 'Neilson Park Trustees' who took over the management of the park using the income from the endowment for its upkeep. The new Trustees jealously guarded their control of the park and ensured that the local authority should not be allowed to have any part in running it. However, by 1948 the income available from capital monies was insufficient to maintain the park and an application was made to the Court of Session to hand over the park and the endowment to the Town Council.

Newton Port

The port or gatehouse at the north-eastern end of the old town provided an entrance across the Hardgate and after the erection of the Town Wall in 1597 this port was resited in the vicinity of St John's Free Church at what is now Alexandra Place. This was 'Newtown Port' as it was then known and the port was removed around 1763. (5. p.7).

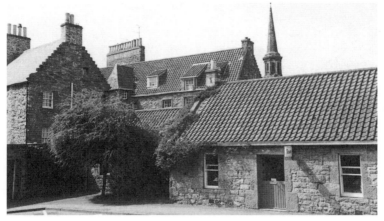

Miller (2.p.226) tells us that 'the north part of the town, leading from the wynd head at the (mediaeval) Tolbooth, was called Newtown.' The street from the North-East Port to the South Port (at Sidegate adjacent to Maitlandfield) was considered to be dangerous to travellers on horseback because of its height in the middle - they had to remember to 'duck' their heads but many a hurrying horseman was unseated.

By 1766 both the South Port and the North-East Port were removed and the bridge at the latter was widened. At the Market Street end of Newton Port a row of six cottages, owned by the butcher of Market Street, George Pringle, were home to six children and their parents in a room and kitchen and in another to seven children plus parents, according to the 1891 census. The occupants of these cottages, almost as many as twelve adults and thirty children, had to share an outside toilet and a water pump. There were three entrances with houses on each side of the passageways and additional outside toilets were added later.

The derelict cottages were demolished in 1955, the vacant space becoming a lawn and eventually a private car park for the staff of the East Lothian Courier when the ground was acquired by D & J Croall Ltd.

The unused square Gothic St John's Church in Newton Port was built originally because St Mary's could not accommodate the excess congregation and they separated in 1838 when St John's was complete. The church was used as a military hospital during the 1914-18 war.

The popular Public Library in Newton Port was built as Knox's Free Church for the 'Anti-Burghers'. The library inherited the precious Gray collection which had been accommodated in the English School at Church Street (1.p.54) was catalogued by Forbes Gray FRSE, FSAScot in 1929. A large wooden plaque in the library is inscribed:

> *Joseph Harper Esquire, sometime farmer at Snawdon, in the Parish of Garvald, who died in Edinburgh on 30th January 1891, by his Trust Disposition and Settlement dated 28th March 1890 GENEROUSLY BEQUEATHED to the Provost, Magistrates and Town Council of Haddington the sum of FIVE HUNDRED POUNDS, to be invested, and the Annual Income arising therefrom to be applied towards the maintenance of this Public Library.*
>
> *November 1895.*

Another church in Newton Port was St John's Free Church which is now Alexandra Place. It was built in 1842 and was vacated in 1890 when the new Free Church in Court Street replaced it.

Nungate Bridge

The year in which this ancient bridge was built is uncertain. Martine simply describes it as 'an old veteran, no doubt built about the same time as the Collegiate Church.' (2.p.85). An early reference by Dr Wallace-James in a letter to the Scotsman of 2nd January 1912 refers to a 13th century deed (Carta Prioratus S. Andrea c. 1282) in which 'the old bridge' is mentioned. In 1293 it is recorded that Sir William Lindsay left money for its repair. Other charters dated 1311 and 1356 leave sums of money for further repairs and in 1350 Hugh de Giffard, Lord of Yester, gifted two pieces of land in Giffordgate 'for the benefit and upkeep of the said bridge, with free ish (egress) and entry to all wishing to use the said bridge.' (1.p.145).

The bridge was severely damaged during the 'Siege of Haddington' in 1548. After 'Black Saturday' (10th September 1547) - the Battle of Pinkie (near Musselburgh), the Scots having suffered a severe defeat at the hands of the Duke of Somerset (Protector of England), the English laid siege to Haddington (1548-9) and the French, at the behest of the Scots, attacked the English at the Sands; it was at this time that the bridge was damaged. Evidence of its repair can still be seen from the difference in the type of stone used (2.p.204). Additional repairs were necessary in 1608 and in 1639. Much of the stone used in these repairs was obtained from the ruined Choir of St Mary's Church; there are some nineteen identifiable masons' marks on the bridge indicating repairs over the centuries.

From minutes of Haddington Town Council dated 27th August 1672 the east end of the bridge was 'built be thame', meaning - built by right of jurisdiction. The 'jougs' - the hinged iron collar attached by a chain to the parapet of the bridge for wrong-doers - were ordered to be replaced with a stone tablet inscribed with the town's coat of arms. In effect the town laid claim to the east end of the bridge

However this seems to have been disputed by the council itself when in 1758, on being asked to contribute £50 towards its repair, stated that the bridge was 'no part of the Royalty'* (1.p.145) - at that time the Nungate and Giffordgate did not form part of Haddington - but it was agreed that because of its use and convenience to the townsfolk the money should be paid. The ownership of the bridge remained in doubt until 1849

This ancient and attractive three-arch (additional arches were added during the 18th century to lessen the slope at each end) stone bridge spans the Tyne over a width of 100 ft and is in regular use for pedestrians.

* The Royalty consisted of land received in gift from the Crown and held under a series of Royal Charters which conferred exclusive rights and privileges relating to markets, customs and dues - powers which were transferred to local governments.

Paterson Place,
Abbeyfield

The name Paterson Place is not shown on Wood's 1819 Plan of Haddington and the Nungate, but it is shown on the 1892 plan. Who then was Paterson? The most likely candidate is the Reverend John Paterson, a United Presbyterian minister, who opened his school in 1831.

This was Paterson Place Academy, a private school of 'tolerably high standard' which opened at a time of considerable dissension between the head of the Burgh School, the Reverend William Whyte, and the Town Council. He was a cruel and vindictive man to his pupils, no-one would serve under him and the number of pupils in his school had dropped from over 200 to 17. Many parents must have removed their children to Paterson Place Academy and to the Parish School.

William Paterson ran an efficient establishment for 23 years in his premises at the back of Lodge Street and when he retired in 1854 the school was taken over by Walter Haig. He ran the academy with efficiency at secondary school level for about twenty-five years until the newly opened Knox Institute attracted most of his clientele. He retired about 1880 to live in Edinburgh where he died in 1904.

Haig's Academy was eventually demolished in 1984 to make way for the modern building of **Abbeyfield** which provides sheltered housing for the elderly; it was opened in 1987 by the Abbeyfield Haddington Society Ltd.

Pegh-de-Loan
Peachdales

Pegh-de-Loan is the area of land behind the Ferguson Monument. Its name, according to Martine (14), is 'thought to be derived from the Pechts or Picts and was 'a narrow, swampy piece of ground, through which a burn ran, well suited for growing willows.' *The Concise Scots Dictionary* defines *Pecht* as Pict or a contemptuous term for a small person or animal. Chambers Dictionary defines *pegh* as the verb to pant and *Peght* as a Pict.

Another school of thought suggests that Pegh is a distortion of the French peche meaning peach from an avenue of peach trees in the vicinity - hence the name **Peachdales** off Station Road. The land above Pegh-de-Loan towards St Lawrence was a campsite for the troops of Sir John Cope in September 1745, two days before the Battle of Prestonpans. They were routed within about ten minutes by the Highlanders of the Young Pretender's army.

An area of land at Pegh-de-Loan Park was sold by the Town Council for £50 to the Gas Company in 1834; the Company being formed in December. Haddington streets were lit by gas from 1836. However, this area was previously known as 'Gallows Green' so called from the fact that criminals were hanged there. Martine in his *Reminiscences* (14.p.3), quoting from a Burgh record of about 1500, described the hanging of a prisoner convicted of stealing cloth. He was hanged for an hour at Gallows Green and taken to be dipped in the water of the Tyne until he was 'clean deed.' A large stone with a square hole, thought to support the gallows tree, was found in 1805 under the ground being excavated for the foundations of Bellevue House.

During the 17th century Gallows Green was the scene of the heinous practice of witch-burning. Miller (2. pps.222-3) records several cases between 1649 to 1677 when John Sleich jnr., son of Provost Sleich, was appointed Commissioner to report the confessions of women suspected of witchcraft to the secret council and to the Assize in Edinburgh.

Poldrate, Poldrate Mill

Poldrate and **Poldrate Mill** can be reached from the east end of the High Street, along Sidegate. There was a Kirk Mill on this site in the Middle Ages and Franciscan monks owned a 'croft at Poldrate'.

Reference to the name Poldrate is made in the 1423 'Auld Register of Haddington' (1.p.81). This early reference negates the notion that the derivation of the name Poldrate is from the French 'poudre', although there was a gun-powder store in the vicinity of the mill during the English occupation of Haddington in 1548. The 'Siege of Haddington' lasted almost two years in 1548-49 and took place when the town was captured by the invading English army whose 2000 soldiers fortified the town against 5000 Scots and French soldiers with 10 cannon. The Poldrate was thus part of a French fortification during the siege. However, the derivation of the name Poldrate is more likely to be from the Scots word 'polder' meaning powder (11.p.514), corn being ground at the medieval mill to make 'powder'.

Another early reference to the name Poldrate which predates the 'Siege' was in 1478 when Sir John Haliburton of Carlowry assigned a tenement to a warden and eight Franciscan Friars in 'Poldrate' to administer his charity for the poor of Haddington (1. p.28)

Poldrate was an early meeting place for members of the Scottish Episcopalian Church which had its precarious beginnings at the start of the 18th century; the building was demolished about 1850. It was at this meeting place that the Rev. John Gray preached after he had been dismissed, in 1689, from his charge at Aberlady for his refusal to read a proclamation of the Scots Parliament and to pray for the new king and queen, William III and Mary II. Gray's precious collection of books, bequeathed to Haddington, formed the basis of Haddington's first library.

In a room above the Episcopal meeting place performances of drama took place during the late 18th century; this activity did not meet with the approval of the established church. Another nonjuring Jacobite minister, Joseph Robertson, preached at this meeting-place and attempted to raise support for the 'Young Pretender' in 1745. He tried to gain permission to preach at St Mary's Parish Church but he was rebuffed with the reason that he was presuming too much too quickly.

Towards the end of the 18th century part of the property at Poldrate was owned by a group of weavers who sold it to George Jack, a mason in 1798; the 1819 Plan shows a building belonging to Mrs Jack.

The 18th century buildings of Poldrate Mill were built on the site of the old medieval Kirk Mill. The mill was reconstructed in 1842 but fell out of use with advent of modern machinery and lay almost derelict for several decades but it was reopened by Mr William Templeton and was known as Templeton's Mill during the 1940s. A major restoration was undertaken by the Lamp of Lothian Collegiate Trust in 1968, the old workers houses being used as a community centre and studios. The Collegiate Clubs of the Trust included a visual arts workshop, the East Lothian Literary Club, the Haddington Camera Club and the Bridge Youth and Community Centre.

Princess Mary Road,
Princess Mary Place

The houses of **Princess Mary Road** were built in 1947-9. It runs off Lydgait and leads into the cul-de-sac, **Princess Mary Place** which was built on the site of the old Auction Mart in 1984/5.

Princess Mary Road and Place were named to commemorate the visits of the Princess Royal, daughter of King George V and Queen Mary who on 15th April 1947 accepted the honour of the Freedom of the Royal Burgh of Haddington on behalf of the Royal Scots (The Royal Regiment) of which she was Colonel-in-Chief.

Princess Mary was born on 25th April 1897 at York Cottage, Sandringham, the third child and only daughter of the Duke and Duchess of York (later King George V and Queen Mary). Her eldest brother, Prince Edward became Edward VIII who renounced the throne to marry an American divorcee, Mrs Simpson; her second brother, Prince Albert, thus became King George VI. Her younger brothers were Prince Henry who became Duke of Gloucester, Prince George who became Duke of Kent and Prince John who died in 1905 aged three years.

During her childhood she was educated by governesses and became fluent in both French and German. She enjoyed the outdoor sports of fishing and hunting. During the Great War her Christmas Gift Fund ensured that troops at the front received gift boxes. In addition she organised help for the families at home of soldiers in France. Towards the end of the war she took a course in nursing and worked at Great Ormond Street Hospital.

Princess Mary married Henry, Earl of Harewood, Viscount Lascelles on 28th February 1922 at Westminster when one of her bridesmaids was Lady Elizabeth Bowes-Lyon (now The Queen Mother); this was her first royal ceremony. They had two sons: George (1923) and Gerald (1924).

In 1926 through her interest in nursing she was appointed Commandant-in-Chief of the British Red Cross and in 1932 she was created Princess Royal. During the second World War, as Commandant of the Auxiliary Territorial Service (ATS), she travelled throughout the country to visit ATS Units and various welfare organisations.

Her interest in the Royal Burgh of Haddington stemmed from the fact that she was Colonel-in-Chief of Haddington's famous regiment - the Royal Scots and the naming of Princess Mary Road is a permanent reminder of the Princess's visit to Haddington in 1947, during the Provostship of Robert Leslie Fortune (ref. Fortune Avenue), when she accepted the invitation of the Town Council on behalf of the Royal Scots to accept the Freedom of the Royal Burgh.

During the 1950s the Town Hall of Haddington was found to be in danger of collapse when dry rot was discovered and it was saved from demolition by the Burgh Surveyor, the redoubtable Mr. William Lee Hogg (1899-1994). Princess Mary again accepted an invitation to Haddington to perform the opening ceremony of the newly restored Town Hall in 1956.

She died at Harewood House on 28th March 1965.

Queen's Avenue

Queen's Avenue, off Hospital Road, runs parallel to Haldane Avenue and was named to commemorate the coronation of Queen Elizabeth II in 1953. The houses of Queen's Avenue were built soon afterwards.

Elizabeth II was born Princess Elizabeth Alexandra Mary on 21st April 1926. Her father, George VI, reigned from 1936 until his death in 1952 and her mother Lady Elizabeth Angela Marguerite Bowes-Lyon was crowned Queen at Westminster in 1937.

On the outbreak of World War II the thirteen year-old Princess Elizabeth and her nine year-old sister Princess Margaret were moved to Birkhall near Balmoral but during the summer of 1940 they returned to Windsor Castle and she made her first broadcast on BBC's *Children's Hour*. In 1942 she became Colonel of the Grenadier Guards and she joined the Auxiliary Transport Service in 1945 in which she qualified as a driver and was promoted to the rank of Junior Commander.

The Princesses toured South Africa with their parents in 1947 for four months before Elizabeth's engagement to the son of Prince Andrew of Greece and Princess Alice of Battenberg, Lieutenant Philip Mountbatten. The Prince and Princess first met in 1939. She never forgot him and after her return from South Africa the king agreed to their engagement. They were married on 21st November 1947 at Westminster Abbey the Prince having been created Duke of Edinburgh the day before the wedding.

It was during their Commonwealth tour of 1952 that the Princess received the sad news of the death of her father. He died on 6th February 1952 and she received the dreaded news in the early hours of that morning at Sagana Lodge in Kenya. She was proclaimed Queen Elizabeth II on that day and crowned on 2nd June 1953. In 1957 her husband was styled Prince Philip. They had three sons and one daughter, Prince Charles Philip Arthur George, born 1948; Princess Anne Elizabeth Alice Louise, born 1950; Prince Andrew Albert Christian Edward, born 1960 and Prince Edward Anthony Richard Louis, born 1964.

During her reign there have been nine Prime ministers: Winston

Churchill (1940-45 and 1951-1955), Anthony Eden (1955-1957), Maurice Harold MacMillan (1957-1963), Sir Alec Douglas-Home (1963-1964), James Harold Wilson (1964-1970, 1974-1976), Edward Heath (1970-1974), James Callaghan 1976-1979), Margaret Thatcher (1979-1991), John Major (1991-). She celebrated her 40th anniversary as Queen in 1992, the year she described as her 'Annus Horribilus' because of unwelcome publicity about the marriages of her family.

During her reign Mount Everest was conquered by Edmund Hillary and Sherpa Tensing (1953), the Open University and many Polytechnics which became universities were created, Rhodesia was given its independence, British forces were withdrawn from Suez, Britain entered the European Common Market, South Africa became a republic outside the Commonwealth (1961), space travel - man landed on the moon (1969), Perestroika and the dismantling of the Berlin Wall, the dismantling of the USSR and the end of communism, the murder of her favourite 'Uncle Dickie', Lord Louis Mountbatten by Irish terrorists in 1979, nuclear disarming, the Falklands War (1982), the Gulf War (1990), aparthied ended in South Africa and the undreamt of divorces of each of her children except the unmarried Prince Edward.

Her Majesty visited the Royal Burgh of Haddington on 12th July 1973 and was accompanied by her Lord Lieutenant, the Earl of Wemyss, the Provost of Haddington, Alexander Fraser Spowage, the Reverend James Riach and other good people of Haddington who had given their talents and time culminating in the opening of the newly-restored St Mary's Parish Church by Her Majesty.

Rosehall Court, Place, Walk

The origin of the name **Rosehall** is unknown. However, elderly residents of Haddington recall a profusion of rose bushes in the gardens of the old houses in the area and suspect that the name Rosehall arrived through common usage.

Rosehall Court off the Haddington-Pencaitland Road was named in 1976; the lane adjacent was known variously as Coal Brae and Donkey Walk on one side of which was Thomson's field and on the other a nine-hole golf course. This was converted into an army training area during the 1914-18 war with trenches and a practice bayoneting area; it is now arable land.

Rosehall Place was named in 1986 and the little complex of houses on the north side of Knox Academy, **Rosehall Walk**, was named in 1995.

Rosehall Dairy farm was tenanted by the McCall family when James McCall arrived from Dalkeith in 1891 where he was a successful farmer having won two trophies for the best yield mare and the best cross cow in the Dalkeith Horticultural Show. With his wife, three daughters and his son, William, he worked the farm for over forty years to supply milk by horse and cart to the people of Haddington. William McCall took over the farm when his father retired but the McCalls left Haddington in 1934. The new electricity sub-station was built about 1923 next to McCall's field and coke storage and workshops were adjacent to the large gasometer.

The farm land, shown as 'Town's Property' on the 1819 Plan of Haddington and Nungate, was used for the building of the new Knox Academy. This plan indicates the position of Rosehall Toll at the corner of Knox Place and Meadow Park.

Rosehall Foundry owned by the Stevenson family was situated west of the farm on the 'Road from Pencaitland' on the property of Jas. Roughead Esq., and supplied wrought iron railings, gates, iron bridges *et cetera* throughout East Lothian. In addition the company carried out repair work for the thriving West Mill.

A well-known feature of Rosehall was Dobie's Well at Beenie Craig's house. Its cool and refreshing chalybeate water was enjoyed by many generations of Haddingtonians until its water from the Garleton Hills was diverted when a deep sewer was laid during the construction of the new houses at Acredales in 1978.

Ross's Close

Ross's Close runs between the High Street and Langriggs and takes its name from a well-known plumber and Provost whose shop was at No.32 High Street and whose premises, T.M. Ross, Plumber, were sited at the rear of the close which came to be known as Ross's Close in late 19th century. Behind Ross's Close the modern housing (1963) by Campbell & Arnott is described by McWilliam as 'a misfire' (29) which has attempted to maintain tradition in its design and the placing of its windows.

Thomas Miller Ross was born in 1860 in the Highlands. He first arrived in Haddington at the age of 14 years and after working in Edinburgh and in America he returned to Britain to work, firstly in London and finally to settle in Haddington in 1889 to start his own plumbing business in his shop in the High Street.

This well-travelled man-of-the-world soon became a popular figure in the Royal Burgh. No job was too small or too large and his cheery disposition led to the success of his small company. He was a plumber of excellence and the quality and reliability of his work led to his membership of the Edinburgh and District Master Plumbers' Association of which he became a leading member.

He took a keen interest in the public affairs of Haddington which led to his election as a Town Councillor in November 1903. Small in stature but big in voice, he expressed himself with force and clarity caring little for criticism which was sometimes severe. He was to serve the Council in every capacity, except that of Treasurer, continuously for a total of 31 years, except for a one year break in 1909. During the 1914-18 War he worked tirelessly for the families of the soldiers of East Lothian on active service. He was elected Provost in 1918 and retired in 1923, a year before the end of his second term of office. He was still serving the Council as Convener of the Water and Lighting Committees in 1937 when he became suddenly ill at home. His died at his home, Stamford Villa in Haddington, on 10th March 1937.

St Ann's Place
St Anne's Gate

St Ann's Place, off Sidegate, is a picturesque little street the houses of which were built in 1814. The Chapel of St Ann's, at the corner of Church Street and Sidegate, had been demolished ten years before and its stone was used for the houses (14.pps.79 & 196). The chapel itself had been used by beggars and tinkers and had fallen into disrepair. The Town Council decided to remove it in order to widen the road and Miller's *Lamp of Lothian* (2) gives some details: -

> 'On the 12th November 1804, the town-council of Haddington purchased the tenement called St Ann's Chapel, which belonged to Thomas Shanks, wheelwright, in order that it, and the contiguous tenements, might be taken down, and an open area formed as an ornament to the street. The town paid £155 sterling for this ruinous tenement, and an equal sum for one adjoining, belonging to Widow Borthwick. This projected improvement, however, was not carried into effect, and the ruins of St Ann's and Borthwick's tenement were sold in 1813, to Mr M'Watt, late builder in Haddington...'

Martine (14.p.79) explains that part of the old chapel was used as a smithy by one George Henderson, known locally as 'Parrot' because of his incessant chatter.

St Anne's Gate which leads from Church Street into St Ann's Place is a picturesque restoration of the old mid-18th century houses by architect John A.W. Grant in 1955. The relief panel above the entrance is that of Haddington's goat.

St Ann's Chapel was one of eight religious establishments in Haddington; the others being:
- St Mary's Collegiate Church the patronage of which belonged to the Prior of St Andrews.
- The Dominican Monastery of Blackfriars which was on the site of the present Episcopal Church and the Elms. Its stones were used for the present wall which surround the church and the house.
- The Abbey of Haddington founded by Princess Ada, mother of William the Lyon and daughter-in-law of David I. There is no trace of the Abbey.
- St Martin's Nunnery in the Nungate the ruins of which still exist
- St Lawrence House and Chapel and Leper Hospital (ref. St Lawrence)
- St John's Chapel of the Knights Templar at the custom stone; no trace of it exists.
- St Catherine's Chapel on the west side of Hardgate - its stone was used to build the house of Andrew Pringle (subsequently owned by Mrs Jamieson.(14)

St Ann (usually spelled Anne, or Anna or Hannah) was the maternal grandmother of Jesus being the mother of the Virgin Mary whose father was St Joachim. As Jesus was a carpenter she became the patron saint of carpenters. Little was recorded of her life, in fact the first mention of it was made in the apocryphal gospel of James in the 2nd century.

In Constantinople a church was built in her honour from which her relics were taken to Jerusalem and to Rome. Many hundreds of years passed until in the 10th century her feast was celebrated at Naples. This was called the 'conception of St Anne' and soon afterwards it was celebrated in England and in Ireland. Then in the 11th century her feast was kept at Canterbury and at Worcester.

Artistic representations of her (possibly English) show her teaching her daughter, the Virgin Mary, to read. The Bodlean Library in Oxford contains examples of 13th century manuscripts pertaining to St Ann and at Croughton in Northants there are wall paintings of her. There are also paintings of her with her husband, Joachim, at their betrothal or marriage.

From the reign of King John (1199-1216) and from the 14th century she was patron of several religious guilds in Bury, King's Lynn, Lincoln and elsewhere.

Martin Luther (1483-1546), the German religious reformer, refuted images of St Ann with Jesus and Mary and he castigated her cult, however, the Holy See extended her feast to the Universal Church in 1584. Her feast day is 26th July.

St Lawrence

The St Lawrence development, off Alderston Road, was named in 1980. It takes its name from the monastery of St Laurence (an adaptation of St Lazerus) which was a leper colony a mile or so outside the boundary of 12th century Haddington.

Martine (14) describes St Laurence House:

> 'a leper house once existed, which was erected by order of an Act of the old Scotch Parliament. The Act narrates "that it was to be built at St Laurence House, bewast the town of Haddington." The old tenement on the north side of the road is supposed to have been the "Leprous House".'

Its hospital was endowed by James V (1513-1542) who appointed one of his Royal Chaplains, Walter Ramsay, as its preceptor. The hospital had about 82 acres and probably included Spittalrig (1). According to the Exchequer Rolls of 1530 the Franciscans of Haddington added the sum of twenty shillings to the funds of the hospital whose revenues amounted to £9 annually.

In 1533 the hospital was incorporated in the monastery of St Katherine of Sciennes of Edinburgh and in 1563 the nuns of St Katherine's sold the land to Sir John Bellenden of Auchenoule and his heir, Sir Lewis Bellenden, sold it to Sir Thomas Craig in 1588, the Scottish writer and the foremost expert of his day on Feudal Law.

The location of the hospital is explained by the fact that leper colonies had to be sited at least one mile outside the town walls. St Laurence House was demolished in 1906 and when the cottages on the site were built the excavations for their foundations revealed several thousand skeletons of sufferers who had died there.

St Laurence (Lazerus of Bethany)

Lazerus was venerated in Jerusalem because of the miracle of Jesus raising him from the dead. The story is told in the New Testament, John (11:1-44) - Jesus arrived in Bethany to find the two sisters of Lazerus, Martha and Mary, mourning over the death of their brother who had died four days before his arrival. Jesus was deeply moved and wept in sympathy with the mourners. He went to the tomb of Lazerus and asked that the stone at the entrance be removed. He astonished his onlookers when he called Lazerus to come out of the tomb. His miracle was performed when the dead man appeared and Jesus asked that his grave cloths be removed. Nothing more is heard of Lazerus in the New Testament after the Resurrection.

The Jews at Jaffa (Tel Aviv-Yafo in Israel), unable to believe in the miracle, were said to have placed Lazerus with his sisters in a leaking boat and pushed them off into the Mediterranean Sea. They landed safely at Cyprus where Lazerus became bishop and lived there until his death 30 years later.

Another 11th century legend emanates from France - in this case the rudderless boat of Lazerus and his sisters was said to have landed at Gaul (the name of ancient France) where they made many converts to Christianity in the vicinity of Marseilles. Lazerus became bishop and was martyred under Domitian. He was thought to have been buried in a cave over which the Church of St Victor was built. However, this version of events was probably a confusion of another bishop Lazerus of Aix in the 5th century who was buried at St Victor.

Lazerus is the patron-saint of Knights Hospitallers and leper hospitals but this is the fictional Lazerus referred to in Luke 16:19-31 in which Jesus relates the parable of the of the rich man and the poor man called Lazerus.

Chichester Cathedral has a sculpture of the Raising of Lazerus whose Feast Day is 17th December.

St Martin's Close, Court, Gate, St Martin's Chapel/Nunnery

The houses of **St Martin's Close** and **St Martin's Court** were built on the Priory grounds in 1978 by builder W.Y.Walker. **St Martin's Gate**, which was originally named East Gate End, is much older and its stone built houses are early 19th century.

The 12th century **St Martin's Chapel** was built on land granted to Alexander de Saint-Martin, a Norman sheriff of Haddington, in 1150. The nunnery was founded by Princess Ada, daughter-in-law of David I and Countess of Northumberland, who became the Queen of William I. She was of French birth and dedicated the Nunnery to St Martin of Tours. Only its nave is intact; it is a roofless ruin about 60 feet (18.3m) long and 15 feet (4.6m) wide.

It was a priory of Cistercian nuns before 1178 from which date it was taken over by the Abbey of the Franciscans (the Lamp of Lothian). The predominance of Nuns had given rise to the feeling in the Church of Rome that a balance was necessary and so came the Franciscan Friary which stood near the site of the present Episcopal Church in Church Street.

After the Reformation (1560) the Town Council took over St Martin's and it was used by Presbyterians for the next one hundred years or so. Sir Walter Scott refers to it as 'Sancte Martine' in his novel 'Quentin Durward'. The election of the

Nungate Bailies was proclaimed upon a consecrated stone at its east end. The custom continued until 1821 when Provost Dods's election was proclaimed there. (14.p.87).

In 1822 the church authorities, looking for a site on which to build a Parish school, proposed its demolition. In 1832 those who died in the cholera epidemic were buried on its north side but the relatives of the dead who were buried on the south side 'protested against their kindred being mixed with infected dust' (15.p.175). It ceased to be used as a burial ground after that year. The ruin was made safe in 1913.

St **Martin** was the first saint who was not a martyr. He is the patron saint of innkeepers and drunkards. The first signs of his goodness and holiness came about quite unexpectedly when he was an army officer. He was so overcome with sorrow for the plight of a beggar that he shared his cloak with him. This was an exceptional act of mercy at a time when army officers were feared by ordinary people and more so by beggars. Shortly afterwards he had a vision of Jesus Christ wearing half a cloak. This so inspired him, he was baptised soon afterwards and he resigned his commission two years later. However, his request to be relieved of his commission coincided with the invasion of the Barbarians into France and Martin was accused of cowardice. He protested firmly that he was a soldier of God and His law would not permit him to remain in the army. He offered to stand unarmed before the enemy advance but in the event this was not necessary; the Barbarians surrendered without a fight and Martin left the army about 339 AD.

Martin was born about 315 AD at Sabaria in Hungary. His father was an army officer and Martin was therefore a conscript. His parents were pagans but they never-the-less had him enrolled for rudimentary teaching in Christianity - he had become a catechumen. Soon after his army service the Bishop of Poitiers, St Hilary, ordained Martin as an exorcist and he travelled widely before becoming a hermit on an island off the coast of Italy.

His mother having been converted to Christianity was distressed when her son Martin was publicly flogged for his opposition to the teachings of Arius (c250-336) whose doctrine of Arianism was condemned by the church as heresy but this merely served to strengthen his belief. Meanwhile St Hilary had returned from exile and Martin rejoined him to found a hermitage near Poitiers. This expanded into a community and Martin's name and fame grew with several miracles attributed to him. He was elected Bishop of Tours but during the election he was opposed by several nobles and other influential people - he was considered too ordinary, perhaps scruffy - not a gentleman. However, he was duly elected in spite of his dirty clothes and unkempt hair - he was consecrated on 4th July 371.

He founded a monastery for hermits outside Tours. During one of his services he gave a beggar most of his clothes and his disgusted arch deacon threw down a rough garment so that he could cover himself; Martin continued the service singing mass and when he blessed his congregation five of them saw a ball of fire surround his head. At prayer he was said to have encountered evil demons which presented themselves in the guise of deities and on one occasion Satan, disguised as our Lord, accused Martin of admitting sinners as monks. Martin answered him, 'if you yourself would, even now, repent of your misdeeds, I have such trust in the Lord Jesus Christ that I would promise you mercy.' He was said to have conversed with St Paul, St Peter and the angels; he raised three men from death, cured a leper with a kiss and he gave a paralytic mobility by pouring oil into his mouth.

During his visits throughout the country he tried tirelessly to convert pagans to Christianity and often destroyed the sanctuaries which they venerated. On one occasion he ordered the felling of a tree which had been venerated by pagans. Disgusted and full of scorn they challenged him to stand in the path of its fall. They were astonished when the tree swerved aside and he stood unharmed. A pagan's sword fell from the hand of the assailant when raised against him. The Emperor's wife served him with humility at table. He refused to communicate with the bishops who were instrumental in having the heretic Pricillian put to death after the Emperor Maximus had promised a reprieve. Martin relented when the order was given to recall a tribune from Spain thus saving the lives of many condemned prisoners. Such was his influence that Count Avitianus, heeding his plea, released many prisoners from torture and certain death.

When Martin lay mortally ill his disciples begged him not to leave them to the mercy of the wolves. Characteristically, he prayed, 'Lord if thy people still need me, I will not shirk the toil, Thy will be done.' His service was not asked for; he died 1600 years ago on 8th November 397 and was buried at Tours three days later on his Feast Day, the 11th November, the day of the Roman Vinalia (wine festival) - the Feast of Bacchus, which accounts for his purely accidental patronage. In art he is portrayed as a young mounted soldier dividing his cloak with a beggar.

St Mary's Parish Church,
St Mary's Roman Catholic Church

It was about the year 1134 that the Priory of St Andrews was granted to the Church of St Mary's at Haddington by King David I and in 1139 he gave the Burgh of Haddington to his daughter-in-law, Princess Ada, who founded the nunnery of St Martin of Tours.

The first church was built on the site of the present St Mary's Parish Church. It was of course Catholic which was then the only religion in Scotland. St Margaret, King David's mother, brought the Church of Rome to Scotland after her marriage to Malcolm III, Malcolm Canmore, in 1070. It was due to her saintly influence that all Scotland became Catholic.

The early church which was built on the site of the present St Mary's Parish Church was known as the Abbey. It was almost totally destroyed in 1356 when Edward III's English armies, in an orgy of religious destruction, levelled this as well as the Franciscan Friary, known as 'The Lamp of Lothian', and on the site of which is the present Episcopalian Church in Church Street. However, this appealing appellation was adopted in reference to St Mary's Parish Church by the 'Lamp of Lothian Collegiate Trust'.

St Mary's was a Collegiate church; the collegiate status allowed the church to train its own priests. The present church building was started about 1370 and was completed by 1486. It gained its collegiate status in 1540 but only eight years later its roof and vaults were almost completely destroyed by Henry VIII's army during the two-year 'Siege of Haddington'. This was part of the process of destruction which came to be called the 'rough wooing' because of Scotland's refusal to allow the betrothal of Mary Queen of Scots to Henry's son Prince Edward (who became known as 'the Hammer of the Scots', Edward I).

After the Reformation (1561) the nave was repaired by the Town Council and the choir and transepts had a barrier wall built. For the next 400 years the church remained in this condition except for the added embellishments of the nine incorporated trades of Haddington who financed their galleries and lofts. In

1810 three new galleries were added after the roofs of the north and south aisles had been raised and the present day Victorian furnishings with the stone pulpit, font and communion table were provided.

It is difficult to imagine that there was opposition to the proposal to restore the choir and transepts of St Mary's. However, in 1960, dedicated men and women of the triumvirate of the Kirk Session (solicitor John McVie was Session Clerk and Town Clerk), the Lamp of Lothian Trust and the Friends of St Mary's, pressed for its restoration which was started by architects Ian G. Lindsay & Partners in 1971 and was completed by 1973.

The result is impressive and of cathedral dimensions; it is the largest parish church in Scotland, just over half a metre longer than St Giles in Edinburgh. Some of its notable features include: the Judas pillar - the one of the twelve pillars without decoration; the flags in the nave - the Haddington Militia (Napoleonic War), 8th Battalion The Royal Scots (1810 and 1914-18); the John Brown Bible and pulpit; the John Brown Memorial window in the South Aisle is a Burne-Jones, Pre-Raphaelite window; 'The Crucifixion' (Burne-Jones, from the Victoria and Albert Museum in London); the Scicluna window by Sax Shaw, commemorating Margaret Helen Cadzow, Samuelston, wife of Sir Hannibal Scicluna of Malta; the Jane Welsh gravestone by Thomas Carlyle; the Scallop Shell which is the badge of the pilgrims to the shrine of St James of Copostella in Spain in 1410 and 1535; the Consecration Cross carved on the pillar, adjacent to the pulpit steps, to mark the completion of St Mary's in 1480; the two

Green Men - one in the west vestibule and the other supporting the west gallery; the east wall tapestries woven by the Edinburgh Tapestry Company and designed by Archibald Brennan; the Lady aisle; the Columba aisle; the Lauderdale Aisle (1595, chapel of the Three Kings) in the north of the Choir.

St Mary's Roman Catholic Church

St Mary's Roman Catholic Church in Poldrate was built in 1862 and designed by Augustus Pugin (who designed the Tolbooth Church, Castlehill, Edinburgh). Its early congregation consisted mainly of Irish farm workers. The wheel window in the west gable gives light to its gallery and the stained glass window commemorates the first Parish Priest, Father Prendergast. A new altar was installed in 1989.

St Mary

Strange though it may seem, little has been recorded about the life of the mother of Christ, the Virgin Mary, but every Christmas, the story of the birth of Christ is enacted in schools and in church Nativity plays.

Mary and Joseph, having travelled long and far, arrive in Bethlehem and having been turned away from the inn, the baby Jesus is born in the adjacent stable. He was wrapped in swaddling clothes and laid in a manger. The angel of the Lord appeared and said,

"Fear not: for, behold, I bring you good tidings of great joy, which shall be to all the people. For unto you is born this day in the city of David a Saviour, which is the Christ the Lord. Glory to God in the highest, and peace on earth, good will toward men."

The three wise men, having followed the star of David, arrived at the stable and presented their gifts of gold, frankincense and myrrh. The flight of Mary and Joseph to Egypt to save the baby Jesus from King Herod and Herod's killing of the children are all part of the Christmas story.

The Gospels describe Mary as humble, obedient, candid and prudent at the Annunciation when the Archangel Gabriel came to her to declare that she was chosen as the Mother of God. The miracle of Mary's Immaculate Conception is clearly stated in the Scriptures and Mary is pre-eminent among the saints.

Thomas of Aquinas described her as 'hyperdoulia', meaning that she 'is venerated above all other saints but infinitely below the adoration, due to God alone.' Her special cult is therefore called Hyperdoulia, the highest of God's creatures.

Throughout the life of her only son Mary remained in the background sharing in his suffering. She did not become involved in teaching and preaching. For his mother Jesus performed his first miracle at a wedding in Cana of Galilee when she remarked, "they have no wine." Initially, Jesus was reluctant to do anything about it but he decided to perform his first miracle for his mother who said to the servants: "Whatsoever he saith unto you, do it." Jesus asked them to fill six stone pots with water and when the 'ruler of the feast' tasted the water he found it to be wine.

Throughout all the sufferings of Jesus, Mary suffered with the anguish of a loving mother to her son but never once did her faith waver. Any ordinary woman would have done anything to prevent his crucifixion and her greatest anguish must have occurred when, standing erect at the cross on which Jesus was crucified, she heard him say, "Woman behold thy son" and then to a beloved disciple, "behold thy mother." This language may seem strange but he, knowing that he would shortly depart this earth, was the loving son making provision for his mother.

Mary lived so quietly and kept in the background to such an extent that there is little record of her life and none of her death. There were claims that she died in Ephesus in Turkey, but Jerusalem was claimed as her last abode by the Eastern Fathers. Nations and diocese of the Catholic Church venerate the Blessed Virgin fulfilling her prophecy: "from henceforth all generations shall call me blessed."

Sidegate,
Sidegate Lane,
Sidegate Mews

S idegate, at the east end of the High Street, runs southwards to Poldrate. Its name, originally 'Sydgate', is ancient and is referred to in the 'Auld Register of Haddington' of 1423 (1. p.81) (as are Hardgate and Poldrate). Miller (2.p.226) gives a 1429 reference to a 'heritable sesing' (sasine) which was granted to John Paterson, cordwanar, "in feferme of a tenement lyand in the Sydgate on the Kyngis Wal." The 'King's Wall' (1429) crossed Sidegate, opposite Maitlandfield, and joined the watch tower of the South Port at the corner of the wall of Maitlandfield.

Sidegate was the address of Provost George M'Call (ref. M'Call Park) whose early 17th century, L-shaped house with its picturesque roundel stood just north of Haddington House. Sadly, it was demolished in the interests of road widening in the 1950s. M'Call was postmaster of Haddington and Provost in 1723 and 1728; he owned the park on which Knox Academy was built.

Fortunately, the three-storey 17th century Haddington House in Sidegate was saved from demolition by the Earl of Wemyss when he purchased the house and gifted it to the East Lothian Antiquarian and Field Naturalists' Society in 1950. Walking along Sidegate, the balustrated stair and canopied door catch the eye and draw you to examine the initials 'AM 1680 KC' engraved in the stone lintel which signifies that a burgess of Haddington (1673), Alexander Maitland and his wife Katherine Cunningham lived in the house from 1680, the year of their marriage. The house and its gardens are best viewed from the rear where its L-shape and central turret with a beautiful bowed fillet can be seen. The house was the headquarters of the 'Lamp of Lothian Collegiate Trust' until 1995 and has been taken over as offices for the new unitary Council for East Lothian.

Sidegate Lane was formerly known as Bedlam Close at the foot of which was an old smithy where the swords and bayonets of the French and Scots soldiers were sharpened during the Siege of 1548. The smith was John Cochrane who was nicknamed 'Hinges' possibly because of the excellent quality of the door hinges which he made. A man of good cheer, he was often heard to raise the toast: "May the hinges of friendship never rust." (14.p.53).

 Maitlandfield House (formerly Bearford's House) at the south end of Sidegate was the home of Lady Bearford in 1657 (1.p.44). In 1754 Francis Charteris, Earl of Wemyss sold it to Lieutenant Thomas Maitland who changed its name to Maitlandfield. The property remained in the Maitland family until the 1840s when the Howden family bought it (Dr Thomas Howden became provost of the Burgh in 1877). The Rayners owned Maitlandfield from the 1930s and during the 1939-45 war it was taken over as offices by the Ministry of Food. After the war British Road Services used it as offices. Mr and Mrs Stan Godek redecorated the house, firstly renting out rooms to homeless young couples, and latterly as an hotel. In 1988 Ivor Reid Craig took over and carried out a complete refurbishment adding a large L-shaped conservatory, the 'Sixteen Kings'Restaurant' and the Bearford bar.

Somnerfield Avenue, Crescent, Grove
Somnerfield House, West Road

S omnerfield Crescent, off the north side of West Road, leads
to Somnerfield Avenue and Grove and were named in 1988.
The modern houses were built by Cala Homes (Lothian) Ltd.

According to the Register of Sasines, 24th September 1816, the
name Somnerfield was given to an area of land of almost
seventeen acres of St Laurence House by Richard Somner when
Elizabeth Boyd, the widow of John Murray, a lieutenant of the
7th Regiment of Foot, sold the land to Somner. John Wood's
1819 Plan of Haddington and Nungate shows "Richard Summers
Esqrs., Property" but this a misspelling.

'Somner Mains' appears on a map of Haddington dated 1854
which shows that the Somner family owned the land immediately
west of the railway station. Somner Mains was demolished
towards the end of the 19th century (it does not appear on the
1892 plan) to make way for the prestigious houses of West Road
which were built soon afterwards. Somnerfield Works is shown
on the north side of the station on the 1892 and the 1906 plans.

Dr Richard Somner, according to Martine (14.p.31), was the
principal surgeon in Haddington about 1790. His dispensary and
drug shop was situated on the west side of Fishmarket Wynd
(now Cross Lane). He was Provost in 1789 and 1793 although
James Miller (2 p. 218) relates:

'In 1793, January 5th, Mr Richard Somner, provost,
was required to accept or demit his office, as he had
never attended the meetings of the council since his
election in October! He accepted.'

It is probable that the Somnerfield streets bear his name. His
son, born in 1760, George Somner Esquire, laird of Hopes, was
also a surgeon in Haddington and partner of Dr John Welsh (father
of Jane Welsh Carlyle). Somner's gravestone, in the Old Calton
Burying Ground in Edinburgh, gives his death in June 1815 age
55 years. His son, also George Somner is named on the same
gravestone.

S omnerfield House at 11 West Road (now The Compass
School) takes its name from the Somnerfield estate and was

built in 1879 for a Miss Farquharson of Paris as a summer residence. She had decided that Paris, having been occupied by the Prussian army, was no longer a fit place for the well-being of a sensible Scotswoman.

The next owner was her cousin, Mrs Johnstone who inherited the house from Miss Farquharson. Her husband, Captain Johnstone, entertained Sir John French, (commander-in-chief of the British army in 1914 who was replaced by Douglas Haig), at Somnerfield.

Colonel and Mrs C.S. Cameron were the next owners. The colonel served in India and was shell-shocked during the 1914-18 war; he died in 1964. Mrs Cameron was member of the Town Council and convened the 'Warmth for War' committee during the 1939-45 war. The ladies met regularly in the bakery department of the 'Co-op' in Market Street and knitted gloves, scarves, *et cetera* for soldiers serving at home and abroad. Their son, Donald, became a lieutenant-colonel in the army and their daughter, Anne, a talented pianist and opera singer with the Glyndbourne, served with the First Aid Nurses Yeomanry during the 1939-45 war.

Part of Somnerfield House was let out as flats for ex-army officers after the war and the last tenant,, Major and Mrs Kelway Bamber, left in 1955 when the house was purchased by Mr and Mrs John Ralston.

John Ralston MRVCS was a veterinary surgeon who with his wife Mrs Jessie Dalton Ralston MA and their four children lived at Somnerfield until 1969 when it was sold to The Compass School. (ref. Appendix II). The Ralston children distinguished themselves academically - Ian Beith McLaren Ralston MA(Hons), PhD, FSA, FSA(Scot), MIFA is a distinguished academic, archaeologist and President of the Institute of Field Archaeologists; Kenneth Charles Ralston MA(Hons), BSc, Dip Arch, RIAS, ARIBA, FSA(Scot) is an architect with several major designs to his credit; Helen Elizabeth Ralston BA(Hons), CA, ACT, MBA, FRSA is an accountant and has held positions as company treasurer and internal auditor of Irvine Development Corporation.

Stevenson Bridge

S **tevenson Bridge**, the footbridge at West Haugh which crosses the Tyne near West Mills, is named after a well-known and long-serving Provost of Haddington, David Stevenson. He served the town for over thirty years and was elected its first citizen on three occasions from 1855.

David Stevenson was the proprietor of the George Hotel and among his guests were Jane Welsh Carlyle and her husband, the great 'Sage of Chelsea', Thomas Carlyle.

At that time (1855) some of Stevenson's business competition was removed when the Blue Bell Inn at Carlyle Court closed. In days gone by the Bell had vied with the George as a welcoming station for the change of horses for the coaches which ran between Edinburgh and London.

David Stevenson was an active and enthusiastic member of the Volunteer movement from its formation in 1859. Francis, 9th Earl of Wemyss was the local Member of Parliament and he expended great energy in exhorting some sixty-seven riflemen to enrol in 'Defence not Defiance' - their motto. One can imagine David Stevenson, resplendent in the uniform of the Haddington Volunteers - a dark green tunic embellished with a bronze star having the cross of St Andrew emblazoned upon it in white and 'with scarlet facings, cuffs, and neck, and a thin scarlet braiding down the outside seam of the trousers.' (1.p.75), marching proudly in what was described as a magnificent sight 'when more than two-and-twenty thousand rifles and many hundred sword blades flashed out the royal salute' (15.Vol.II p.321) - this was the Royal Scottish Volunteer Review before Queen Victoria on 7th August 1860 which was held in front of over 100,000 spectators in the Royal Park below Arthur's Seat from the summit of which floated the mighty Royal Standard of Scotland, 25 square yards in area.

David Stevenson died in 1890 and was survived by his son, George H. Stevenson, who became Town Clerk of Haddington and County Sheriff Clerk. Stevenson's grandson, A.C.Stevenson, followed in his father's footsteps when he in turn became Town Clerk.

Tenterfield
(formerly Sunnybank)

The 1819 Plan of Haddington and Nungate shows Sunnybank on the west side of 'Hardgate Street' as the property of A. Donaldson Esqr. Alexander Donaldson was the Town Clerk of Haddington and lawyer of Dr John Welsh. In addition to his property in Haddington he owned 'a Tenement of land in Dirleton' which he purchased in September 1823.

Sunnybank was probably renamed Tenterfield when the Donaldson family arrived and extensions were added at the rear and sides about 1864

His three daughters, the 'Misses Donaldson of Sunny Bank' receive a complimentary mention from Martine in his *Reminiscences* in which he describes them as : 'kind, friendly and genial disposition, and for their unostentatious and benevolent deeds of charity for the poor.' They were born, as were most of the Donaldsons, in Provost M'Call's old baronial house at the foot of Sidegate Lane, their father having married a daughter of Provost M'Call.

Haddington born Jane Welsh Carlyle, wife of the illustrious Thomas Carlyle, during her last visit to Haddingon from London in 1849, was a guest of the Misses Donaldson at Tenterfield (one of whom was her Godmother) when she wrote a letter of gratitude to the new owner of her father's old house, Carlyle House, in Lodge Street for the gift of some pears from the trees in the old garden. She invited this Haddington lady to Tenterfield to meet the Misses Donaldson and to thank her personally for her thoughtfulness.

The name Tenterfield is probably derived from the fact that Messrs Davies had their dyeworks in the Hardgate and dried their yarns et cetera on the tenters at Tenterfield. The name Tenterfield first appears in the Burgh Records of May 1897 and was described as:

> 'Tenterfield and garden extending to five and a half acres bounded on east partly by the Great Post Road from Haddington to Dunbar, on the south side partly by the Town Wall and on the west by Newton Port to Harperdean and Aberlady.'

By 1903 the halcyon days of Tenterfield were over; the last of the Donaldsons had gone and Tenterfield became a Christie Female Industrial Home - an orphanage for girls. In December 1912 the house with 1.498 hectares (3.7 acres) was sold to the trustees of John Christie of Cowden near Dollar. In 1950 the Governors of the Lothian Homes Trust sold Tenterfield House, offices, the adjoining garden and parks (5.5 acres) to the County Councils of the Counties of Midlothian, East Lothian and Peebles for £6500 and the house became a Children's Home. It was taken over by the Lothian Regional Council's Social Work Department in 1974. Internally, it was allowed to fall into disrepair and was vacated in 1992 to be put on sale. The house lay empty for almost two years and was subjected to occasional vandalism.

In January 1994, Tenterfield House with 1.5 hectares (3.7 acres) of land was sold to John Ferguson of the Sports Tune Motor Co., Ltd., for conversion into luxury flats and work started in January 1995. Whilst the layout of the interior has been redesigned many of the original features have been carefully restored at a cost of almost £0.5 million.

The Town House

The 16th century Tolbooth of Haddington had a thatched roof and accommodated the Sheriff Court, prison cells and the offices of the Town Council. A clock for its tower was proposed in 1539 and again in 1540 but it was not until 1687, in fact on 7th April of that year that, 'John Elliot, surgeon-apothecary, deposited 800 merks for buying a clock for the use of the burgh, to be set up in the Tolbooth. It cost L25. The monument of John Elliot, chirurgeon, may still be seen about the north centre of the churchyard.' (2 p.227).

The judicial court met in the large dining room of the Provost, James Lauder, in 1691.

By 1732 the condition of the Tolbooth had deteriorated to such an extent that, for reasons of safety, the steeple, clock and bell had to be taken down and meetings of the Town Council were held in the town-library.

In 1741 a public subscription was taken up for the erection of a new Tolbooth. The estimated cost was £500 for a building 60 ft long by 36ft broad to the design of the famous architect, William Adam 'to be finished by Whitsunday 1744' (2. p.227). It is interesting to note that a local painter, John Learmouth, was given five guineas for the land and that £100 was borrowed by the Town Council to pay contractors. Miller (2) also notes that the council agreed, on 10th June 1745, that £30 should be paid for a clock for the Town House. Nothing remains of Adam's work.

New buildings were erected on the south side of the old building providing three prison cells, a spacious hall and a new steeple, 150ft high, designed by James Gillespie Graham (1777-1855), the architect of the Tolbooth Church, Castlehill and other churches in Edinburgh. His design replaced the old Dutch type construction which had developed a dangerous lean.

The foundation stone of the new building was laid in June 1830 and it was completed in September 1831. In the foundation a written record of events, several silver and copper coins, the *Edinburgh Almanac, The Scotsman, the Edinburgh Evening Courant,* The Shorter Catechism and the Rev. John Brown's Explication were placed in a stone jar and left for posterity.

In 1843 the weather cock had seized-up; no matter how windy the weather, it was immovable. A young sailor offered to scale the steeple using a rope-ladder, a kite was said to have been used to pass a rope over the top and the rope-ladder was then pulled up.

The Steeple was re-pointed in 1921 but by 1950 the Town Hall was in danger of internal collapse when dry rot was discovered. The easy solution was to demolish it but the Burgh Surveyor, the redoubtable Mr. William Lee Hogg (1899-1994), with the Town Clerk, Mr John McVie, put a strong case to the Town Council to save it. Restoration work was carried out by architect Peter Whitson in 1952 and Princess Mary (ref. Princess Mary Road and Place) accepted an invitation to perform the opening ceremony of the newly restored Town Hall in 1956.

Traprain Terrace,
Dunpender Drive

Traprain Terrace, between Dunbar Road and Riverside Drive, is so named from the fact that it faces Traprain Law, the horizontal columns of which are of basalt and its trap rests in a basin of Sandstone; the basin being man-made due to quarrying, a trap was formed in which rain water made a small loch which no doubt is the simple explanation of its name - a trap for rain - Traprain. Sadly the clay bottom of the small loch so formed was punctured by falling rocks and has now drained away. The village of Traprain lies just south of East Linton.

Dunpender Drive, off Garleton Drive and running parallel to Davidson Terrace, is named after Dunpender Hill which is the ancient name of Traprain Law and this street name was suggested by Bailie Mary Taylor in 1952 for the new houses which were built in 1953.

The change of name of the hill from Dunpender to Traprain took place between 1682 and 1736; Adair's map of 1682 shows the name as Dunpender whereas the Adair/Cooper map of 1736 shows the name changed to Traprain Hill.

There is evidence of an ancient iron age settlement on Traprain Law which is a Scheduled Ancient Monument with a long history dating back some 8000 years. Around the time of the birth of Christ, during the Iron Age, a tribe known as Votadini lived on the then densely populated hill. This was a major manufacturing site during the 3rd and 4th centuries and the Votadini had peaceful contacts with the Romans when Agricola invaded Scotland. Traprain was on the edge of the Roman empire and several Roman artefacts found on the site provide the evidence of trade.

In May 1919 a hoard of Roman silver, thought to have been buried by the Votadini, was discovered on Traprain Law. This was the finest treasure find in Europe and Traprain Law was now the centre of Scottish pre-history. Magnificent silver cups, chalices, spoons, plates and many other objects were packed into three large boxes and taken to Edinburgh for cleaning and further examination. This hoard was probably a gift from the Romans. This silver is exhibited in the National Museum of Antiquities in Edinburgh.

Recently, (August 1996) a heath fire on Traprain Law uncovered some additional fragments of Iron Age pots and dishes as well as the remains of wattle-and-daub walls. Archaeological excavations continue under the National Museums of Scotland.

Early in the 6th century King Loth (from whom Lothian is said to take its name) had his palace situated at the top of the Law on forty acres of fairly flat surface. This was an example of a hill-top enclosed town where the villagers were mainly farmers whose cattle grazed the plains below. The 8ft (2.4m) high Loth Stone on Traprain Law is said to mark the grave of the legendary king.

He and his Queen Anna, daughter of King Arthur, ruled over his people, some of whom lived at the foot of the Law. In the event of attack they simply moved to the summit and lived within the stout walls of the palace grounds until the enemy was dealt with.

Scotland had not yet achieved its identity and consisted of Pictish Alba, Dalriada and Strathclyde. Legend has it that King Loth had tried Christianity but had reverted to paganism. His daughter, Princess Thania (or Thenew), was strongly Christian and when, in 517, her father insisted that she marry a pagan prince, Owen Ap of Rheged in Galloway, she refused. The King, accustomed to total obedience, was furious and he banished her to the Lammermuir Hills as a shepherdess.

However, Thania found herself completely contented with her new life of peace and solitude but it was rudely and viciously interrupted when the jilted prince, on his way home, found her in the hills and raped her. She became pregnant and retired to a nunnery at Whittingehame but when King Loth discovered her plight he ordered that she be stoned to death which was the penalty of the time.

Such was the respect in which she was held, no one would lift a stone against her and so her father decreed that she be tied to a type of sled and flung from the top of Traprain Law. However, during her fall her voluminous gown was caught by the branches of an overhanging bush. Her cries for help were eventually heard by a passing noble who took pity on her. Her father, now in a state of confusion and fearing to offend her Christian God decided that she should be sacrificed to the God of the sea, Mannan (from which Clackmannan takes its name). The tide carried her across the Forth and gently along the coast of Fife until she was washed ashore at Culross.

She was taken in and cared for by the monks of St Serf's monastery and she gave birth to a baby boy in the year 518. Her son was baptised by St Serf and educated in the monastery and he was named Kentigern.

Many years later she, with her son, travelled westwards and Kentigern (which means 'Chief Lord') was so well loved that he became known as Mungo meaning 'dear friend'. He founded a monastery in a place called Cathures, now Glasgow. St Mungo was consecrated bishop of Cumbria in 543.

Another legend associated with Traprain Law relates to it as a meeting-place of fairies. Martine (14) describes it:

'When the country folks saw a light on the west side, near Green Loaning row of houses, there was sure to be a fairy tournament. The light sparkled like a bright star, which the folk alleged was the reflection of a bright diamond they had, but when the place was approached by inquisitive folks, the light instantly vanished. Lizzie's (Richardson) legend of the fairies of Traprain Law, derived from old tradition, and firmly believed in olden times, is quite in accordance with traditions scattered over the whole of Scotland.'

Tweeddale Monument

The monument to the 8th Marquis of Tweeddale stands opposite the County Building - the Burgh Court and offices of the East Lothian Council - in Court Street. This red sandstone monument by David Rhind (1880) is specially attractive with its crown top on pillars forming a votive temple with the marble portrait bust of the Marquis, by G.B. Amendola on its five-foot high base. It is inscribed:

Erected by Public Subscription
AD 1881
In Grateful Remembrance of
The Public Services in War and Peace of
George, VIIIth Marquis of Tweeddale FM,KT,GCB
Lord Lieutenant of Haddingtonshire
Born February 1st 1787
Died October 16th 1876

George Hay (Hay being the family name of the Marquis of Tweeddale) was born on 1st February 1787 at Bonnington and, at the age of seventeen years, he acceded to the title of 8th Marquis of Tweeddale and the East Lothian estates at Yester (ref. Yester Place). He was a powerfully built young man and decided upon a military career, following a family tradition. In fact, he entered the army as an ensign (sub-lieutenant) only two months before his father's death in August 1804.

In 1806 he was sent to Sicily and by May 1807 he was given his own company. Soon afterwards he was sent to the Iberian Peninsula to serve in the Peninsular War (1808-1814) under Sir Arthur Wellesley (later Duke of Wellington) who landed at Mondego Bay on 1st to 8th August 1808 with 12,000 men to advance to Lisbon. Tweeddale was twice wounded, firstly at the British success over the French at Busaco (27th September 1810) and then at Vitoria (21st June 1813), a final and great strategic victory for Wellington. Immediately following the latter in which British losses totalled 5000 out of 79,000 men, he was promoted to Lieutenant-Colonel and invalided home. However, as soon as he was fit again he rejoined his regiment in the American War (1812-15) and distinguished himself as a cavalryman but he was again wounded at Niagara in 1813 where he was captured after a great struggle in which he refused to surrender.

At the end of the American war he returned home to Yester and was made a Companion of the Most Honourable Order of the Bath (CB) for his heroic military service. Whilst he saw no further active service he remained on the employed list and during the rest of his life he was steadily promoted: Colonel, 27th May 1825; Major-General, 10th January 1837; Lieutenant-General, 9th November 1846; General, 20th June 1854; Field Marshall 29th May 1875. His honours included a Knighthood of the Most Ancient and the Most Noble Order of the Thistle (KT) in 1820. Queen Victoria knighted him in 1862 as Knight Commander of the Most Honourable Order of the Bath (KCB) and he was awarded the Knight Grand Cross of that Order (GCB) in 1867.

On 28th March 1816 he married Lady Susan Montagu, third daughter of the 5th Duke of Manchester. They had seven sons and six daughters. One of his daughters, Lady Elizabeth Hay, married the son of the Duke of Wellington in 1839. Gray and Jamieson (1.p.73) note that the disproportionately high amount of money collected by the ladies of East Lothian towards the statue of the equestrian 'Iron Duke' in Edinburgh was due in no small measure to this relationship (£1153 out of £10,000).

Tweeddale was East Lothian's war hero and he was invited to lay the foundation stone for Waterloo Bridge, the new bridge over the Tyne. This duty he carried out amid masonic honours in 1817 on the anniversary of the great victory of Waterloo - 18th June.

The Marquis was Lord Lieutenant of East Lothian from 1822 to 1842. While resident in East Lothian at Yester he maintained a strong interest in farming; he pioneered deep ploughing and tile-draining. He spent considerable sums in farming experiments and he developed and invented several farm implements.

A man of great energy, and to prove his expertise as a coachman, he drove the mail coach non-stop and without relief from London to Haddington (20). He was vice president of the elite Agricultural Society of East Lothian whose membership consisted of fifty-five nobles and other gentry.

His interest in the affairs of the Royal Burgh of Haddington extended to the proposal to build a new Court House in what was then called King Street and renamed Court Street. He was appointed chairman of the committee to oversee its erection in 1833 after its foundation stone was laid by Sir John Gordon Sinclair of Stevenson 'in presence of the beauty and fashion of the neighbourhood' (2.p.229). The committee membership included: the Marquis of Tweeddale, Lord Lieutenant; Sir John Gordon Sinclair; Sir David Kinloch; David Anderson of St Germains; James Hamilton of Bangour; and Robert Riddell, Sheriff-Substitute.

He demitted the office of Lord Lieutenant in 1842 on taking up the Governor-Generalship of Madras in India where he was Commander-in-Chief of the armed forces; the latter command was given by special arrangement of the Duke of Wellington because of the poor state of the local army. The select membership of the East Lothian Agricultural Society (founded in 1819) gave their vice-president, the departing Marquis, a public dinner in his honour. It was held on 20th May 1842 in the Assembly Room of Haddington and over 150 'gentlemen' attended. It was presided over by Lord Elcho who, in extolling the virtues and accomplishments of the Marquis, referred to his 'glorious career', his 'signal military talents that were afterwards developed in the Peninsular War, where the Marquis of Tweeddale had the good fortune to attract the attention of that illustrious commander (Wellington), who repeatedly placed him in offices of trust and responsibility, and by his heroism gained that distinguished commander's good opinion, which, on a recent occasion, he took a public and memorable opportunity of expressing.' (2.p.167). The Marquis replied:

"This going to India was no seeking of mine: I was commanded by my sovereign. I was asked by the East India Company, in these times of difficulty, to serve them in a civil capacity, and also in a military capacity; and sorry would I be to think that anyone bearing my name, when such a call was made upon him, would refuse the last drop of his blood in the service of his native country. My noble friend has alluded to the compliment paid me on a late occasion, as well as to my services under that great man (Wellington) whose career commenced in India. I, a humble imitator, go to follow in his steps..."

He returned home from India in 1848 and for the next twenty-six years he followed his farming pursuits at Yester, his work and expertise being recognised in his presidency of the Agricultural and Highland Society. His eldest son, the Earl of Gifford, died in 1862 and his wife died on 5th March 1870.

In 1876 at the age of eighty-nine years he suffered an accident from which he died on 10th October. He was succeeded by his second son Arthur. The monument in Court Street therefore commemorates a great soldier, a man of many accomplishments in farming and the new science of meteorology and one who took great pride in his community as well as his colonelcy of the 30th Foot (1830), the 42nd Foot (1862) and of the Lifeguards (1863).

Vert Memorial Hospital - Vert Court

The **Vert Memorial Hospital** and its 1950s maternity extension , having been closed for several years, has been redesigned internally to form private flats and renamed **Vert Court**.

It was built from the red sandstone obtained from the demolished mansion house of Amisfield. It was named in memory of its principal benefactor John Vert who, having amassed his fortune in America, gifted the sum of £7000 (about £250,000 today) for the erection of a cottage hospital in 1927. As building progressed it soon became apparent that although local subscription equalled Vert's generosity there would be insufficient funds for its completion and Vert unhesitatingly provided the outstanding amount of a further £3000 (£110,000 today).

John Vert was born in Haddington in 1852. His father, Francis Vert (1821-1888), an auctioneer, was elected Provost of Haddington from 1866 to 1869 and during his Provostship he campaigned successfully for the removal of road tolls. This involved a change in legislation and previous attempts by the Town Council objecting to additional tollbars in 1792 had failed. For his service he was presented with a magnificent piece of silver plate which his son John took with him to America after the death of his father.

John Vert married Jessie S.S. McLean of Kirriemuir and the young couple emigrated to America where he worked hard in the estate agency business in the town of Pendleton in Oregon. Towards the end of his life he decided to make a tangible gift to the town of his birth, Haddington. He gifted a substantial proportion of the money to build the cottage hospital and in addition he presented to the Town Council his father's silver plate and a valuable 18th century clock. He returned to Haddington for the opening ceremony of the hospital in 1929 and was accorded the Freedom of the Royal Burgh. In Kirriemuir he contributed the funds required to build a cottage for the local nurse in memory of his wife and her parents.

He died in 1934 at the age of eighty-two in America.

Vetch Park

Vetch Park, off Victoria Park, is named after the illustrious Vetch family of Haddington several of whom had distinguished military careers. The father was **Robert Vetch** who owned land in the vicinity of Vetch Park and several acres between Aberlady Road and Station Road (as shown on the Survey Plan of 1819). His residence was at Hawthornbank House which became Caponflat House.

The land between Aberlady Road and Hospital Road which was the property of Robert Vetch Esq. of Hawthornbank was sold by Miss Vetch to the Town Council for the Caponflat, Hopetoun Drive, Baird Terrace, Davidson Terrace development of 1938.

The second of Robert Vetch's sons was **Lieutenant-Colonel George Anderson Vetch** born in Haddington in 1789. He was educated for military service and in 1809 at the age of twenty he became a cadet of the Bengal Presidency of the East India Company. For the next 27 years he served with distinction in India.

As a young subaltern with the 54th Regiment of Native Infantry his first baptism of fire was at the Siege of Comone in India where he was wounded. Soon afterwards he led an incredibly brave attack against the rebels and succeeded in taking them prisoner in a Mosque. During the peace that followed he supervised the construction of new roads and in 1816 the people of Barreily presented him with a magnificent sword and silver scabbard for his 'brave and humane qualities and the protection he had afforded them during the war.'

His next responsibility was as keeper of the native Prince at Delhi. He greatly admired the work of the new Governor-General, Lord William Bentinck, who had boldly outlawed the Hindu practice of bride burning known as *suttee* and in addition had tackled head on the murderous and secret society of *Thugees*. George Vert, now promoted to the rank of lieutenant-colonel, had the honour of entertaining Lord Bentinck at his residence at Burdwan.

In 1836 he returned home to his estate in Haddington. He was now able to pursue his lifelong interest in the study of literature.

He had already written a volume of poems which had been published during his army service. Now, he wrote of his experiences in India in a fictitious novel, *Gregory's Gong* which was published in Edinburgh. Between 1848 and 1850 he wrote and published his most ambitious dramatic poem *Dara, or the Minstrel Prince* which was again based on Indian native legend. One critic wrote of it: 'There are many passages of surpassing beauty. The language is lofty and appropriate, the verse harmonious, and the sentiments give utterance to all that is noble and generous.' He was particularly touched when his publisher informed him of an old lady's enquiry about one of the characters in his serialised book *Gregory's Gong;* she was most anxious to learn more of 'Tibbie' the old nurse with whom she identified.

This warm-hearted, patriotic veteran became active again in military matters when in 1859, with the threat of invasion by Napoleon III after his invasion of Italy, he, with Provost Roughead, championed recruitment into the Rifle Volunteer Movement and his powerful plea before a huge audience in the Assembly Rooms of Haddington was largely responsible for the formation of two Volunteer Corps.

His large family of 16 children, by his second wife, mourned his death in October 1873 at the age of 86 years.

Another Son of Robert Vetch was **James Vetch** who was born on 13th May 1789 at Haddington. He served under the great Glasgow general Sir John Moore during the Peninsular War (1808-14). James Vetch was then a military engineer of distinction, well-known for his assiduous and competent work.

In civilian life one of his early tasks after the war was the first full survey of the Orkney and Shetland Islands which he followed by the triangulation of the Western Isles.

In 1824 he was offered and accepted the post of manager of silver mines in Mexico. He returned twelve years later to become resident engineer of the Birmingham to Gloucester Railway Company. A man of considerable vision, he proposed the building of a ship canal to link the Mediterranean Sea with the Red Sea but his design was opposed by Lord Palmerston who considered it to be against British interests. However, in 1855 the great French engineer, Vicompte de Ferdinand Lesseps, included Vetch's proposals in his own report to the French government.

At that time Lesseps was at the height of his fame having completed the design and construction of the Suez Canal.

Vetch went on to design the sewage and drainage systems of Leeds; Prince Albert had exerted great influence over the government by his exhortations for improved sewage and drainage systems in London and at Windsor Castle. The Prince was disgusted by the smells and described the Thames as 'Aqua Mortis'. He appointed Vetch to design and install the drainage system for Windsor Castle and for Southwark.

In 1846 Vetch was appointed by the Admiralty as consulting engineer to advise on harbours, rivers and railway bridges to ensure their safety. He was a member of several learned societies and he retired in 1863 having published several learned papers including: *Account of the Island of Foula (1821), Monuments and relics of the ancient inhabitants of New Spain (1836), Political Geography Nomenclature of Australia (1836), On the Structural Arrangements most favourable to the health of Towns (1842), Havens of Safety (1844).* He published reports on the harbours of Ramsgate, Tyne, Isle of Man, Holyhead, Portpatrick, and in South Africa - Table Bay and Port Natal (Durban). Sadly, his wooden pier at Durban fell over having been designed in London without knowledge of the severe tidal conditions of the Indian Ocean - the derelict 'Vetch's Pier' can still be seen today.

Such was his reputation and his highly valued expertise he was elected to membership of many learned societies and to the highest academic honour in Britain - his election as a Fellow of the Royal Society (FRS).

He died in London on 7th December 1869 and was buried at Highgate Cemetery.

Victoria Bridge,
Victoria Road, Terrace,
Victoria Park

The newly-built Bermaline Mill at the east end of Haddington had restricted access to the town over the narrow Nungate Bridge and the old and rickety Gimmersmill wooden bridge. The mill owners (the Montgomerie family) petitioned the Town Council to build a wide and substantial bridge over the Tyne. This would provide a wide access road to the east from Market Street. The new bridge and road required the demolition of Provost Main's shop adjacent to Gowl Close. The Council eventually agreed but only if the mill owners would pay half the cost. This was agreed after a lengthy petition to the House of Lords and in 1900 the **Victoria Bridge** was opened to link Victoria Terrace to Market Street.

The old Gimmersmill wooden bridge was now redundant and was demolished. The total cost of the new bridge was £9237 of which £2824 was raised by means of a bazaar which attracted subscribers from town and country.

Victoria Park is the continuation of Newton Port and its houses were completed on the sixtieth anniversary of the reign of Queen Victoria. Following a celebration of her Diamond Jubilee in 1897, the wife of Provost A. Mathieson Main accompanied a procession of Town Councillors and she formally named the street Victoria Park.(1.p.78)

Victoria Bridge and Victoria Park, Road and Terrace commemorate the long reign of Queen Victoria. She was born on 24th May 1819, only four years after the Duke of Wellington finally defeated Napoleon Bonaparte at Waterloo (ref. **Waterloo Bridge**). Raffles had acquired Singapore in 1819 as a trading centre and, with the Cape, Ceylon and Mauritius, the route to India was secure. Two years after her accession to the throne, in 1837, the British (mainly Scots) had colonised New Zealand and Australia had been colonised since 1787, mainly with English and Scots convicts; the British Empire seemed invincible. The industrial revolution had led to the recapture of Continental markets after the Napoleonic War during which trading links in South America had been opened. Hong Kong received its colonial charter in 1843, Natal was annexed in 1843, by 1879 the Zulu nation had been subjugated and Transvaal and the Orange Free State had been annexed in South Africa, the Crown had taken over the Gold Coast and in 1875, through a Disraeli master stroke, the Suez Canal was obtained for Great Britain. The Queen had been declared Empress of India which Prime Minister Gladstone described as 'flummery'. This was only part of the great empire of Victoria's sixty-three year reign.

She was the only child of Edward, Duke of Kent (fourth son of George III) and Victoria Maria Louisa of Saxe-Coburg (sister of King Leopold of Belgium). Young Victoria had a somewhat sad and lonely childhood but she fell madly in love with her cousin, the handsome Prince Albert of Saxe-Coburg and Gotha. As Queen of Britain she proposed to him and they were married on 10th February 1840. She was twenty and deliriously happy. She was crowned on 28th June 1838 aged only nineteen in succession to her uncle, William, IV, and because of her sex she was excluded from the sovereignty of the House of Hanover.

As a young Queen she became immediately authoritative and quickly demonstrated a maturity of outlook, a sound understanding of constitutional principles and a quite remarkable ability to put certain Prime Ministers in their place. She disagreed with Peel but Melbourne was a good friend and mentor whose advice tended to balance that of her Uncle Leopold, King of the

Belgians. She detested the formal, austere and haughty "firebrand Palmerston".

She had little idea of the conditions of the poor or of the unrest throughout the country. Even the attempt on her life as she drove through London in 1840, seemed not to affect her. At Court her straight-laced aloofness made her unpopular especially when she insisted, quite unjustifiably, that one of her spinster ladies-in-waiting should be medically examined for pregnancy; the poor woman was not only a virgin but was suffering from cancer of the liver which had caused swelling of the abdomen from which she died shortly afterwards.

A devoted wife, she had four sons and five daughters but she disliked babies as messy. However, with Prince Albert she took a keen interest in their education.

Albert worked himself to the point of exhaustion for the government and in close harmony with his beloved wife. He was made Consort in 1842 and he encouraged the arts and promoted industrial and social reforms. The Great Exhibition of 1851 in Hyde Park was his dreamchild. He was made Prince Consort in 1857 but tragically he died of typhus at Windsor Castle on 14th December 1861 aged only forty-two. Victoria was grief stricken. She mourned in seclusion for too many years during which there was criticism, even doubts, about the monarchy itself. Her young family lived in an atmosphere devoid of laughter. Her golden jubilee brought her, at long last, before the public eye and all criticism dissipated into a series of tumultuous welcomes; she was surprised and touched by the love and concern of her people - considering she had shown little interest in them.

Several of her family married Royals of other European countries; Victoria, (1840-1901), the Princess Royal, married Frederick III, Emperor of Germany; her eldest son, Albert Edward, Prince of Wales, (1841-1910) who became Edward VII, married the beautiful Princess Alexandra, daughter of King Christian IX of Denmark. Her second eldest daughter, Princess Alice Maud Mary (1843-1878), married Prince Frederick William Louis of Hesse-Darnstadt who succeeded as the Grand Duke of Hesse, (their fourth daughter married Nicholas II, the last Tzar of Russia who was shot with his family by the Red Guards). Queen Victoria's youngest and favourite daughter, Princess

Beatrice May Victoria Feodore (1857-1944), married Prince Henry of Battenberg. Queen Victoria's influence on foreign affairs was therefore considerable.

Her reign from 1837 to 1901 saw many changes in society - most of which she disapproved; the start of compulsory education; Disraeli's second Reform Bill of 1867 and Gladstone's third Reform Bill of 1884. She was the first monarch to travel by rail - from Slough to Paddington with Isambard Kingdom Brunel himself on the footplate - and in 1876, Bell demonstrated his new telephone to her.

In 1848 the Chartists riots, which were quelled by the Duke of Wellington, caused Victoria to flee from London with her six children. There was an attempt upon her life in 1849 and another in 1850. The potato famine and trading restrictions in Ireland caused over two million deaths and rebellion. This was temporarily alleviated with the vote by Parliament of large sums of money and a visit from Victoria and Albert during which they were given a great welcome. The lesson of over-dependence on home grown food had led to the repeal of the Corns Laws in 1846 to allow the importation of tax free foreign corn.

Her love of Scotland was obvious from the regularity of her visits especially after she acquired Balmoral Castle in 1852 and through her personal attendant, the Highlander, John Brown. She enjoyed his kilted presence and forthright manner for thirty-four years, although some members of her family disapproved of his coarse tongue; he died in 1883 at Windsor Castle.

Britain with France declared war to repel the Russian invasion of Turkey and in 1856, near the end of the Crimean War, at the instigation of Prince Albert, Queen Victoria introduced the Victoria Cross for very exceptional gallantry. At her insistence its design was simple and the Cross was made from a bronze cannon captured at Sebastopol. She presented 111 VCs at a parade in Hyde Park in June 1857.

After the meeting of the Indian Sepoys in 1857, the relief of Lucknow and the end of rule by the East India Company the British government ruled that continent. By 1850 Britain had transformed itself from an agrarian society into the greatest manufacturing country in the world, and in 1851, when gold was discovered in Australia, two new colonies were created to be called Victoria and Queensland. In Africa massive land areas were taken under British protection; diamond and gold discoveries brought thousands of colonists. Cecil Rhodes made his fortune from diamond mines and added to British lands - Rhodesia, now Zimbabwe. David Livingstone, the Scottish medical missionary and explorer, in charting the Zambesi River, discovered the 5700 feet wide falls which he named after his Queen - the Victoria Falls.

When gold was discovered in the Transvaal the Boers, who occupied the territory, objected to English colonisation. War broke out in 1899; the Boers immediately took the offensive. Ladysmith and Mafeking were under siege for many months; the latter held by a small force under Colonel Robert Baden-Powell until its relief in May 1900 which was a great morale boost at home. The Queen was now eighty; she was delighted with the great news but sadly she did not live to celebrate the British victory in 1902.

She died at Osborne, her Royal residence on the Isle of Wight, on 22nd January 1901 aged eighty-two in the arms of her grandson, the Kaiser of Germany. Her lifespan was a few days longer than that of her grandfather, George III. Her funeral was majestic, magnificent; it was the greatest Royal procession of mourning ever seen in Britain. It was the occasion of not simply national mourning but of global grief. This was the end of an age - the Victorian age. She had become a symbol which represented the Victorian values of stability during a period of great change and of reassurance through times of war. Life without Victoria seemed unimaginable.

Waterloo Bridge

Leaving Haddington via the Sidegate to Poldrate, the Waterloo Bridge crosses the Tyne on the way south to Gifford and the Lammermuirs. This road bridge was opened in 1817 by the Marquis of Tweeddale accompanied by Archibald Fletcher (Lord Milton), the Grand Master of the Masons, Provost Thomas Pringle, Bailies and many other dignitaries who formed a grand procession. The opening ceremony took place on the anniversary of the Duke of Wellington's great victory over the French at Waterloo on 18th June 1815.

Until 1817 the only crossing for carts and carriages over the Tyne was over the pre-13th century Nungate Bridge; there were, in addition, a couple of wooden footbridges.

Many towns and cities had named streets, pubs and bridges to celebrate and to commemorate the 'Iron Duke's' victory of Waterloo which finally brought to an end the Napoleonic War against France. The Town Council of Haddington decided to name its new road bridge to commemorate the great victory.

The Battle of Waterloo:

Just as it seemed that peace in Europe had been achieved the Allies, having signed the Treaty of Paris with Louis XVIII and Napoleon having abdicated to the Island of Elba, started quarrelling amongst themselves over boundaries. A million French soldiers were suspicious of the Bourbon throne which was now supported by their recent enemies.

Prussia threatened war having lost Poland to the Russians and Lord Castlereagh, the British War Minister, took on his greatest responsibility by signing a secret treaty with Austria and France against a Prussian attack.. On the same day that Castlereagh returned to England, Napoleon landed in the South of France - lst March 1815.

Louis XVIII fled when his army deserted him to support Napoleon who struck quickly knowing that the British were weak after the American war.

Wellington was given only 20,000 men and was dependent on the Prussians to give him a total of 67,000 men and 184 guns against Napoleon's 74,000 men and 246 guns; they were thinly stretched from Ostend to Liege, a distance of 150 miles. Napoleon attacked their centre at Charleroi, thirty miles south of Brussels, and after two days (16th and 17th June) and two tough battles he advanced to the north east. But Wellington had to retreat to join the Prussians. However, he had planned exactly where he would make his stand; he knew every ridge, valley and woodland around the little village of Waterloo, ten miles to the south of Brussels in the middle of the forest of Soignies. He placed 17,000 men ten miles north west at Hal under the command of the eighteen-year-old Prince Frederick of the Netherlands. This was a precaution in case Napoleon tried a turning movement. Napoleon had already defeated the Prussians at Ligny and was confident that they had given up in retreat. He wasted valuable time and 30,000 men in following them.

At Waterloo, Wellington, having hardly slept for three nights, realised that this would be a close run battle. It was Sunday, 18th June, a dull, wet day. At 6.0am Wellington, astride his chestnut horse, 'Copenhagen' was resplendent; the sight of him gave confidence to the men. He ordered a chequer board formation of squares behind a ridge and ordered the men to lie down. Wellington's policy was to move around and to show himself everywhere spreading goodwill and encouragement. He exuded calm confidence, he was well-named 'the Iron Duke'; he had nerves of steel.

The artillery on both sides opened fire just before noon. Napoleon assumed wrongly that the Prussians were well beaten and could not possibly reach Wellington for at least another two days. He had jeered at Marshal Soult's advice to recall the Marquis de Grouchy's 33,000 men from his eastern flank as reinforcements with the remark: 'this affair is nothing more than eating breakfast.'

At 11.30 am Prince Jerome, Napoleon's younger brother, sought glory with an attack on the chateau at Hougoumont but Wellington ordered his Howitzers to fire over the heads of the defenders which allowed the Allied infantry to counter-attack. The French were repulsed after three attacks and Wellington was to state afterwards that 'the success of Waterloo depended on the closing of the gates of Hougoumont.'

At 1.30 pm French infantry under Marshal Ney attacked the centre and burned all before them as an act of revenge for Quatre Bras two days before. They drove off the Germans and Prince Bernhard's troops, then the 92nd rifles followed by Bylandt's light brigade were swept aside but the Gordons, the Black Watch and the 44th flung themselves into the fray. Then the Scots Greys thundered through carrying many Gordons on their stirrups. Wellington led the Life Guards like a torrent into the now exhausted French Cavalry. By 3.0 pm not a Frenchman was to be seen on the ridge.

By 4.0 pm the French artillery had slackened and Wellington moved back part of his line one hundred yards to allow the evacuation of the wounded. Ney misinterpreted this as a withdrawal and sent 4500 cavalry in pursuit. This was heaven sent; Wellington was completely prepared. His infantry formed into squares and were ordered to hold their fire until the last moment. From a distance Napoleon imagined victory - the English were falling back. Wellington seized his chance, the French cavalry was shot and cut to pieces by veterans of the Peninsular War.

Wellington, always vigilant, heard the Prussian guns at the edge of Paris Wood and he knew then that he was the victor. He rode up and down his lines encouraging his men. The tough, crude Prussian Prince Blucher attacked the French right and another Prussian corps supported the British at the French rear.

Marshal Ney decided that La Haye Sainte must be won and win it he did. Now the Allied centre was in danger and Ney sent for reinforcements which were refused. This was Napoleon's great error which he compounded by a pause; this allowed Wellington to bring up all his reserves. However, Napoleon brought up his Grenadiers as far as La Haye Sainte to hand them over to Ney. Wellington's 1st Foot Guards lay in wait and he rode quickly to rally two battalions of Brunswickers. The French Imperial Guard were brought to a sudden halt when the order to stand up and fire was given. They fled towards Hougoumont and Wellington gave them no time to rally. The Prussians joined in the rout and captured the fleeing Napoleon. After the capitulation of Paris, Ney was found guilty of high treason and shot. Napoleon abdicated on 22nd June in Paris and ended his days on St Helena where he died six years later.

The losses at Waterloo were horrific: 15,000 British, over 7000 Prussian and 25,000 French. Wellington wept when he learned of the loss of life which was much worse than he had imagined. To the doctor who dressed his wounded hand he said, "Well, thank God, I don't know what it is to lose a battle; but certainly nothing can be more painful than to gain one with the loss of so many of one's friends." (3.p.584) After Waterloo, Wellington grew to detest war.

Wemyss Place

Wemyss Place is a small cul-de-sac off Victoria Road and commemorates the Earldom of Wemyss and March. John Wood's 1819 Plan of Haddington and Nungate shows the land on the east side of Haddington stretching from Dunbar Road, across the Tyne, the Nungate and southwards as the 'Property of the Earl of Wemyss and March', although the earldom owned much of the land 'from the sea to the hills', that is from Aberlady Bay to the Lammermuir Hills as well as lands in Fife (East and West Wemyss and Wemyss Bay bear the family name), Elcho Castle and estates in Peeblesshire including Neidpath Castle.

Situated in the centre of magnificent parkland, east of Haddington town centre, was Amisfield House, described by McWilliam (26.p76) as 'the most important building of the orthodox Palladian school in Scotland.' It was rebuilt in 1755 for Francis Charteris Wemyss, second son of the 5th Earl of Wemyss (ref. **Amisfield Park, Place**) who inherited the estate from his grandfather, the notorious Colonel Francis Charteris. Most of the Park is now Haddington Golf Course.

This story of the Wemyss family starts with the creation of Lord Wemyss of Elcho as the 1st Earl of Wemyss in 1633 during the visit of Charles I to Scotland when he was crowned and ordered that Edinburgh be the capital of Scotland.

The **1st Earl** was born in 1586 and was created a Baronet of Nova Scotia in 1625 and Lord Wemyss of Elcho in 1628. Fearful of a return to Roman Catholicism he was one of many thousands of signatories of the "National Covenant" on 28th September 1638 and he attended the conference in Edinburgh with Oliver Cromwell in 1648 when the reinstatement of the ultra-Presbyterian party in government was discussed. He married Jane, a daughter of Patrick, 6th Lord Gray. The 1st Earl died in 1649.

The **2nd Earl**, David, known as the 'Great Earl', was born on 6th September 1610. He became Master of Wemyss in 1628 and Lord Elcho when his father was created an Earl in 1633. He succeeded to the Earldom in 1649 and married three times. By his first wife, Anna who was the eldest daughter of Lord Balfour, he had eleven children but his eighth and last surviving son David died unmarried in 1671. Knowing of the existence of coal in his estates in Fife he built and paid for Methil harbour in preparation for the coal to be mined. He sunk several pits, the first of which was called the 'Happy Mine'. These pits were owned by the Wemyss family until nationalisation of the coal industry in 1947. The 2nd Earl died in June 1679 and his titles and estates were inherited by his 6th and only surviving daughter by his third wife, Margaret, the widow of the 2nd Earl of Buccleuch.

Margaret, Countess of Wemyss, is counted as the '**3rd Earl**' (16). She was six months old when she became the sole successor on the death of her father; she was born on 1st January 1679. She married her third cousin twice removed, Sir James Wemyss, who was created Lord Burntisland in 1672. He died ten years later and his title became extinct. The countess's second husband was George MacKenzie, 1st Earl of Cromarty. The countess died on 11th March 1705 and her first son, David, by her first marriage, succeeded her.

The **4th Earl**, David Wemyss, was born in 1678 being styled Lord Elcho. In 1703 he became an Ensign of the Royal Company of Archers; he was elected MP in 1705 in which year his mother died and he succeeded as the 4th Earl. He was appointed Lord High Admiral of Scotland but this office was abolished after the Union in 1707, of which he was a strong supporter and Commissioner. He was appointed Vice Admiral of Scotland, a Privy Councillor and representative peer until 1710. He took no part in the uprising of 1715. His first wife, Lady Anne Douglas, was the only daughter of the 1st Duke of Queensberry and sister of the Hon. William Douglas, 1st Earl of March. She was burned to death in an accident only two years after her marriage in 1699/70. She had two sons the second and only survivor of whom succeeded to the titles and estates. The Earl's second wife, Mary was the first daughter of Sir John Robinson. She died in 1711 after three years of marriage and the Earl died in 1720.

The **5th Earl**, James Wemyss, was born on 30th August 1699. He was a member of the Royal Company of Archers (1714) and he inherited the earldom and estates in 1720. He was a brigadier in 1724, lieutenant-general in 1726 and captain-general in 1743 of the Royal Bodyguard in Scotland. In 1720 he married secretly,

Janet, the very rich heiress and only daughter of the notorious Colonel Francis Charteris of Amisfield (who gave Amisfield its name). The 5th Earl's concerns over money were as a result of the spendthrift ways of the countess (they separated in 1732) and his eldest son's support of the '45 Rebellion. The Earl, although sympathetic to the Jacobite cause, had little interest in politics preferring to give his time to his interests in coal-mining and salt manufacture. He made his estates over to his third son James, passing over his attainted second son, Francis Charteris Wemyss. He died on 21st March 1756.

David Wemyss, the eldest son, became known as 'Lord Elcho of the '45'. He assumed the title de jure '**6th Earl of Wemyss**' but being attainted in 1746 his claim to the title was forfeited. He was born on 21st August 1721 and educated at Winchester and at the military school at Angers in France immediately following which (1740) he visited the Old Pretender (who, had he succeeded the throne would have been James VIII of Scotland, III of England) in Rome who made him a Colonel of the Dragoons. He was a member of the Royal Company of Archers but his ardent support of the Jacobite cause was aided by his younger brother, Francis Charteris Wemyss, who advanced him 1500 guineas (£1575) for the cause.

On his return to Scotland in 1744 David Wemyss collaborated with Sir John Murray of Broughton (who was to become Prince Charles Edward's secretary during the '45 and to betray the Jacobites after Culloden) in the Jacobite cause in France. David joined Prince Charles Edward to become his ADC and a member of his Council. He fought at the Battle of Prestonpans (21st September 1745) and gave distinguished service in command of the 1st Troop of Horse Guards during the advance through England. After the defeat at Culloden he escaped to France never to return to Scotland. In later years Lord Elcho's nephew, Sir James Stewart Denham, described his uncle's dissatisfaction at Culloden when the Chevalier rode off the field with Elcho's words ringing in his ear: "there you go for a damned cowardly Italian." (28. p190).

In France Lord Elcho continued to distinguish himself militarily becoming a captain of the Regiment of FitzJames and a Colonel of the Royal Scots from 1756 to 1763. He was awarded the Order of

Military Merit from Louis XV. He married the daughter of Baron d'Uxhull in Switzerland and died in Paris on 29th April 1787.

The de jure **7th Earl**, Francis Charteris Wemyss, succeeded his brother David in 1787 but he too was not officially recognised as the Earl of Wemyss because of the attainder of his brother. He was born on 21st October 1723 and in 1731/2 his wealth increased considerably when he inherited his maternal grandfather's estate including Amisfield. On 13th September 1745, at Preston Hall, he married Catherine, 6th daughter of Alexander, Duke of Gordon (ref. **Lady Kitty's Doocot**). The story is told of the bridal party's arrival at Amisfield when a sudden warning was given that the Jacobites were advancing upon them. It was a false alarm which amused the bride and groom but embarrassed Sir John Cope. (1. p.57)

Lord Elcho bought the Elcho estate from his father in 1750 for £8500 (the old nunnery, Elcho Castle near the River Tay, four miles from Perth) and in 1771 he adopted his maternal grandfather's name Charteris through an Act of Parliament - this was a condition of the infamous colonel's Will. He did not inherit Wemyss Castle and was wrongly known as Earl of Wemyss. He rebuilt Amisfield (1755 by Issac Ware) and Gosford (1790 by Robert Adam) having bought the old Gosford House and estate in 1784.

He was elected MP in 1780 and 1784 in the Tory government of William Pitt. Francis Charteris died at Amisfield on 24th August 1808 six months after the death of his only son, also Francis Charteris Wemyss, who was born on 31st January 1748/9 in Edinburgh. He was a Member of the Royal Company of Archers (11th December 1786) and was wrongly known as Lord Elcho after 1787 (the attainder of his uncle David who died in 1787 passed to his father and the forfeiture of 1746 was still valid). He was elected MP for Haddingtonshire in three Parliaments between 1780 and 1787. On 18th July 1771 he married Susan, 2nd daughter of Anthony Tracy-Keck and Susan, daughter of the 4th Duke of Hamilton. It was through this marriage that the Stanway estates in Gloucestershire were eventually inherited by the Wemyss family. As a wedding present his father moved to Gosford and gave him Amisfield. Following a long and painful illness at Amisfield he died aged fifty-eight on 20th January 1808. His ageing father was undoubtedly affected by his son's protracted illness and died six months afterwards. The estates now passed to his grandson.

The **6th Earl**, (sometimes counted as the **8th Earl**), Francis Charteris (grandson of Francis Charteris (1713-1808)), was born on 15th April 1772 and educated at Eton from the age of eight until he was fifteen years. In 1793, when France declared war, he became ADC to his great uncle, Lord Adam Gordon, who was commander of the army in Scotland. When his father died in January 1808 he became Lord Elcho and a few months later, on the death of his paternal grandfather (24th August 1808), he styled himself Earl of Wemyss, although it was not until the 'reversal' of 1826 when three peerages were restored (the plea for which had been made by Sir Walter Scott to George IV) that he became officially recognised as the 6th Earl.

On the death of a distant cousin he became heir to considerable estates in Peeblesshire. The cousin was William Douglas, 4th Duke of Queensberry. Francis Charteris was the surviving male heir of his great-great grandmother, Lady Anne Douglas, the only daughter of the 1st Duke of Queensberry who married the 4th Earl of Wemyss. Now Earl of Wemyss, Viscount Peebles, Lord Douglas of Neidpath, Lyne and Munard, he styled himself Earl of Wemyss and March in 1810 and took the name Francis Charteris-Wemyss-Douglas. He was Lord Lieutenant of the County of Peebles from 1821 until his death. On 31st August 1794 he married Margaret, 4th daughter of Walter Campbell of Shawfield, who died at Gosford House in 1850. He died there on 28th June 1853 aged eighty-one years

The **7th Earl**, (sometimes counted as the **9th Earl**) Francis Wemyss-Charteris-Douglas, was born on 14th August 1795. He matriculated for Christ Church, Oxford in 1812. He became a Member of the Royal Company of Archers in 1824 in which he attained the rank of Lieutenant-General in 1842. He was Grand Master Mason of Scotland from 1827 to 1830 and Lord Lieutenant of Peebles from 1853 to 1880. He was a trustee of the National Portrait Gallery from 1856 to 1866.

On 22nd August 1827 he married Louisa, 4th daughter of Richard Bingham, 2nd Earl of Lucan. She died at Gosford in 1882; her effigy in marble is in Aberlady Church. He died eight months later on 1st January 1883 aged eighty-seven and is commemorated by the large window on the south transept of St Mary's Church, Haddington (1892 by his son). He was buried at the Holy Trinity Church of Haddington.

The **8th Earl** (sometimes counted as the **10th Earl**), Francis Wemyss-Charteris-Douglas, was born in Edinburgh on 4th August 1818. He was educated at Edinburgh Academy and Eton (1832-35) and matriculated for Christ Church, Oxford where he gained his BA degree in 1841 and befriended John Ruskin (1819-1900), the writer and art critic. He was a member of the Royal Company of Archers (1838), Conservative MP for Gloucestershire (1841-6) and for Haddingtonshire from 1847 until 1883 when he succeeded to the Earldom on the death of his father and took his seat in the House of Lords.

In April 1848 the 8th Earl purchased the anchorage in Aberlady for £375 (1). As an MP he was a strong Conservative at first but his disenchantment with the Conservatives led him towards Liberalism and latterly he described himself as a Liberal/Conservative. He was the power behind the Act of Parliament of 1859 which created the General Medical Council but his main interest was in military matters. He was appointed Lord of the Treasury from 1853 to 1855 in Lord Aberdeen's coalition ministry of 1852-55. He was acutely aware of the government's total neglect of the army and navy at the start of the Crimean War in March 1854 and of the 'panic', as it was described in 1859 by Cobden, of the War Office in the belief that the French planned invasion. Because of this the Earl strongly promoted the Rifle Volunteer movement from its beginning in 1859 when he was instrumental in the creation of the London-Scottish Regiment becoming its Lieutenant-Colonel. Such was his influence and enthusiasm in Haddington that Provost Roughhead and Lieutenant-Colonel Vetch of Caponflat convened a public meeting to raise subscriptions for the uniforms and equipment for the 67 riflemen of Haddington who enrolled within the next fortnight.(1) By 1860 the Haddington contingent, commanded by Captain Roughead, consisted of almost 300 volunteers and took part in the review of Scottish Rifle Volunteers on 7th August by Queen Victoria. Grant's *Old and New Edinburgh* refers to:

'The whole force was commanded by Major General Alastair Macdonald; and perhaps none were more applauded in the march past than the London Scottish, led by Lord Elcho.'

He was the first chairman of the National Rifle Association to which he presented the Elcho Challenge Shield awarded annually to the winner of a competition of marksmanship. When, in 1879, he became ADC to Queen Victoria he relinquished command of the London-Scottish Regiment. He was ADC to two further monarchs, Edward VII and George V and for his services to the Crown he was created a Knight Grand Cross of the Royal Victorian Order (GCVO). He never lost interest in military matters and in 1907 he strongly opposed the army reforms of Viscount Haldane (1856-1928) (ref. Haldane Avenue) who amalgamated yeomen and volunteers to form a Territorial force of fourteen divisions and fourteen cavalry brigades in addition to many other reforms.

The 8th Earl's interest in art was undoubtedly influenced through his friendship with John Ruskin. He was a discerning collector with an eye for a bargain; he painted in water colour and practised sculpture as a leisure activity. His death in 1914 was widely mourned. His obituary in the Times of 1st July 1914 described him, 'a lone individualist, protesting vigorously against every kind of social legislation that debarred men from making use of what they liked of their liberty.'

His marriage to his first wife, Anne Frederica, 2nd daughter of Thomas William Anson, 1st Earl of Lichfield gave them four sons: Francis (1844-1870) died accidentally of gunshot wounds, Arthur (1846-47) died in infancy, Alfred Walter (1847-1873) was a lieutenant of the 71st Foot and while serving under Sir Garnet Wolseley in the Ashanti War he became seriously ill of dysentery and fever and died at sea on his way home. The only surviving son was Hugo Richard who succeeded to the titles and estates.

The **9th Earl** (sometimes counted as the **11th Earl**), Hugo Richard Charteris, was born on 25th August 1857 and was educated at Harrow (1871-74). He matriculated at Oxford (Balliol 1876) having become Lord Elcho on the death of his brother in 1873. When his grandfather died in 1883 and his father took his place in the House of Lords, Hugo was elected Conservative

MP for Haddingtonshire. This was the year of his marriage (9th August 1883) to Mary Constance, 1st daughter of Hon. Percy Wyndham who was Conservative MP for West Cumberland for twenty-five years. They lived at the Wemyss Gloucestershire estate at Stanway. Lady Wemyss's A Family Record (1932) gives an insight of their family life, especially the lives of her two sons both of whom were killed during the 1914-18 War. Their eldest son, Francis, Lord Elcho (1884-1916) married Lady Violet Manners, a daughter of the 8th Duke of Rutland. They had two sons, Francis, the present Earl of Wemyss KT, Hon.LLD, JP, BA born in 1912 and Martin, Baron Charteris of Amisfield OBE, MVO, KCVO, PC, KCB, GCVO, GCB, born 1913. Their father, Lord Elcho, was a captain of the Gloucestershire Hussars and was killed during the Great War in 1916.

In 1886 until 1895 the 9th Earl was MP for Ipswich and a member of London County Council from 1904 until 1910. He succeeded his father as 9th Earl in 1914. After the first year of the 1914-18 War losses were so devastating that a recruitment drive was necessary (there was no conscription at this stage) and the Earl of Wemyss addressed a public meeting in Haddington to try to overcome what he referred to as, 'the orgy of pessimism.' (1.p.79). After the war he was Lord Lieutenant of East Lothian and honorary colonel of the 7th Volunteer battalion of the Royal Scots. His wife died on 29th April 1937 and he died less than three months later on 12th July and was buried at Aberlady.

The **10th Earl** of Wemyss and March (sometimes counted as the **12th Earl**) Francis David Charteris, is the present and longest holder of the Earldom. He was born on 19th January 1912 and educated at Eton and Oxford (Balliol) where he took his BA degree in 1933. His titles include the Knighthood of the Most Ancient and the Most Noble Order of the Thistle (KT), Viscount Peebles, Lord Elcho and Methil and Baron Douglas of Neidpath, Lyne and Munard and Baron Wemyss of Fife. He entered the Colonial Service to become Assistant District Commissioner of Basutoland from 1937 to 1944 during which he was a lieutenant of the Lovat Scouts and a Major with the Basuto troops in the Union Defence Force in the Middle East (1940-44). He was less interested in politics than his predecessors but his record of public service is enormous and on his return to Scotland in 1948 he, with the East Lothian Antiquarian and Field Naturalists' Society, was instrumental in saving Haddington House from demolition. His presidencies and chairmanships give an indication of the breadth of his interests - The Royal Scottish Geographical Society, The National Trust for Scotland, The Thistle Foundation for Severely Disabled Scottish Ex-servicemen, The National Bible Society of Scotland, The Society of the Friends of St Mary's in Haddington, the Scottish Churches Council, the Royal Commission on Ancient and Historical Monuments of Scotland and the Scottish Committee of The Marie Curie Memorial Foundation. He is Vice-President of the East Lothian Antiquarian and Field Naturalists' Society. He was twice Lord High Commissioner to the General Assembly of the Church of Scotland. He was a director of Scottish Television (1964), Lord Lieutenant of East Lothian (since 1967), Lord Clerk Register of Scotland and Keeper of Her Majesty's Signet, Ensign in the Royal Company of Archers (The Queen's Bodyguard in Scotland). His honours include the Knighthood of The Most Ancient and the Most Noble Order of the Thistle (KT) (which is restricted to sixteen distinguished Scotsmen) and an honorary Doctorate of Laws of St Andrews University. Most recently, on 12th November 1996, he was appointed one of the Commissioners 'to safeguard, repair and preserve' the Stone of Destiny which is housed with the Regalia of Scotland at Edinburgh Castle

On 24th February 1940 he married Mavis Lynette Gordon Murray BA, elder daughter of the late Edwin Edward Murray of Hermanus, Cape Provence. They had two sons:

Iain David, Lord Elcho who was born on 20th June 1945 and died tragically aged nine on 3rd April 1954 as a result of a car accident.

James Donald, born in 1948, is the present heir and was given the courtesy title of Lord Douglas of Neidpath after his elder brother's death. He was educated at Eton and Oxford where he graduated BA (1969), MA (1974) PhD (1975). He is an acknowledged historian. He married Catherine Guiness, elder daughter of the Hon Jonathan Guiness. They reside at Stanway House in Gloucestershire with their son, grandson of the present Earl, Hon Francis Richard Charteris born in 1984.

The 12th Earl, following the example of his grandfather, married again at the age of 83 in 1995 to Canadian born Shelagh Kennedy at Aberlady Parish Church.

Wilson's Close (or Opera Close)

The name **Wilson's Close** could be the cause of a little controversy - its name was changed almost as often as its residents. It has been called Faunt's Close when Fred Faunt's fruit shop traded there; it was also called Crowe's Close after Francis Crowe who had his plumbing business in the Close. Haddington's Dramatic Club held their rehearsals in the rooms now occupied by the Labour Club and the Haddington Amateur Operatic Society rehearsed their productions during the 1950s in the same rooms, previously the old Scottish Co-operative Wholesale Society bakehouse - then it was known as **Opera Close**.

It is the narrow entrance between Nos. 20 and 24 Court Street which leads to the Labour Club and to Tesco's supermarket beyond. The Close was named after a local grain merchant who owned several of the buildings in the close. These buildings, which were, successively, the premises of a minister, millwright, spirit dealer and wig-maker and were used by one Mr Thomas Wilson, a grain merchant.

The Register of Sasines of June 1934 makes reference to Wilson's Close in which a two-storey tenement and two stables were disponed to Haddington Co-operative Society in May 1884 and in 1887 'with right to the well, granaries and stable, the common entry being part of the Malt barn and loft above the malt kiln.'

The buildings at the rear were demolished except for the Court Street frontage to make way for the William Low's supermarket, now McKays Stores Ltd. New buildings were erected on vacant ground to accommodate the enlarged Low's Supermarket, now Tescos. The East Lothian Register of Sasines as recently as April 1960 also makes reference to Wilson's Close.

Yester Place

Yester Place, off Davidson Terrace, takes its name from the seat of the Gifford family of Yester Castle and the Marquis of Tweeddale of Yester House. The latter is reached via a stunningly beautiful avenue of trees in Gifford; the castle is about 1.5 km south-east of the house.

Yester Castle was built for Hugh de Giffard (original spelling) who died in 1267. It is famous for its subterranean 'Hobgoblin Hall' noted in Scott's 'Marmion' and was said to have been created by magic.

Hugh de Giffard (ref. Giffordgate) was one of fifteen of the nobility who were appointed Regents after the Earl of Gloucester had 'captured' Alexander II and his Queen. Henry III, having returned from warring against the French, was aggrieved that Alexander II of Scotland had married (his second wife) the daughter of a French magnate (said to be even richer than the dauphin) and felt it justified to invade Scotland in 1244. Another of the Regents was Sir Gilbert de Haya, an ancestor of Hay, the Marquis of Tweeddale.(2. p.8).

In 1418 the old barony of Yester passed to the Hay family through marriage. A 15th century reference to the ownership of Yester relates to a charter of Yester, Morham, Duncanlaw, and Giffordgate of 6th April 1434 in which **Sir David Hay** of Yester was served heir of his brother Thomas Hay in exchange for the barony of Teyling (Tealing) in Forfarshire. (2.p.230). In 1452 Sir David gained the remaining share of the Gifford lands from one Robert Boyd of Kilmarnock in exchange for other lands.

In 1670 the **2nd Earl of Tweeddale**, John Hay, proposed the building of a new house near the Collegiate Church of Bothans and about 1.5 km north-west of the castle. This was Yester House and he engaged Sir William Bruce (1630-1710), the King's Surveyor-General, to design the new house, but Tweeddale, now **1st Marquis**, died in 1697 and his son engaged James Smith (who designed the Parish Church of Gifford in 1710) and Alexander McGill to design the new 'large, austere box of a house.' (26.p.211) It was about this time that the village of Bothans, near the old Parish Kirk of Bothans, was resited and given a new name - Gifford. Alexander MacGill's contribution started in 1710 and the house took almost 30 years to completion. The interior of the house is largely Adam (father and son - 1789). In 1830 the entrance was moved from the central north to the west side.

John Hay, the **1st Marquis of Tweeddale** (1626-97), was the eldest son of the 1st Earl of Tweeddale. His grandmother, Lady Margaret Ker, left him the house at Tweeddale Court in Edinburgh's 'Royal Mile' in 1645. He supported the Royalists joining Charles I at Nottingham on 22nd August 1642 - the start of the Civil War against the Parliamentarians. However, Tweeddale, appalled at the treatment of Covenanters, joined the Scots army to command the East Lothian Regiment.

He succeeded his father in 1654 and represented Haddington in the Scots Parliament. He was made a Privy Councillor but again, in support of the Covenanters, he refused to pass sentence on a Covenanting minister, James Guthrie. By Royal command he was imprisoned in Edinburgh Castle but was released after eight months. He persuaded the Duke of Lauderdale, who had just made himself Commissioner (1668), to issue a 'Letter of Indulgence' which allowed peaceable 'outed' ministers to be restored to their churches.

Tweeddale however disagreed with the all-powerful and tyrannical Lauderdale administration over many issues and was dismissed from office and expelled from the Privy Council. After the cruelties against the Covenanters following the Battle of Bothwell Bridge (2nd July 1679) Lauderdale lost support and he died in 1682. That year Tweeddale was reinstated to the Privy Council but Charles II died three years later and Tweeddale, unable to tolerate the 'Killing Time' of James II (VII of Scotland), gave his support to William of Orange during the Revolution of 1688-9.

He was now appointed High Chancellor and elevated to Marquis in 1694. After the Massacre of Glencoe (13th February 1692) he was a member of the commission of enquiry. He was appointed Lord High Commissioner to the Scots Parliament in 1695 but his support of the disastrous Darien Scheme lost him his Chancellorship. He died soon afterwards on 11th August 1697.

John Hay, **2nd Marquis of Tweeddale** (1645-1713) was fifty-two years old when he succeeded to the title in 1697. He had married Lady Mary Maitland, daughter of the Duke of Lauderdale and they had three sons and two daughters. During the 'Revolution' to oust James II (1688-9), he was colonel of the East Lothian regiment against the invasion of Scotland by the Duke of Argyle. Tweeddale was a Privy Councillor, Sheriff of Haddington and Commissioner to the Scots Parliament. As leader of his new party he failed to persuade the Scots Parliament to agree to a Hanoverian succession. Tweeddale became head of the 'Squadrone Volante' (flying squadron) administration on the failure of the Islay/Milton group to deliver sufficient Scottish votes to Walpole's government. Tweeddale's group of thirty gave its support to the Union of Parliaments of 1707 and Tweeddale became a representative peer for Scotland.

John Hay, **4th Marquis of Tweeddale** (c1690-1762) was appointed an Extraordinary Lord of Session in 1721. He was Principal Secretary of State for Scotland until the office was abolished after the '45 Rebellion. Tweeddale had joined the Carteret Party. Carteret, the Earl Granville, was Tweeddale's father-in-law, Tweeddale having married Lady Francis, the Earl's daughter, by whom he had two sons and four daughters. Pitt denounced Carteret as the 'Hanoverian troop-minister'. In 1761 Tweeddale was appointed Lord Justice-General. He was a governor of the Bank of Scotland and Principal Keeper of His Majesty's Signet. He died in London on 9th September 1762 and was buried at Yester.

George Hay, **8th Marquis of Tweeddale** (1787-1876) was the soldier of the family who rose to the rank of Field Marshal. He served with distinction during the Peninsular War (1808-14) and the American War (1812-15). He was Governor-General of Madras in 1842 where he commanded the Army. At Yester he pioneered many new farming techniques and was president of the Agricultural Society. As Lord Lieutenant of the County he took a strong interest in local affairs including the construction of the Court House in Haddington in front of which is his red sandstone monument. Following an accident he died on 10th October 1876.

Arthur Hay, **9th Marquis of Tweeddale** (1824-78) was born at Yester and aged seventeen he enlisted in the Grenadier Guards. He was aide-de-campe to Lord Hardinge, Governor-General of India. In the Crimean War (1854-56) his conscientious service earned him the rank of lieutenant-colonel and after the war he concentrated his whole energy to the study of ornithology and zoology publishing many articles which were collected and published privately after his death. He was President of the Zoological Society of London and a member of the Royal and Linnean Societies. He inherited the title in 1876, on the death of his brother, and made his home at Yester having lived in Chiselhurst. Locally he was known and loved for his munificence in the provision of several amenities including a library and reading room, improvement of schools and the provision of a medical officer for his tenantry. He died at Chiselhurst in December 1878.

The present owner of Yester House and grounds is **Gian-Carlo Menotti** who purchased the estate from Peter Morrison 1984.

He is a world-famous composer whose works include several operas two of which won Pulitzer prizes in 1950 and 1954 and for which he wrote his own libretti.

He was born in 1911, one of eight children, at Milan where his early love of opera led him to a career in music. A child prodigy, he composed his first opera at the age of 11 and, on the advice of the greatest conductor of his time Arturo Toscanini (1867-1957), at the age of 17 he was sent to the conservatory in Philadelphia where he produced his opera, *Amelia goes to the Ball in 1937*. Several others followed: *The Medium* in 1940, *The Consul* in 1950 for which he won the Pulitzer Prize*, *Amahl and the Night Visitors* in 1951 for television, *The Saint of Bleeker Street* 1954 for which he won another Pulitzer Prize, *Maria Golovin* 1958, *The Most Important Man* 1971 and many others. Although he spent many years in America he remained an Italian citizen. He founded the world famous festivals of Spoleto (north of Rome) and Charleston in USA and he is director of the Rome Opera where he produced his exceedingly successful *Lucia di Lammermoor* in 1994. Although he travelled world wide for many years he has made his home at peaceful Yester where his

Theatre School gives tuition and encouragement to young musicians, dancers and directors.

* The Pulitzer Prize is awarded annually by the Trustees of Columbia University for distinguished works in journalism and letters and for a larger musical work.

Appendix I

Churches of Haddington

The earliest reference to Christianity in Haddington dates to about 518 AD when Princess Thanea (or Thenew), daughter of the legendary King Loth (from whom Lothian is said to take its name), was said to have defied her semi-pagan father by refusing to marry Owen Ap, a Welsh prince. She was banished from her father's palace, on Traprain Law, to the Lammermuir Hills to become a shepherdess. The spurned prince, on his way back to Galloway, found Princess Thanea in the hills and raped her.

On discovering her pregnancy the Princess took refuge at the Nunnery of Whittingehame but her father ordered that she be stoned to death. No one would lift a stone against her. He had her tied to a type of sled and thrown over the cliffs of Traprain Law. However, she was not to die, she was caught on an over-hanging bush. King Loth, now fearful of offending her Christian God, had her placed in a coracle and left her to the mercies of the sea - he imagined that the pagan god Mannan (the god of the sea and from which Clackmannan takes its name) would decide her fate. Thanea was washed up at Culross in Fife where she gave birth to her son Kentigern.

It was through Kentigern's preaching in Lothian at the end of the 6th century that the King of Picts was converted to Christianity. Kentigern (meaning 'chief lord') founded a monastery at Cathures (now Glasgow) and became St Mungo.

St Baldred

One of St Kentigern's disciples, the earliest Christian priest to be stationed in East Lothian, was St Baldred. He died in 607 and 'a Saxon monastery of St Baldred was established at Tyningham' (2.p.172). It was destroyed by the Danes in 941. During the 6th and 7th centuries no successor to Baldred is recorded except for the bishopric of Lindisfarne in 635 under the guidance of St Aiden who belonged to the Irish Church as did St Columba. St Cuthbert was a shepherd boy in Northumbria and was said to have shepherded his sheep in the Lammermuirs. He left Melrose in

664 to become prior of the island monastery of Lindisfarne. The Lindisfarne Gospels were written there about the year 700.

St Martin's Chapel/Nunnery

In the year 1020 Lothian was ceded to Malcolm II and came under the jurisdiction of the Bishop of St Andrews. In 1139 David I's eldest son, Prince Henry, married Ada, daughter of the Earl of Warrenne and Surrey, and as a wedding present he gave her the lands of Haddington. She founded a priory of Cistercian nuns whose nunnery was dedicated to St Martin. This is the ruin on the consecrated ground between Bullet Loan and Park Road which was made safe from collapse in 1913.

From 1178 St Martin's Chapel belonged to the Abbey of Haddington and after the Reformation of 1560 the Town Council took it over. For the next one hundred years or so it was used by the Presbyterians but it was abandoned and fell into disrepair by the end of the 18th century. In 1822 it was threatened with demolition when the Church authorities were seeking a site for a new Parish School but fortunately they built it in Lodge Street. After a dispute over the burial of those who died of cholera in 1832 the burial ground ceased to be used.

Lamp of Lothian

The *Lamp of Lothian* was the Franciscan Friary which lay just east of the Holy Trinity Church in Church Street. The Franciscans arrived in Scotland during the reign of Alexander II (r.1214-1249) when the monastery was established (the precise year is not known but it was shortly after the death of their patriarch St Francis of Assisi in 1226). Their richly endowed church was magnificent; its light could be seen for miles around and it became known as *Lucerna Laudoniae* or *Lamp of Lothian*. It was badly damaged in 1356 by Edward III but it was sumptuously re-endowed with fifteen altars dating from 1314 to 1572-73 (2.p.177). Such embellishments were detested by the Reformers.

St Laurence

The earliest mention of the Chapel of St Laurence is in 'the ancient taxatio of Lothian in 1176' (2.p.172) in which the chapel was rated at five merks (the Church of Haddington was rated at 120 merks). The leper hospital of St Laurence was endowed by James V (1513-1542) who appointed one of his Royal Chaplains, Walter Ramsay, as its preceptor.

The hospital had about 82 acres (33 hectares) and may have included Spittalrig (1.p.26). According to the Exchequer Rolls of 1530 the Franciscans of Haddington gave twenty shillings to the funds of the hospital which totalled £9 annually. In 1533 the hospital was incorporated in the monastery of St Katherine of Sciennes of Edinburgh and in 1563 the nuns of St Katherine's sold the land to Sir John Bellenden of Auchenoule. His heir, Sir Lewis Bellenden, conveyed it, in 1588, to Sir Thomas Craig the Scottish writer and foremost expert of his day on Feudal Law.

The location of the hospital is explained by the fact that leper colonies had to be sited at least one mile outside the town wall. St Laurence House was demolished in 1906 and when the cottages on the site were built the excavations for their foundations revealed several thousands of skeletons of sufferers who had died there.

St Mary's Parish Church

On the site of St Mary's there was an ancient place of worship which was dedicated to the Mother of Christ. In 1134, ten years after David I became king, he granted St Mary's Church with its chapels, lands and tithes to the Priory of St Andrews. The Augustinian monks arrived in Haddington in 1139 when David I granted them the Church and Priory and the lands of Clerkington with the tithes of the mills.

The nave of the present St Mary's is thought to be built upon a burial ground which belonged to the old church. This was confirmed in 1891 when many skeletons were found during repairs to the floor.

The construction of St Mary's started after the destruction of the original by Edward III in 1356 (5.p.8). The 1426 'Auld Register of Haddington' refers to it as the 'Paroche Kirk' (1.p.24). Its ninety-foot tower was thought to have had a crown spire (as St Giles of Edinburgh) and the building was completed by 1480 but it was partially destroyed during the Siege of 1548-9 when its bells were removed and carried away by the English. Henry

VIII's ambition to have his son married to the daughter of James V (who became Mary Queen of Scots) had been thwarted by Cardinal Beaton and Henry wreaked his vengeance (the 'Rough Wooing') for the insult by destroying all before him. The destruction of St Mary's was perpetrated by his son Edward VI (his father died in 1547) and St Mary's lost its Choir but the Nave was usable. After the Reformation (1560) the nave was refurbished for Presbyterian use. The choir and transepts fell into decay. Four hundred years passed, until 1972, when the old choir and transepts were restored to their former glory and the Church today is the largest Parish Church in the country renowned for its music and its welcoming atmosphere.

St Mary's Roman Catholic Church

St Mary's Roman Catholic Church in Poldrate was built in 1862 and designed by Augustus Pugin (who designed the Tolbooth Church, Castlehill, Edinburgh). Its early congregation consisted mainly of Irish farm workers. The wheel window in the west gable gives light to its gallery. The stained glass window commemorates the first Parish Priest, Father Prendergast. A new altar was installed in 1989.

Haddington West Church

Haddington West Church was built as **St John's United Free Church** in 1890. It was designed by Sydney Mitchell and built on land which had been sold to the Trustees of the Free Church for £500 by John Farquharson of Hilton Lodge (now a Nursing Home) in Court Street. In 1932 the minister, Rev. Dr Fleck, died and St John's United Free Church amalgamated with the nearby **West United Free Church** whose minister, Rev. Mr. Duncan, had decided to retire. The tower of the old West Church can be seen in the narrow lane next to Hilton Court.

The story of church amalgamations starts much earlier: during the 18th and 19th centuries there were at least six churches in Haddington, each with a different emphasis in their Christian belief.

The first 'Secession' from the Church of Scotland occurred about 1733 over the thorny issue of patronage. The 'Breach' of 1747 split the church into 'Burghers' and 'Anti-Burghers'. The latter refused to take the 'Burgess Oath' which required them to renounce the Pretender and to declare their loyalty to George III and with their minister, Rev. Robert Archibald, this small Secession congregation met in a malt store on the site of the present town library. The Seceders, as they were known, joined the **Burghers' Church** at John Brown Court and appointed the scholastic Rev. John Brown *qv* as their minister in 1751. Their 'meeting house' was demolished in 1765 and replaced by new building which lasted until 1806 when the present church was erected (it is now converted into flats). This church became the **East United Presbyterian Church** in 1847. An unsuccessful attempt at union between the East and West United Presbyterian Churches in 1903 resulted in the dissolution of the East Church. Some of its members joined the West Church, the others joined the Free Church.

In 1805 another split occurred over a question put to ministers and elders at their ordination: this brought about the 'Auld Lichts and the 'New Lichts'. The Anti-Burghers under their minister, Robert Chalmers, and two elders in support of the Auld Lichts were sacked but most of the congregation supported them (the 'original seceders') and Chalmers remained their pastor until his death in 1837. In 1852 the Anti-Burghers ('Auld Lichts') joined the **Knox Free Church** in Newton Port.

In 1838 a new church called **St John's Church** by David Bryce was built in Newton Port to accommodate the excess congregation of St Mary's Church and five years later, following the 'Disruption' of 1843, many of the congregation, objecting to patronage in the church, decided to form **St John's Free Church**. The two churches were adjacent to each other; St John's, which was retained by the Church of Scotland, had seating for 872 whilst St John's Free Church provided 650 seats.

In 1852 St John's Free Church and the Knox Free Church united to form **St John's United Free Church** and Knox Free Church became the town's library in 1881. A new church was built in Court Street in 1890; this was the church which became Haddington West Church.

By 1929 old divisions in the church had become somewhat blurred and many Free Churches joined with the Church of Scotland. In 1932 the congregation of the **West United Free**

Church, previously the West Presbyterian Church (shown on John Wood's 1819 Plan of Haddington and Nungate as 'the Anti-Burgher Meeting House') decided to amalgamate with St John's Free Church and adopted the new name **Haddington West Church**.

In 1987 the bicentenary of the death the Rev. John Brown was celebrated at the West Church which celebrated its own centenary in 1990 with the addition of a new entrance to the east side to form easy access for the handicapped.

Holy Trinity Church

The Holy Trinity Church, built on the site of the Franciscan Friary 'Lamp of Lothian', is the Episcopalian Church of Haddington in Church Street. It was built on workmen's yards in 1769-70 and half its cost was met by the Earl of Wemyss. Its parsonage was built in 1820. It is a simple Scottish country church in design and its eastern apse which forms the choir was added in 1930.

In the 1670s, John Maitland of Lethington (now Lennoxlove), Duke of Lauderdale, drove the Episcopalians into complete subservience with his militia of 20,000 men in his aim to ensure the absolute power of the crown over church and state. Only forty Episcopalians were left at the end of the 17th century and after the '45 Rebellion they were restricted under penalty to a maximum of five worshippers under English Chapel conditions. They had to meet in a small room in the Sidegate. Certain conditions had to be satisfied before an Episcopalian Church could be built: allegiance and loyalty had to be sworn to the king, the English Prayer Book had to be followed and curates could only be ordained under Presbyterianism. Some early founders included the 1st Earl of Wemyss, John Dods, Margaret Gourlay and others; The Earl of Wemyss subscribed a chapel which came to be called the 'Wemyss breakfast room'. In 1930 the 10th Earl of Wemyss contributed the chapel. Following the fire of 1988 the church was restored to its present splendid condition.

Church of Christ

The Church of Christ in Newton Port was established in Haddington about 1955. Previously the members travelled to Tranent where the Church of Christ celebrated its centenary (1992). The members of Haddington obtained the use of the

Buffet Room in the Town Hall and this small group of worshippers bought the old 18th century derelict property at Newton Port, previously 'the Granary', which contained wash houses and laundry rooms on either side of a passageway with a large room upstairs which was used for the storage of cattle feed etc.

Members of the congregation completely restored and transformed the interior of the building into its present pristine state. The two rooms and passageway of the ground floor level were combined to form a chapel in which the traditional pine pews and dais were obtained and modified from the Parish Church in Dunbar which had been partially destroyed by fire some years before. A toilet block was added and the upstairs room, previously used by the Camera Club of Haddington, was converted into a hall and meeting room.

This small church for the worshippers of the Church of Christ is additionally a popular meeting-place for the committee of Haddington's History Society and the Haddington Remembered Group. Its church services are conducted by members themselves who follow the sharing precepts and teachings of the book of The Acts of the Apostles.

Churches in Scotland

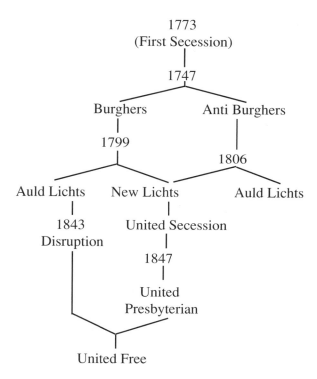

- The First Secession of 1733 opposed the Patronage Act of 1712 and supported the Solemn League and Covenant of Hanoverian monarchy.
- New Lichts against State connection; concerned with personal salvation.
- Auld Lichts favoured State connection and Covenant cause
- United Secession opposed State connection and held with the voluntary principle and anti-Covenanting

(Adapted from Churches in Scotland by JHS Burleigh A Church History of Scotland 1960)

Appendix II

Education in Haddington

The earliest mention of a grammar school in Haddington dates to around 1270 when Johannes Duns Scotus (c.1265-1308), one of the greatest of the medieval theologians, attended there. A further early reference to a school in Haddington appears in the Exchequer Rolls of 1378 which states 'that £3.15.2d (£3.76) was paid to the master of the school of Haddington by command of Robert II' (1.p.128).

Another famous theologian who attended the **Grammar School of Haddington** was John Major (1469-1550) of Gleghornie, the historian and scholastic divine who "imbibed the pure milk of Latyn." Before the Reformation (1560) monks performed teaching duties and encouraged their pupils to follow in their footsteps. John Knox was such a pupil. He was educated at the Grammar School of Haddington and wore clerical clothing. He was said to have spoken Latin with ease, but he was probably not the only one to have gained such a facility; pupils were punished for speaking in their mother tongue. This 'auld schule' was sited opposite the old bowling green behind the south side of what is now Church Street. Knox was a devotee of Major and followed him to Glasgow University.

In 1559 Knox had returned from his long exile in Europe and he preached against worship of the Church of Rome in the Parish Church of Perth. That year Robert Dermont was appointed the first Protestant teacher in Haddington's 'auld skule'. His annual salary was 24 merks ie £16 (1 merk = 13/4d = 66p) plus '12d termly of schoolhouse fees, and 4d termly from the parents or friends of the bairn.' (14.p.181).

In 1579 a new school was built alongside the old one which was converted into a house for the schoolmaster, the parish minister and some other employees of the town. This school was in continuous use until 1755; it is shown as the **'High School'** on the 1819 Plan of Haddington and Nungate in St Anne's Street (now Church Street).

In 1560 John Knox's First Book of Discipline laid down that every town should have a school, every parish a schoolmaster and that all children, from the richest to the poorest, should receive education according to their capacity. This ideal was not fully realised because of the appropriation of the revenues of the Medieval Church by the Crown (13).

In 1563 Mr Thomas Cumming was appointed schoolmaster at 90 merks annually to instruct the children of the burgh in English grammar, Latin and moral virtues by 'good life, honest behaviour, and conversation, example to others, as well as in his instruction and doctrine, as God will give him grace during all the days of his lifetime.' (14.p.182). In 1571 the minister of the Kirk of Haddington, Mr James Carmichael, performed the duties of schoolmaster until 1577 when Mr James Panton became schoolmaster.

In 1583 a **Song School** was established in Haddington and John Buchan, the first music teacher, was given a house and 'ane chalmer' (chamber) in which to teach about 60 children. In 1610 Patrick Dunbar was appointed to teach singing and playing the virginal, lute, gutharie and other instruments. He led the psalm singing in the kirk. Greek was first taught in 1591.

In 1606, there was a rival, unauthorised **school in the Nungate** and the burgh schoolmaster complained that parents had withdrawn children from his school preferring instead the Nungate one. The magistrates ordered the Nungate school closed. Disciplinary problems led the Town Council to agree 'to assist, maintain and defend ye said Mr. Alexander in correcting and repressing ye insolence of ye scholars.' (1. p.130). In 1623, Alex Seton became schoolmaster with a greatly enhanced salary plus two shillings per pupil which he collected from their parents; he was the father of Sir William Seton who was Provost of the burgh from 1661 to 1671 and 1682 and lived at Northrig.

In 1696 the Scottish Parliament enacted that heritors (landowners) of every parish should provide the salary for a teacher and a "commodious house for a school." At that time the school day began at 6.0 am but in 1699, from Hallowmas to Candlemas (first week of November to 2nd February), the assembly hour was 9 o'clock and some relaxation was permitted in the form of play-acting in the open-air. The boys of the

Grammar School were encouraged to develop their acting talents and in 1729 the town treasurer was instructed 'to provide trees and deales (a deal being a stretching board for a dead body) and other materials for the stage.' The plays were *Julius Caesar* and *The Gentle Shepherd* the latter by the poet Allan Ramsay (1685-1758) who was present and who supervised the performance (his statue can be seen at the Floral Clock in West Princes Street Gardens, Edinburgh). John Leslie was the schoolmaster and a friend of Allan Ramsay.

Latin and Greek were important subjects in the curriculum but in 1731 English was given prominence with writing and arithmetic. However, about this time there was pressure to drop Latin and Greek for subjects of a more vocational nature. The medieval grammar school had outgrown its usefulness and the English school was its modern counterpart. There was a gradual move away from the old Scots tongue after the Union of Parliaments in 1707 and the 'literati' strove to remove Scots from their works of prose.

In 1755 a new **Grammar School** and house of red sandstone were built for £5906 Scots (£481 sterling) on the south side of Church Street. It was extended in 1761 for the teaching of English and allied subjects under the supervision of John Abernethy, former schoolmaster of Gifford - the school was given a new lease of life. His pupils included many well-known Haddington names which appear on the 1819 Plan of Haddington - Wilkie, Roughead, Martine, Donaldson, Neill, Forrest, Veitch, Pringle, Haldane, Smith, Brown, Banks, M'Claren, Carfae and many others.

Ball games were introduced in 1799 at the Sands and on 'Fastern's E'en' (Shrove Tuesday) a football match was held between masters and scholars. The grammar school was the sole educational establishment in Haddington but after 1731 there were attempts to open private schools.

Miss Janet Halyburton's School at Bothwell Castle in the Hardgate flourished about 1786. She was appointed by the Council as a teacher of sewing. Her disciplinary methods included the banishment of recalcitrants to the old kitchen school for young ladies.

Towards the end of the century the English master of the new **Academy at Paterson Place** was Richard Hay whose main interest was in teaching arithmetic being the author of a book entitled *Beauties of Arithmetic*.

In 1801 William Graham of Dirleton was schoolmaster and Martine said of him: 'he was a very successful teacher and although a little pedantic, was much esteemed in society' (14.p.184); he was rector for 38 years. He had 27 boarders under his care and each Sunday the scholars in residence were marched to the parish church where they occupied a large square pew.

In 1809 a new building adjoined the English school and was called the **Mathematical School**. Its first teacher was Edward Irving who taught Jane Welsh and introduced her to Thomas Carlyle. Irving encouraged the study of astronomy and took his pupils out on dark nights to study the stars. In 1814 the Mathematical School was affiliated with the English School.

In 1821 a **School of Arts and Sciences** was established and the Town Council voted the sum of £10 towards the purchase of scientific apparatus. In 1822 the heritors approved the establishment of a Parish School but the scheme was discouraged by the Town Council on grounds of economy. Two years later it was again mooted but not until 1826 was it realised. A **Parish School** was erected in Lodge Street - though when sites were being considered it was suggested that St Martin's Chapel be pulled down and the Parish School erected there.

The 1833 Act of Parliament voted a grant of £20,000 for education in Britain and the Government inspection of schools followed in 1836 with the first appointment of Government Inspectors of Schools. Their report of 1841-42 gave a favourable mention to:

> *The Burgh School of Haddington, attended by about 180 children, and in which an English, Commercial and Classical Education is imparted with great Ability and Skill. Its schoolroom measured 40ft x 25ft and was 14ft high, was sufficiently ventilated and warmed, but with no lobby or closet for bonnets and cloaks, and no exercise ground.*

The only master was Thomas Henderson whose appointment lasted seventeen years. He was paid £34 annually plus school fees totalling £95 (English Reading, 2s 6d; Writing, 3s 6d; Arithmetic, Geography and Grammar, 4s 6d).

By 1843 the old Grammar School had suffered a gradual decline under the Rev. William Whyte who was constantly in dispute with the magistrates and the council over his salary. He thought himself to be the most important man in Haddington being qualified for the ministry and in classics. Many parents lost confidence in him and withdrew their children until only 11 pupils occupied the school which could accommodate 200-300 pupils. He was vindictive and cruel being known to 'strip, expose and abuse' his pupils (35). One of his pupils died some time after a blow on the head by Whyte - he was fortunate to escape a charge of murder. Only two dozen pupils attended the school examination in 1866 and the *Haddingtonshire Courier* alluded to 'the melancholy spectacle now annually presented at what is still called the Examination of..... the once famous and flourishing Burge School of Haddington'. Whyte was asked to resign. He was offered £60 to sever his connection with the school and to vacate the rector's house but there was no response - he remained for another six years being dismissed in 1873 as 'unfit and inefficient.' This was the end of the Haddington Burgh Schools which were sold in 1879. (35).

Around 1850 there was a "**Ragged School**" at the **Poldrate Mill**. This was a charity school the head of which was a Mr Reid who may have been a mill-worker. The curriculum was very restricted due to lack of skilled teachers and money and was confined to cleanliness, discipline and attendance.

Under the Education (Scotland) Act of 1872 the administration of education was transferred from church to secular authorities and School Boards were elected for all parishes and burghs. These Boards had powers to prosecute the parents of non-attenders; the main aim of the Act was the elimination of illiteracy. Exemption from school attendance could be obtained if ability to read, write and perform elementary arithmetic could be proved. Denominational schools were now allowed and a school at St Mary's Roman Catholic Church was opened.

The Parish School in Lodge Street came under the direction of the newly appointed School Board. Its name was changed to the **Landward Public School** and was responsible for the education of the great majority of the youth of the town. Private schools now existed for both sexes; two of them were Paterson Place

Academy and **Flora Bank private school**. Several small schools also existed for young ladies.

In 1876 there was a proposal to unite the Burgh and Parish Schools but the education department did not approve it. However, the historic school of Haddington was nearing its end. Three years later, in April 1879, the old grammar school building in Lodge Street was advertised for sale with the English School, where Edward Irving taught mathematics. The Grammar and English Schools were sold in May and June, the former for £600. Both buildings were converted into houses. Thus ended the old Grammar School of Haddington which had existed continuously from the 14th century and probably earlier, a period of 500 years.

About 1870 a memorial to John Knox was proposed in the form of an educational establishment. In October 1879 the **Knox Memorial Institute** (now Knox Court) was opened; its rector was J C Graham, MA, previously a classics master of Merchiston Castle School in Edinburgh. The formal opening ceremony was performed by A.J.Balfour of Whittingehame, afterwards 1st Earl Balfour. D W Stevenson's life-size statue of John Knox was a gift of the Misses Traill of Aberlady. A dedicated and talented teacher was John Dow Porteous (1852-1937) who was appointed to the school in 1883 and became its Rector from 1894 to 1919. His two sons, Alexander and Norman Porteous, who attended the Knox Institute were to become distinguished classical scholars.

Walter Haig's Academy in Paterson Place found a powerful rival in the Knox Institute. Walter Haig, who had taken over from the Rev. John Paterson in 1854, was now elderly and the seminary, of which he had been the respected head for many years, was closed.

The advance in educational methods affected the town's schools and when an elementary school was built at the rear of the Knox, built on the site of the school garden in Meadowpark - **Haddington Public School**. Its well-loved and highly respected headmaster, from 1890 to 1925, was Mr Alex Burnett. It afforded the same teaching provided by the burgh and parish schools but with superior equipment and greater efficiency.

By 1938 the old Gothic Knox Institute was too small. A new school was built at a cost of £30,000 at Rosehall for the senior pupils. The infants and the primary school moved into the old building. The new senior school for 400 pupils was opened on 7th February 1938; its first Rector was James Black. In 1946 free education was introduced in State schools and two years later the Memorial Institute was renamed **Knox Academy**. Its roll was 368 pupils whilst that of the primary school was 167. In 1968 the school leaving age was raised to 16 years. In 1970 the old Knox Institute was finally vacated, a new school having been built at Neilson Park Road- **King's Meadow Primary School**; the head teacher was Mr D, McGillivray. Knox Academy has been extended and today it accommodates 800 pupils under the headship of Anthony B Ellis BA(Hons), DipEd, MEd.

The Compass School in West Road is the only independant Primary School in East Lothian. It started life in the hall of Holy Trinity Church 1963 for 11 pupils. Mrs Alny Younger was the originator of the school which, within a few years, had outgrown the church hall. In 1969 Somnerfield Lodge at 11 West Road was purchased and today the school accommodates 94 pupils in the age range of 4 to 11 years under the Headmistress Miss CR Budge BA(Hons), PGCE(Moray House). There are 6 full-time teachers and several visiting teachers whose specialisms add an interesting breadth to the curriculum; pupils as young as four years have French conversation lessons. Music, drama and sport all add to the core subjects of reading, writing and mathematics and science, technology, history and geography are often linked in the development of pupil projects.

Some famous men and women educated in Haddington:

Johannes Duns Scotus (1265-1308), one of the greatest medieval Franciscan scholars, attended the Grammar School of Haddington.

Walter Bower (c1400), an eminent scholar who continued Fordun's Latin *Scotichronicon*, was elected Abbot of Inchcolm in 1418.

John Major or Mair (c1470-1550) of Gleghornie near North Berwick - a distinguished historian and writer of scholastic theology, a boarder at the Grammar School.

John Knox (c1505-1572) the famous leader of the Reformation, born at Haddington (or Morham), was educated at the Grammar school of Haddington.

John Maitland of Lethington (1616-82), 2nd Earl of Lauderdale, 1st Duke of Lauderdale, Scottish Commissioner at Westminster, Scottish Secretary of State after the Restoration.

Adam Cockburn, Lord Ormiston (1656-1735) a Commissioner for the Union of Parliaments in 1689, Privy Councillor, Commissioner on the Inquiry into the Massacre of Glencoe, Lord Justice Clerk and a Lord of Session.

John Cockburn (-1758), (son of Adam Cockburn above) MP, Lord of the Admiralty and agricultural 'improver' in East Lothian.

Rev. Dr. John Witherspoon (1723-94) born in the manse of Yester, President of the college and Pastor at Princeton, New Jersey. He was a signer of the American Declaration of Independence - plaque in Gifford.

Dr. Andrew Mylne - minister of Dollar - author of several educational works.

Rev. John and Ebenezer Brown - sons of the Rev. John Brown of Haddington and later their brothers: Thomas, minister at Dalkeith and George, minister at North Berwick and Samuel, merchant in Haddington who instituted the 'itinerating libraries' in 1817. He was one of the founders of the Haddington School of Arts.

Sir Peter Laurie (1778-1861) - Lord Mayor of London in 1832

Colonel Vetch of Hawthornbank - distinguished Indian officer.

Jane Welsh Carlyle (1801-66), wife of Thomas Carlyle (1795-1881), the 'Sage of Chelsea'.

Samuel Smiles (1812-1904) educated at the Burgh School under Patrick Hardie. Graduated MD at Edinburgh and became a celebrated author and social reformer - author of Self Help - plaque in High Street.

Professor George Harley FRS (1829-1896) - educated at the Burgh School of Haddington, gained his MD at Edinburgh and became Professor of Medical Jurisprudence of University College, London.

Sir James Black Baillie (1872-1940) - educated at the Burgh School of Haddington and the newly opened Knox Memorial Institute. He was Professor of Moral Philosophy, Aberdeen University for 22 years and Vice-Chancellor of Leeds University.

Professor Alexander Porteous (1896-1981) - educated at the Knox Memorial Institute who became Professor of Philosophy at McGill University, Montreal, Professor of Education at

Liverpool University and Professor of Moral philosophy at Edinburgh University.

Professor Norman Porteous (1898 -) - educated at the Knox Memorial Institute who became Professor of Hebrew and Oriental Languages at St Andrews University, Professor of Hebrew and Semitic Languages at Edinburgh University and Principal of New College, Edinburgh.

Sir William George Gillies KBE, CBE, RSA, RA (1898-1971) - educated at the Knox Memorial Institute who became Principal of the Edinburgh College of Art.

Sir Alastair Grant Kt (1937-) chairman of the Argyll Group plc and chairman of the Agricultural and Food Research Council and visiting professor at Stirling and Strathclyde Universities. He is currently Chairman of Scottish and Newcastle Breweries.

Appendix III

Provosts of the Royal Burgh of Haddington

The first recorded reference to the title of 'Provost of the burgh of Hadingtone' appears in the Ragman Rolls of 1296 (1.p.94). These were the returns to the inquest of 1274-5 (so named from their ragged appearance; dozens of pendant seals were attached to the document). As far as Scotland is concerned this was the roll of professions of homage and fealty made by the Clergy and nobility to Edward I ('the hammer of the Scots') in 1297.

There is a long gap in records but James Miller (2) records the provostships of William Clerk and James Ayton in 1454. The first elected provost was William Broun of Stottencleuch who was elected on 9th October 1543 before the assembled community at the Tolbooth. Then followed James Oliphant in 1554 but he delayed his appointment for three years, the expense incurred being something of a disincentive - the Provost could be required, by Royal command, to lead townsmen into battle or to carry out other thankless tasks. Several members of the Sleich family served as Provosts during the 17th century - John Sleich senior and his two sons John and Henry were Provosts and at one stage no fewer than four members of the family served on the council together.

The following list is an adaptation of that by Miller (2.p.216-217) with additional information gleaned from Martine (14), The Transactions of the East Lothian Antiquarian and Field Naturalists' Society, Vol.VII p.4 and brought up to 1974 by ex-provost Alexander Fraser Spowage JP (the year of the formation of Regional and District Councils) when most provostships, including that of Haddington, were ended.

Years	Name	Occupation
1296	Alisaundre le Barker	Barker (or Tanner)
1454	William Clerk	
	and James Ayton	Bailies
1530	Patrick Hepburn	Master of Hailes
	Thomas Sinclair	
	Alexander Hepburn	Bailies
1532	Patrick Lawson	Bailie
1543	William Broun	
1552 &1554	James Oliphant	
1568	James Puntoun	
1569	John Forrest	Owner Gimmersmill
1570	John Aytoun	
1579	Robert Nesbett	
1585?	Thomas Vass	
1588-90?	Francis, 5th Earl of Bothwell	
1594-98 & 1605-08	Sir William Seton	Sheriff of Midlothian, Postmaster for Scotland, and MP in 1661
1630	John Sleich	Merchant
1631, 1649	John Cockburn	Wester Monkrigg
1658	William Hatton	
1661-1671	Sir William Seton	(imprisoned in Tolbooth in 1667)
1680	John Sleich snr.	(b. 1595, d.1686)
1681,1698	Henry Cockburn	
1686	Sir William Paterson	Clerk to Privy Council
1688	Alexander Maitland	Acting Provost
1689	William M'Call	Merchant
1691	James Lauder	Merchant
1701	John Sleich jnr. (14.)	
1700,1703, 1707	Alexander Edgar	Burgess
1705,1708, 1712,1718	Richard Millar	
1710,1714, 1714,1720	David Forrest	Owner Gimmersmill

1719	Alexander Hay	
1722	James Dods	
1723,1728	George M'Call	Postmaster
1725	George Smith	
1730	Archibald Millar	
1732	James Erskine	Cordwainer
1733,1736, 1750,1754 & 1758	Andrew Dickson	Merchant
1734	George Heriot	Sheriff-clerk
1736	Robert Forrest	
1738,1748, & 1752	William Ray	Merchant
1739	Col. Charles Cockburn of Clerkington	
1742	James Rutherford	
1746,1762, 1766, 1770	James Lundie MD	Surgeon
1756,1760	Robert Thomson	
1761 1772, 1764, 1776 & 1780	James Dudgeon	Surgeon
	Henry Hepburn	
1774,1778	Robert Burton	Grocer & Tobacco Merchant
1781,1809, 1813 & 1817	John Martine	Postmaster
1783	Patrick M'Claren	Grocer and Merchant
1785	David Smith	Candlemaker
1787,1791	James Banks	Merchant
1789,1793	Dr Richard Sumner	Surgeon
1795, 1824	Alexander Hislop	Draper (depute-lieutenant)
1797	Alexander Maitland	Surgeon
1799	Robert Roughhead	Innkeeper
1801	James Roughead	Merchant
1803	William Cunningham	Merchant
1805	George Banks	Seed Merchant and Bank Agent for East Lothian
1807	George Martine	Currier
1809	James Deans	Painter

1811	George Haldane	Manufacturer (weaver)
1815	Thomas Pringle	Tanner
1819	Thomas Pringle	Tobacconist
1821	Peter Dods	Nurseryman
1825,1829	William Dods	Seedsman
1827,1831	Archibald Dunlop	Distiller
1833	John Ferme	Banker and Writer
1834-36	Samuel Brown	Ironmonger
1836,1839,1842	Thomas Lea	Draper
1848-54	George More	Proprietor, Gimmersmill
1855-65	David Stevenson	Hotelier, The George
1866-69	Francis Vert	Auctioneer
1870-76	William Davidson	Tweedmill worker
1877	Dr Thomas Howden	Medical Practitioner
1894	John Brook	Merchant
1900-02	A Mathieson Main	Draper (Hardgate)
1903-06	William Aitchison	Manager, West Mill
1907	Mark Ormiston	Stonemason
1911-18	George Younger	
1918-19	Thomas M Ross	Master Plumber
1931-34	Alexander Phail	Ironmonger
1935	W. Rattray	Solicitor
1936	William Binnie	Brewer
1936-38	William Davidson	Weaver, West Mills
1939-46	Alexander Aitchison	Weaver, West Mills
1947-56	Robert Fortune	Warehouseman, West Mills
1956-59	Hugh Craig	Farmer, Harperdean
1959-62	William Crow	Hotelier (The George)
1962-65	Harvey Gardiner	Chemist
1965-68	John Barbour Wood	Road Surveyor
1968-71	John Halliday Scott	Insurance Co. Head
1971-74	Alexander F Spowage	Licensing Officer - Motor Taxation
1974-75	William Grant	Company Director

Appendix IV

The Town Wall of Haddington

M ost of Haddington's Town Wall has disappeared with the passage of time. It was built between 1597 and the early 1600s as a defence against lawlessness and the plague (23.iii 178) rather than a fortification against invaders. It was built partly by property owners at the edge of town as a series of "yaird dykes" and earthern works; it was 'a haphazard affair at best.' (1.p.83)

Miller's 'Lamp of Lothian' (2.p.33) gives a description of its route around the town. It is described in relation to the 1819 Plan of Haddington and Nungate. The following route is that of Miller with details of that described in the Scottish Burgh Survey, 1977, *Historic Haddington* (5) and Forbes Gray (1.p84-85). It is described in relation to present day streets, although its exact course is not known with precision.

Starting at its western extremity, that is at the Ferguson Monument, there was the gateway of WEST PORT from which the town wall ran north for a short distance up Hope Park. It then turned east behind the West Church and Hilton Lodge to another gate which was called SALLY PORT, situated approximately behind the Post Office. Its pillars were removed in 1803. The wall continued east and fifty or so metres of the original wall can be seen at the north end of the car park at Tesco's Supermarket. The wall continued to the north end of St John's Church at Newton Port and on to the NORTH WEST PORT (or NEWTOWN PORT) at the head of Newton Port; it was demolished in 1763. The wall continued on to the NORTH EAST PORT at Hardgate just south of Tenterfield.

Following a southerly direction the wall skirted the Tyne to Gowl's Close where there was another gateway. It continued along the east side of Holy Trinity Church (the present day wall surrounding this church, in Church Street, was constructed from stone of the original Town Wall).

The route of the next section is open to question; Miller describes it as passing by the site of Elm House, along by Peter

Potter's teashop to the Nungate Bridge where there was another gateway. The wall continued along Ba' Alley to the north side of St Mary's Churchyard. At Sidegate, opposite the entrance to the Maitlandfield Hotel, was SOUTH PORT, and the wall continued along the south side of the Maitlandfield Hotel along Mill Wynd to Millfield, turning north at Tynebank where there was a watch-tower. The wall continued northwards along Meadowpark to Rosehall. However the 'Scottish Burgh Survey' of 1977 (5) and Forbes Gray (1.p.85) shows it turning northwards round the back of Maitlandfield and along the line of the Butts to Victoria Road. Its final stage was eastwards along Knox Place to WEST PORT at the junction of Station Road and Knox Place.

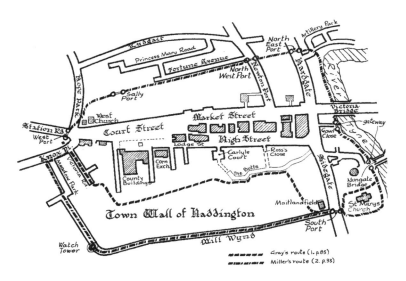

References

1. A Short History of Haddington, by W. Forbes Gray and James H. Jamieson, Pub. Spa Books Ltd., Stevenage, Herts.
2. The Lamp of Lothian or, the History of Haddington, by James Miller. Pub. William Sinclair, 1900.
3. Wellington The Years of the Sword, by Elizabeth Longford, Pub. World Books, London.
4. From Threshold to Rooftree The Haddington Home of Jane Welsh Carlyle, Pub. The Pentland Press, Edinburgh.
5. Historic Haddington the archaeological implications of development, by Robert Gourlay and Anne Turner. Scottish Burgh Survey. Pub. Department of Archaeology, University of Glasgow.
6. Statistical History of Scotland, 1853. by James Hooper Dawson. Pub. W.H.Lizars, Edinburgh & Samuel Highley & Son, London.
7. A Short History of Scotland, By P.Hume Brown, Pub. Oliver and Boyd Ltd.
8. Scotland. A New History, by Michael Lynch. Pub. Century Ltd, 20 Vauxhall Bridge Road, London.
9. East Lothian Biographies by Gray and Jamieson; 4th vol. of Transactions of the East Lothian Antiquarian and Field Naturalists' Society.
10. Memories Yesteryear in and around Haddington, by Haddington Remembered Group 1991.
11. The Concise Scots Dictionary, Ed. Mairi Robinson. Pub. Aberdeen University Press.
12. Scottish Place Names, by Nicola Wood. Pub. W & R Chambers Ltd, Edinburgh.
13. Public Education in Scotland. HMSO. 1961.
14. Reminiscences of the Royal Burgh of Haddington by John Martine. Pub. John Menzies, Edinburgh & Glasgow 1883.
15. Old and New Edinburgh, Vols. I-III, by James Grant. Pub. Cassell & Co., Ltd.
16. The Complete Peerage, Vol.XII, pt.II, Ed. GH White and RS Lea. Pub. The St Catherine's Press, London. 1959.

17. The Lives of the Kings and Queens of England, Ed. Antonia Fraser. Pub. Macdonald Futura Publishers.

18. Late Great Britons. Pub. Brook Productions for the BBC. Chambers Biographical Dictionary, Pub. W & R Chambers Ltd.,

20. Dictionary of National Biography, (1885)

21. Scottish Kings, by Gordon Donaldson. Pub. Book Club Associates, 1977.

22. The Holy Bible with Notes and Observations by the Rev. John Brown - Memoir of the Rev. John Brown.

23. Lennoxlove, Home of the Duke of Hamilton and Brandon, Pub. Pilgrim Press Ltd., Derby.

24. The Exchequer Rolls of Scotland 1878-1908. Ed. J. Stuart and others (Edinburgh).

25. The Buildings of Scotland, Lothian except Edinburgh by Colin McWilliam. Pub. Penguin Books Ltd., London.

26. Itinerating Libraries and their Founder, by Samuel Brown. Printed by William Blackwood & Sons, Edinburgh. 1856.

27. Lothian Except Edinburgh, by Colin McWilliam. Pub.Penguin Books Ltd.

28. The Transactions of the East Lothian Antiquarian and Field Naturalists' Society Vol. VII.

29. East Lothian Studies by David Louden and Rev. William Whitfield. Pub. John Hutchison, 81 High Street, Haddington. 1891

30. The Poetical Works of Sir Walter Scott Bart., Pub. Adam & Charles Black, Edinburgh.

31. A History of Morham Parish by Mary Stenhouse. Pub. Garvald and Morham Church and Garvald and Morham Community Council.

32. Obituary of The Late Lieut.-Colonel Vetch of Caponflat, Haddingtonshire Courier, 17th October 1873.

33. Placenames of Edinburgh and the Lothians, by John Milne. First published by McDougall's Educational Company Ltd.

34. Facsimile edition published by Lang Syne Publishers Ltd. Haddington Burgh Schools and the Rev. William Whyte by Irene MacDonald.

36. Haddingtonshire Courier and East Lothian Courier, pub. D & J. Croal Ltd., 18 Market Street, Haddington - 22nd September 1911
37. The East Lothian Courier 27th June 1980
38. The Lovable Craft, 1687-1987 by George Dalgleish and Stuart Maxwell, Incorporation of Goldsmiths of the City of Edinburgh.
39. The Story of the Hays by Kenneth McLennan Hay
40. Register of Seisins (Sasines): Haddington 1781-1868, East Lothian 309-699, Search Sheet 440 Alderston
41. Festival of the North, The Story of the Edinburgh Festival, by George Bruce. Pub. Robert Hale & Co London
42. The Edinburgh Evening News, 4th December 1954
43. The Evening Despatch, 6th March 1954

The author: **DAVID DICK OBE**

Former Hydro-Electric Power Engineer
Former Depute Principal of Napier College of Science &
Technology (now Napier University of Edinburgh).
Former Principal of Stevenson College, Edinburgh, Scotland.
Currently Lay Inspector of Fire Services, Scotland.
Author of *Capital Walks in Edinburgh - The New Town*, and
several magazine and newspaper articles for *East Lothian Life,
Scottish Memories, The Scotsman, The Glasgow Herald* and other
technical magazines.
Historical Advisor to Videosynchratic, Edinburgh.

Edinburgh born David Dick was awarded the OBE in 1982 for
his services to the Scottish Fire Service and to Education in
Scotland. He is a Post-Graduate Diplomate of the Imperial
College, London, a Fellow of the Institution of Electrical
Engineers and a Chartered Engineer.

His interest in history is based mainly on what he refers to as
'Street Biographies' - i.e. where a street is named after someone
he has an insatiable curiosity to find out why; he finds it
impossible to pass a monument without firstly examining its
inscription. He has completed over 500 street biographies of
several towns and cities at home and abroad.